LEARNING PYTHON

3 Books in 1: Ultimate Beginners guide Including Data Analysis and 50 Step-By-Step Coding Projects in Games, Art and More

Mark Slatkin

presented without assurance regarding its prolonged validity or interim quality. Trademarks that are mentioned are done without written consent and can in no way be considered an endorsement from the trademark holder

Contents

PYTHON FOR BEGINNERS

A complete beginner's guide to learning python 3.0 quickly

Mark Slatkin

INTRODUCTION

Most students opt for online video training courses and python programming tutorials. It helps to understand Python better. Thanks to online courses, students can learn from anywhere and have a career in Python programming.

What are the important things we need to understanding concerning ball pythons we make them pets at home? What are the primary points that ball pythons require to confinement? Before trying to make pythons as dogs and cats, you need to learn more about these kinds of snakes that you will read in this book about ball python knowledge.

Python is a programming language that offers several benefits, particularly for start-ups. Read on to see why Python is so much preferred by startups.

CHAPTER ONE -UNDERSTANDING OF PYTHON

Guido van Rossum develops Python. In 1989, Guido van Rossum began to implement Python. Python is indeed a very simple programming language, so you can learn python without problems even if you are new to programming.

Interesting fact: Python is decided to name after Monty Python's Flying Circus comedy TV show. It's not really named after the snake of Python.

What can you do about Python?

You may wonder what all of Python's applications are. There are so many Python applications, some of them here.

1. Web development – Python is based on web frameworks such as Django and Flask. They help you to write server-side code that helps you manage your database, write backend logic, map URLs, etc.

Develops the Web Application

Python is designed as a general programming language and has no integrated features for web development. However, web developers in Python use a range of add-ons to write modern web applications. During Python, programmers may use several top-level web frames including web2py, Reahl, Django, CubicWeb, and TurboGears while writing web applications. These web structures help programmers to carry out several operations, including URL routing, database manipulation, session storage and recovery, and output template formatting, without writing additional code. You can also make use of the web frameworks to protect the web application against cross-site scripting, SQL injection, and cross-site forgery.

2. Machine learning – Python has many machine learning applications. Machine learning is just a way to write a logic for a machine to learn and solve its specific problem. The product recommendation on websites such as Amazon, Flipkart, eBay, etc. is a user interesting machine learning algorithm, for instance. Another example of machine learning is face recognition and voice recognition on your phone.

3. Data analysis – Python can also be used to develop data analysis and data visualization as charts.

4. Scripting – Scripting means that small programs are written to automatically send automated response emails, etc. Such applications can also be written in the programming language of Python.

5. Game development – You can use Python to develop games.

6. Embedded applications can be developed in Python.

7. Desktop applications – You could use a library such as QT or Tkinter to develop desktop applications in Python.

Why Is Python Here to Stay?

The large popularity shows the efficiency of Python as a modern programming language. Python 3 is currently used for a variety of desktop GUI, Web, and mobile applications by developers worldwide. There are also many reasons why Python's enormous popularity and market share will remain intact for a longer time.

8 reasons why Python's massive popularity remains intact in the future

1) Supports multiple paradigms of programming

Good developers often use various paradigms to reduce the time and effort needed to develop large and complex applications. Just like other modern programming languages, Python supports several commonly used styles including functional, subject-oriented, procedural, and imperative programming. It also features automatic memory management and a dynamic system type. Programmers can therefore use the language to develop large and complex software applications.

2) Do not require programmers to write long-lasting code

Python is designed with full coding readability focus. So the programmers can create a readable code base for distributed team members. At the same time, they can express concepts without writing any long lines of code through the simple syntax of the programming language. The feature simplifies large and complex applications for developers within a fixed time. Because they could easily skip certain tasks that require another programming languages, maintaining and updating their applications is easier for developers.

3) Provides a standard comprehensive library

Due to its extensive standard library, Python scores further over other programming languages. These libraries can be used by programmers to perform a variety of tasks without writing longer lines of code. Python's standard library is also designed with a large number of highly useful programming tasks. This helps programmers perform tasks such as string operations, web service development and implementation, working with Internet protocols, and operating system interface.

5) Facilitates high-quality GUI, scientific and numerical applications development

Python is currently available with Mac OS X, Windows, UNIX, and Linux. The desktop GUI applications can therefore be deployed on multiple platforms in the programming language. The programmers can speed up GUI application development across platforms through frameworks such as Kivy, wxPython, and PyGtk. Several reports have shown that Python is widely used for numerical and scientific applications. During Python's scientific and numerical apps, developers can use tools such as Scipy, Pandas, IPython, and the Python Imaging Library.

6) Simplifies application prototyping

Each organization now wants to overcome competition by developing software with distinctive and innovative features. For this reason, prototyping has become an integral part of modern software development. Before writing code, developers must create an application prototype to show various stakeholders its features and functionality. Python enables programmers to develop the final system in a simple and fast programming language without any additional time and effort. The developers also have the option to start developing the system by simply rebuilding the code directly from the prototype.

7) Can also be used for the development of mobile apps

Frameworks such as Kivy also allow Python to be used for mobile app development. Kivy can be used as a library to create both desktop and mobile applications. However, it enables developers to write code once and deploy the same code on several platforms. Alongside interfaces with mobile device hardware, Kivy includes built-in camera adapters, rendering, and playback videos, and user input modules with multi-touch and gestures. So programmers can use Kivy for various versions of the same iOS, Android, and Windows Phone applications. Besides, developers do not need to write longer lines of code during the creation of Kivy programs. You can package the app separately for each app store after creating different versions of the mobile app. This option facilitates the creation of different versions of the mobile app without using separate developers.

8) Source Open

Although Python is classified as the most popular 2015 coding language, it is still available as an open-source and as free software. Startups and freelance software developers can also use programming language, together with large IT companies, without paying fees or royalties. Thus, Python makes it easier for companies to significantly reduce development costs. At the same time, programmers can also use the help of the large and active community to add extra features to the software application.

PYTHON PROGRAMMING FOR BEGINNERS

Despite what assembly code and C-coders might tell us, high-level languages have a place in any toolbox of the programmer and some are much more than a curiosity in computer science. Python appears to be the best of the many high-level languages we can choose from today for those who want to learn something new and do real work at the same time. Its unreasonable implementation of object-oriented programming and its clean, easy-to-understand syntax make it a language that is fun to learn and use.

In Python Training, you learn how to write apps using command-line options, read and type pipes, access ambient variables, handle interruptions, read and write files, create temporary files, and write system logs. In other words, instead of the old boring Hello, World, you will find recipes for writing actual applications! Stuff.

Start

Initially, if you haven't installed your system with a Python interpreter, it's time. To make this easier, install the latest Python distribution with Linux-compatible packages. You may also use rpm, deb, and tgz on your Linux CD-ROM or online. You should not have any problems if you follow standard installation procedures.

I also advise you to use the Python Library Reference; you might want it if the explanations given here are not appropriate for your needs. It can be found in the same locations as the Python Tutorial.

Scripts can be created using your favorite text editor as long as they save the text in ASCII format and do not insert it automatically line breaks if the line is longer than the window width of the editor.

Always start your scripts with either

```
#! /usr/bin/python
```

or

```
#! /usr/local/bin/python
```

If your system has a different access path to your binary python, change that line and leave the first two characters (#!) intact. Be sure that this line is the first line in your script; it will save you a lot of frustration not only the very first non-blank line.

Use chmod to set your script for file permissions to be executable. If the script is alone for you, typ chmod 0700 scriptfilename.py. If you want to share it with others in your group, but don't have it edited, use 0750 as a chmod value. Type man chmod for help with the chmod command.

Reading options and arguments on the command line

Commandline options and arguments are useful when telling our scripts how to comply with or pass on arguments (file names, directory names, user names ...). All programs can read these options and arguments, and your Python scripts are no different.

WHAT ARE THE IMPORTANT REASONS TO LEARN THE PYTHON PROGRAMMING LANGUAGE?

Python is a high-level open-source programming language developed for use in a wide range of operating systems. Due to its dynamic and diverse nature, it is called the most powerful programming language. Python is easy to use with simple syntax and it is easy for people who first learn to capture concepts. With pioneering websites like YouTube, DropBox, Python has a high level of market demand. If you want Python to benefits, register for Python Training.

Let us now learn the main reasons why Python is used in a broader range of people.

• Object-oriented programming

One of Python's powerful tools is Object-oriented Programming, which allows creation and reusability of data structures. Due to such reusability, the work is carried out efficiently and time is reduced. Object-oriented programming relates to classes and many interactive objects in recent years. Object-oriented programming techniques have been employed and implemented in any programming language in either software.

• Readability

The Python coding language is very easy to understand with simple syntax. Therefore, after testing the code, Python can be used as a prototype and implemented in other programming languages.

• Python is free

Since Python is an open-source programming language, it is free and free of charge. It can be modified, redistributed, and commercially used with this open-source license. The license is available free of charge even for full source code. In all operating systems, CPython, the most widely used Python implementation, can be used. The well designed, robust, and portable software has become a widely-used programming language.

• Programming at a faster rate

Python is a high-level language and is much faster when programming with this language than runtime with the other low-level languages.

• Cross-platform operating Ability

All major operating systems such as Microsoft Windows, Mac OS, Unix and Linus are capable of Python execution. This language provides the best experience to work with any OS.

Integration Capabilities

The following are Python's remarkable integration capabilities:

- The capacity for process control is powerful
- Capability to be integrated into the programming script language
- Easy web service development
- Helps implement many protocols for the Internet

If you are interested in working with Python, register for a Python Training Institute where the candidates benefit from the training.

WHY LEARN THE PYTHON PROGRAMMING LANGUAGE? 9 FEATURES OF PYTHON

Python is Guido van Rossum's programming language. It is a dynamically characterized language with very high data structures. It is used in several locations, including Google and Nasa.

Python features.

1. dynamically Typed.

Variables in the python programming language have no type. You don't have to say that

int x = 10

Rather, you'd write

x = ten

2. Data structures of a very high level.

Lists, dictionaries, and sets are built into data types that permit very high abstraction levels in a language such as a python.

3. Functional programming support.

Functions are first-class objects that can be used as any other variable. This provides functional programming with other functions such as map, filter, and reduce.

4. The programming of multiple paradigms.

Python supports several paradigms, such as object-oriented programming, functional programming, and iterative programming.

5. Quick prototyping.

High-level data structures and dynamic typing make the prototyping of a Python freeze quick

6. Included batteries.

Python believes in the philosophy of the included batteries. This means that many libraries have python programs written in python that are much shorter than in other languages.

7. Meaningful white spaces.

In the Python programming language, whitespaces are important. This makes code readable in Python very easily.

8. The number of keywords is limited.

There are very few keywords in the python language. This makes it easy for beginners to learn. The core of the language is very small and other modules provide features.

9. Spaces for names.

Python attempts to maintain as much namespace as possible.

ROLE OF PYTHON IN IMAGE APPLICATIONS

We will know in this section how Python plays a significant role in image applications. Python is a high-level programming language that enables you to work faster and integrate your systems more efficiently. Because of its simplicity, reliability, and simple interfacing, 90 % of people prefer Python over other technologies. This is often compared with Lisp, TCL, Perl, Ruby, C #, Visual Fox Pro, Scheme, or Java. It can be interfaced easily with C /Obj C/Java /

Fortran. It works on all key operating systems like Windows, Unix/ Linux, Mac, OS/2, Amiga, etc. Day by day, the growth of Python Development is rapid.

Python supports multiple paradigms and modules of programming. The Internet Communications Engine (ICE) and many other integration technologies are also supported by Python. It is packed with rich libraries and numerous add-ons for specific tasks. Python is a friendly language that you can easily learn. Python has been used in many businesses, government, NGOs, Google Search Engine, YouTube, NASA, New York Stock Exchange, etc. Python is being used as the scripting language, but also in a variety of non-script contexts. It provides an easy-to-read syntax. This language allows you to easily write programs. For most applications, the Python code works more than fast enough. It is used in a wide range of applications. Python is a great language for the orientation of objects.

Python applications are Applications

- Web apps (Django, pylons)
- Games(Eve Online-MMORPG).
- CAD / CAM 3D.
- Applications Image.
- Applications for science and education.
- Project Management Software Development (Trac).
- Databases of objects (ZODB / Durus).
- Network (Bittorent) Programming.
- Mobile apps.
- Audio / Video apps.
- Office application. Office application.
- Applications console.
- Company applications.
- Formats of files.

Internet applications. Internet applications.

• Image Application Python

Images always play a major role in reaching the public than words in the field of web apps. Because an image is a thousand words worth. Users can generally satisfy existing images, but some users want to create an image or change it. To meet their requirements, Python offers various programs. Let's see how Python used it in imagery.

• **Gnofract 4D** is a flexible fractal generation software that enables the user to create beautiful fractal images. The computer created the images automatically, including the Mandelbrot and Julia set and much more, based on mathematical principles. This does not mean you have to do mathematics to create the pictures. You can instead use your mouse to create more pictures according to your desire. It runs on Unix-based systems, such as Linux and FreeBSD, and can also be run on Mac OS X. The unlimited number of fractal capabilities and a wide range of options are very easy to use, very fast, and flexible. It is an open-source program that is used extensively.

• **Gogh** is a PyGTK-based image editor with support for tablets/devices with pressure sensitivity.

16

• ImgSeek is a content-based search photo collection manager and viewer. It has many characteristics. You simply design the image or you can use another image in your collection if you want to find a particular item. It gives you exactly what you need.

• **VPython** is the programming language of Python plus the "visual" module for 3D graphics. By using it, you can easily create 3D space objects and animations, etc. You can view the objects in a window. VPython enables programmers to focus more on their programs' computational aspects.

• **MayaVi's** a science-based Visualization Toolkit (VTK) program supports data volume visualization using texture and ray cast mappers. It's simple to use. It can be imported from other Python programs as a Python module and can also be written from the interpreter Python.

ENTER INTO THE PROGRAMMING WORLD WITH PYTHON TRAINING

The engineering curricula in India propose that colleges begin programming courses for students with C, followed by C++ and Java. This has led to the assumption that 'C' starts coding lessons for new coders. A simple metaphor would help you understand the difference between starting C and Python programming lessons. Learning C or C++ programming is like trying to drive by learning how to build, assemble, and then use a car.

You will eventually learn to drive, but too soon at the expense of unnecessary pressure and information. If you begin Python training, however, it would be like learning to drive automatically. You don't need to know how the engine works, how you can and can't assemble your car, and so on. The only thing you can do first is what you should do, i.e. programming. The technical aspects come later.

You can use Python to process anything that is stored on your computer, such as numbers, text, data, images, stats, etc. Its easy-to-use feature keeps programmers committed and excited as they learn Python. Its features like naming conventions, easy indentation, modularity, etc. have made it renowned. In NASA, Google, New York Stock Exchange, and the favorite YouTube Python, video-sharing website, is widely used. Not only in the big shots industry, but Python is also widely used even in enterprises, government, and non-governmental organizations.

The interpreted language is called Python. This means that the code written in Python is converted to computer-readable code during runtime of the program. First, Python was called the Scripting Language, which only suggested its use in trivial jobs. As time progressed, however, its user-friendly functions became the most common language used to write large programs. The four characteristics that have generated such high demand for Python training are:

High level Language: Python is a language of high level. It means it provides an abstraction level that allows you to concentrate on algorithms and code functionality. You do not have to worry about low-level data such as manual storage, etc. There is also a huge library of pre-coded features for nearly every requirement.

Dynamic: Python's main aspect of the language is its runtime. Features such as dynamic typing, easy introspection, and reflection all facilitate coding and reduce the programming time.

Expressive Syntax: Expressive syntax contains how easy and concisely you can express an idea. Python training enables you to write complex codes in just a few lines and keep them readable.

Readability: This is Python's key strength. Instead of curly braces, indentation helps to make the program easy to read and understand. Comprehensive code delimites the code blocks in a program. It is very important to write code or to understand it.

WHY STATISTICS AND PYTHON TO BECOME DATA SCIENTIST?

You can take the right courses to become a data scientist if you're into statistics and pythons. Data encompasses a large number of machines, including cars, robots, and smartphones, just to name a few. The amount of data produced by these units requires the use of specialized decision-making and analysis tools and procedures. Let's find out why statistics and python are important to learn to be a data scientist. Read on to learn more.

Python is becoming increasingly popular in schools, colleges, and universities as an important programming language. This language is agile with many libraries and other supporting materials such as game development and network automation. The good thing is that the Python eco-system has led many libraries to analyze the data. It is therefore part of the courses in data science.

The life cycle of data science: firstly, data science has a life cycle used to conduct analysis worldwide. The objective of the life cycle is to provide ways of developing and then testing hypotheses.

Python helps to conduct basic statistical analysis on a given data set. And these analyses could include hypothesis testing measurements, probability distribution, and central trend measurements.

Python also helps to learn more about output/input operations and variables using another sample program. Besides, the program shows how different variables and data types can be named. The good thing about this language is that it does not have any case declarations.

Although it is not used in data science, it is also presented with object-based design and analysis. This design and analysis aim to organize the programs around the modules in question.

For libraries, TensorFlow, Keras, sci-kit-learn, Scipy, and Numpy can be among the courses. These libraries create the database with Python's help.

You can check Data Science Central, which is a great platform, for more information. You can choose from many eBooks on this site to learn more about this topic. They also have a forum to help you participate in the discussions. This can improve your knowledge further. Apart from that, many YouTube channels are for the same purpose. You can look at them.

The good thing is that many libraries have sandboxes online. You can test the library features. You can follow the tutorials to begin coding. All you have to do is examine various Python modules to learn more. You can learn more about the passage of time.

That is why Python is so important in the field of data science. To be a data scientist, we suggest that you take the right courses to improve your skills in the field of Python

THE REASON BEHIND THE HUGE DEMAND OF PYTHON DEVELOPERS

Python was conceived in the early 1980s and introduced to the industry in the late 1980s. Because of the lack of proper marketing, for more than decades, it could not collect the notice of the industry. Moreover, it has some built-in problems with the core concept and it is an obstacle to its success. In the first 20th century, Google brought it out of dirt and modified it and its configurations. As a result, it has gained the power and performance it has within itself but secretly comes to the industry. Google changed the core language logic to make it lighter and smoother, and also removed all repeated modules and procedures from the library. Now, its performance has been increased twice or three times. This makes it one of the industry's most powerful languages. In the last decade, developers and technology experts have received tremendous popularity and have proven to be a gem in the IT industry.

Python developers could build powerful and efficient Web applications: a Python developer can develop enterprise standard high-performance software applications in various fields due to its huge power and efficiency. Python's tag line is "Batteries Included," all required modules, methods, and classes are available through different libraries inside the language. Well, the development process is much easier than before due to the presence of all these resources. Besides, these built-in resources are highly optimized and therefore can provide better miles for the Python developer. To add this, the resources are highly compatible with other language components, which makes them even powerful.

Python allows software developers to build modern applications across a variety of domains: Python is strongly inspired by C++ and Java and we can therefore expect many features similar to C++ or Java within python. In other words, a Python developer can create desktop software, web application, hardware program, or even smartphone gaming. Python can build any kind of application like Java. This is indeed an excellent feature of python and allows its developers not to limit their talent in any given field. You can develop any application regardless of the domain, device, and platform.

Trustworthiness and quality are paramount: Python is well known for its efficiency, speed, and reliability. Under every circumstance, you can project a Python application and achieve an incredible performance there. It is also very safe and safe. It has the potential to develop highly secure enterprise standards using 128-bit encryption technology. Besides, multi-tier security measures can also be implemented in your application.

Many support environments are available: there is much support in the IT industry. Fortunately, in the industry, there is a huge Python developer community. You can therefore get immediate online support during your difficulties.

CHAPTER TWO - THE PYTHON INTERPRETER

Byterun has been implemented in Python as a Python interpreter. I was surprised and pleased to discover through my work on Byterun that the fundamental structure of the Python interpreter easily fits into the 500-line size restriction. This chapter goes through the interpreter's structure and gives you sufficient context to explore it further. The aim is not to explain everything about interpreters, you could devote years to developing a deep understanding of this topic, like so many interesting areas of programming and computing.

Based on the work of Paul Swartz, Byterun has been written by others and Ned Batchelder. The structure of Byterun is similar to Python, CPython's primary implementation, so understanding of Byterun helps you understand interpreters in general and CPython in particular. Throughout its length, Byterun is able to operate the simplest of Python programs1. (This is probably CPython).

A Python Interpreter

let us just narrow down how much we mean by "the Python interpreter " before we begin. The word "interpreter" could be used on Python in a variety of ways. At times, the interactive prompt you get by typing python in the command line is the Python REPL. Sometimes people use the "Python interpreter" to talk about Python code executing from the beginning to the end. "Interpreter" has a narrower meaning in this chapter. It's the last step in the execution of a Python program.

Python takes three other steps before the interpreter takes over: lexing, parsing, and compiling. These steps together transform the software programmer's code from the text lines into structured code objects that can be understood by the interpreter. Taking these code objects and following the instructions is the job of the interpreter.

You might become surprised to hear which compiling is a step in Python code execution. In contrast to a "compiled" language like C or Rust, python is often known as a "interpreted" language like Ruby or Perl. However, the terminology is not as accurate as it might appear. Most languages, including Python, have to be compiled. The reason why the compilation step is called "interpreted" is that it works relatively less than in the compiled language (and the interpreter does relatively more). The compiler Python has much less information on the behavior of a program than a compiler C does, as we will see later in the chapter.

A Python Python interpreter

In Python, Byterun is a Python interpreter. This may strike you as strange, but it is no stranger than writing a C compiler in C. (Indeed, the commonly-used Gcc C compiler is written in C.) In almost any language you can write a Python interpreter.

Python's writing has both advantages and disadvantages. The main drawback is speed: code execution via Byterun is far slower than executing in CPython, where the interpreter is written in C and carefully optimized. But Byterun was originally designed as a learning exercise, so the speed is not important for us. The biggest advantage of using Python is that it is easier to implement only the interpreter, not the rest of the runtime of Python, especially the object system. For example, if Byterun needs to create a class, it can fall back to "real" Python. Another advantage is that Byterun is easily understood, partly because it is written in a highly proficient language (Python!), which is readable by many. (In Byterun, we also disregard interpreter optimization — again promoting simplicity and clarity over speed.)

Building an Interpreter

Before we begin to look at the Byterun code, we need a higher level context for the interpreter's structure. How does the interpreter Python work?

The Python interpreter is a virtual machine that emulates a physical computer. This particular virtual machine is a stack machine, manipulating several stacks (as opposed to a register machine that writes and reads from specific memory locations).

The Python translator is bytecode interpreter: This input is a bytecode instruction set. The parser, compiler, and lexer, generate code objects to operate on when you type Python. Each code object includes a set of instructions – the bytecode – and more information the interpreter needs. Bytecode is a Python code intermediate representation: it expresses the source code which your interpreter has written in such a way that it can understand. How assembling language acts as an intermediate representation between C code and a piece of hardware is analogous.

A Tiny Interpreter

Let's start with a very minimal interpreter to make this concrete. This interpreter can only add numbers, and only three instructions are available. All code can execute consists of these three instructions. The following are the three instructions:

- LOAD_VALUE
- ADD_TWO_VALUES
- PRINT_ANSWER

Since in this chapter we don't deal with the lexer, parser, and compiler, it does not matter how the set of instructions are created. You can imagine that you write 7 + 5 and have a compiler emit these three instructions together. Or, you can write a Lisp syntax that has turned into the same combination of instructions if you have a right compiler. The translator doesn't care. All that matters is that our interpreter has a well-formed instruction arrangement.

Real Python Bytecode

We're going to give up our toy instruction sets at this point and switch to real Python bytecode. The bytecode structure is similar to the verbose instructions of our toy interpreter except that it uses one byte to identify each instruction instead of a long name. To understand this structure, we are going through a short function bytecode.

Conditionals and Loops

To date, the interpreter just used the instructions one by one to execute code. This is a problem; we often have instructions that we want to execute or skip under certain circumstances. The interpreter must be able to jump around in the instruction set if we can write loops and statements within our code. In a sense, Python uses GOTO bytecodes to handle loops and conditionals! Look at the dismantling of the cond function.

Frames

We learned so far that the virtual Python machine is a stacking machine. It steps on and off a stack and jumps through instructions, push and shoot values. However, there are still a few gaps in our mental model. The last instruction in the above examples is RETURN VALUE, which matches the return declaration in the code. But where is the instruction coming back?

We must add a complexity layer to answer this question: the frame. A frame is an information and context collection for a chunk of code. Frames are created and destroyed on the fly while executing your Python code. Each function call has one frame — while each frame has a code object associated with it, a code object can have many frames. If you had a function, which was called recursively ten times, you would have 11 frames — one for each recursion level and one for the module from which you started. In general, in a Python program, there is a framework for each scope. Each module, function call, and class definition, for example, contains a frame.

Frames live on the call stack, a different stack than the one we have discussed so far. (The call stack is the most widely known stack you've already seen printed in the tracebacks of exceptions, each line in a traceback starting with "File 'program.py, line 10" corresponds with one frame in the call stack.) We're going to call the stack that we examined, the stack that the interpreter manipulates while running bytecode. The third stack is also called the block stack. For certain types of control flow, especially looping and exception handling, blocks are used. Each call stack frame has its data stack and block stack.

Let's give an example to make this concrete. Assume that the Python interpreter runs the line marked 3 below. In the middle of a call to foo, the interpreter is calling a bar. The diagram shows a schematic of the frame call stack, block stacks, and data stacks.

Byterun

The Python interpreter now has enough context to start examining Byterun.

In Byterun, there are four types of objects:

• A VirtualMachine class, that manages a highest level of structure, especially the Frames call stack, and which includes the mapping of operating instructions. This is a more complex version of the above object Interpreter.

• A-Class Frame. Each frame instance has one code object and manages some other required state bits, particularly local and global namespaces, a call frame reference, and the last byte code command executed.

• A function class that is used instead of real Python functions. Remember that calling a function creates a new interpreter framework. We use the function to control the creation of new frames.

• A Block class that wraps the three-block attributes. (The block details are not central, we will not spend much time on the Python interpreter, but they are included here so which Byterun could run real Python code.)

PYTHON VARIABLES

Variables are nothing but fixed storage places. This means that you reserve some room in the memory when creating a variable.

Depending on the variable data form, the interpreter assigns memory and determines what can be stored in the allocated memory. Therefore, you can store integers, decimals, or characters in these variables by assigning various data types to the variables.

Assigning variables values

Python variables do not require explicit memory space reservation declaration. The declaration automatically occurs when a value is assigned to a variable. To assign values to variables, the equal sign (=) is used.

The operand on the left is the variable name of the = operator and the operand on the right is the variable value.

Multiple assignments

Python allows you to simultaneously assign a single value to multiple variables.

Standard types of data

There can be several types of data stored in the brain. For instance, the age of a person is stored as a numerical value, and its address is stored as alphanumeric characters. Python has different basic data types used to describe the possible operations on them and the storage method for each.

Python Numbers

The numerical values are contained in numerical data forms. When you assign a value to them, numbers of objects are generated.

Python Strings

Python strings are marked in the quotation marks as a contiguous set of characters. Python makes either one or two quotes. String sub-sets can be taken from a slice] ([] and ([:])

operator, with indexes starting with 0 at the starting of the string and running from -1 to the end.

Sr. No.	Function & Description

The plus (+) sign is the concatenation string operator and the asterisk (*) is the repeater.

Python Lists

Lists are the most powerful compound data forms in Python. A list of things is used in square brackets, separated by commas ([ ]). Lists are to some degree identical to arrays in C. Several of the differences are that all objects in a list can be of various data types.

The slice operator ([ ] and [:]) are available to access the values stored in a tuple, with indexes starting with 0 at the start of the tuple and moving towards the end of -1. The plus (+) symbol is the list operator and the repeat operator is the asterisk (*).

Tuples of Python

A tuple is another type of sequence that is identical to the set. A tuple consists of multiple comma-separated values. However, as opposed to lists, tuples are in parenthesis.

– Lists are found in brackets ([ ]) and can be modified to their elements and size whereas tuples are placed in parentheses(( )) and cannot be revised. Tuples can be viewed as only read lists

Conversion of data type

Often conversions between built-in types are required. You simply use the type-names as a tool to differentiate between types.

There are multiple interconnected functions to migrate from one data type to another. These functions return a new object that displays the value transformed.

1.	int(x [,base]) Conversion of x to an integer. The base specifies the foundation if x is a string.	
2	float(x) Converts x to a number of floating points.	
3	complex(real [,imag]) Creates a complex number.	

25

4	**str(x)** Converts object x to the representation of a string.	
5.	**repr(x)** Converts object x to a string expression.	
6.	**eval(str)** Returns a string and checks a string.	
7.	**tuple(s)** Convert s into a tuple.	
8.	**list(s)** Converts s into a list.	
9.	**set(s)** Converts s into a set.	
10.	**dict(d)** It's creating a dictionary. d must be a sequence of tuples (key, value).	
11.	**Frozenset(s)** Converts s into a frozen set.	
12.	**chr(x)** Converts an integer into a character.	
13.	**Unichr(x)** Converting of the integer to Unicode character.	
14.	**Ord(x)** Converts single character into its integer value.	
15.	**hex(x)** Converts an integer into a hexadecimal string.	
16.	**Oct(x)** Converts an integer into an octal string.	

Even though you thought you know that a large amount about variables and data types, we would suggest you read this chapter since you have lower-level languages programmed such as C, C++, or other similar languages. In some respects, Python data types and variables differ from other programming languages. There are integer numbers, floating dot numbers, strings, and more, but things don't match C or C++. If you want to use C lists, for example, you must construct the data type list from scratch, i.e. the memory structure of the design and management of the assignment. You will also need to implement the required search and access methods. Python provides power data types such as lists as an authentic language part.

As the name implies, a variable can be altered. A variable is a way to refer to a computer program's memory location. For this physical location, a variable is a symbolic name. This location of the memory contains values such as numbers, text, or more difficult types.

A container (or some say pigeonhole) to store certain values may be seen as a variable. During running, variables are accessed and changed sometimes, i.e. the variable is assigned a new value.

The way Python works with types is one of the main differences between strongly-type languages such as C, C++, or Java. Each variable must have a single data type in strongly typed languages. E.g., if a variable is an integer type, only the whole variable can be saved. Each variable must be declared in Java or C before it can be used. Declaration of a variable means that it is linked to the type of data.

In Python, the declaration of variables is not required. If a variable is needed, you think about a name and start to use it as a variable.

Another noteworthy aspect of Python: not only can a variable change its value during the execution of the program but the type too.

PYTHON OPERATOR – TYPES OF OPERATORS IN PYTHON

Python Operator – Target

In this Python Operator tutorial, we explore what a programming language operator is in Python. On the other hand, with their syntax and examples, we can learn various types of Python operators: Arithmetic, Bitwise, Assignment, Relational, Membership, Logic, and Identity.

The operator of Python is a symbol performing an operation on one or more operands. An operand is a vector or a value on which the procedure is performed.

Before beginning with python operators, let's update Python's basics.

So, let's begin the tutorial for Python Operator.

Python Operator Introduction

Python Operator is divided into seven categories:

- Python Relational Operator
- Python Arithmetic Operator

- Python Logical Operator
- Python Operator Assignment
- Python Identity Operator
- Python Operator Membership
- Python Bitwise Operator

Python Arithmetic Operator

These Python operators include Python operators for fundamental mathematical operations.

- Addition (+)
- Subtraction (-)
- Multiplication (*)
- Division (/)
- Floor Division (//)
- Modulus (%)
- Exponentiation (**)

a. (+)

Adds the operator values on either side.

b. Subtraction (-)

Subtracts the right value from the left value.

c. Multiplication (*)

Multiplies the operator's values on each side.

d. division (/)

Divide the value to the left by the value to the right. Notice that division leads to a floating-point value.

e. Exponentiation (* *)

Enhances the first number to the second's value.

f. Floor Division (/)

Divides and returns the quotient integer value. After the decimal, it dumps the numbers.

g. Modulus(%)

Divides and returns the remaining amount.

Relational Operator of Python

Let's see the Relational Operator of Python.

- Less than (<)
- Equal to (= =)
- Greater than (>)
- Greater than or equal to (>=)
- Less than or equal to (<=)
- Not equal to(!=)

The Python Relational Operator compares the operands. You tell us whether an operand is bigger, smaller, equivalent, or a mixture of those.

a. less than (<)

This operator tests if the value to the left of the operator is less than the value to the right.

b. Greater than (>)

It checks whether the operator's value on the left is higher than that on the right.

c. Less than or equal to (<=)

It tests whether the value at the left of the operator is lower or equal to the value at the right.

d. Greater than or equal to(>=)

It tests if the value on the left of the operator is higher or equal to the value on the right.

e. Equal to(==)

This operator tests if the value on the left is equal to the value on the right. 1 is the boolean True value, but 2 is not. 0 is identical to Wrong, too.

f. Not equal to(!=)

It verifies if the value on the left side of the operator is not the same as on the right side. The Python operator < > does the same role, but in Python 3 it was abandoned.

If a relative operator's requirement is met, it returns Valid. It returns False otherwise. This return value may be used in an additional statement or expression.

Python Assignment Operator

- Assign (=)
- Add and Assign (+=)
- Subtract and Assign (-=)
- Divide and Assign (/=)
- Multiply and Assign (*=)
- Modulus and Assign (%=)
- Exponent and Assign (**=)
- Floor -Divide and Assign(//=)

Assignment Python Operator explained –

A job operator assigns a variable value. The value may be influenced by a factor until it is allocated. We have eight assignment operators-a simple and seven for seven operators with arithmetic pythons.

a. Assign(=)

Attributes a value to the left expression. Note that for contrast = = is used, but = is used for assignment.

b. Add and assign(+=)

Adds the values on both sides and assigns them to the left expression. A+=10 is equivalent to a = a+10.

The same applies to all the next job operators.

c. Subtract and assign(-=)

Subtracts the right value from the left value. It then assigns it to the left word.

d. Divide and Assign(/=)

Divide the value to the left with the value to the right. It then assigns it to the left word.

e. Multiply and assign(*=)

Multiplies on both sides the qualities. It then assigns it to the left word.

f. Modulus and Assign(%=)

Performs modulus on both sides of the values. It then assigns it to the left word.

g.Exponent and Assign (**=)

Exponentiates the ideals on both sides. Then it is transferred to the left expression.

h. Floor divide and assigning(//=)

Performs floor division on both sides of the principles. Then it is transferred to the left expression.

Python Logical Operator

These variations can be used to combine more than one condition. We have three logical Python operators – and or not python operators.

- and
- not
- or

a. and

If both sides of the operator have conditions, then the whole expression is valid.

b. or

The expression is false only if the operator's two statements are false. If not, it's real.

c. not

This inverts an expression's boolean value. It transforms Real into False and False into Reality. The boolean value is Incorrect, as you can see below. So, it doesn't reverse it to True.

Python Operator Membership

These operators evaluate whether a value is part of a sequence. A list, a string, or a tuple may be the sequence. We have two representatives - 'in' and 'not in' - python operators.

a. in

This checks whether a value is part of a sequence. In our example, the 'fox' string is not included in the list of pets. But the string 'cat' is part of it, so it's real. The string 'me' is also a substring of the string 'deception.' That's why it's back real.

b. not

Contrary to 'in,' 'not in' determines when a value is not a part of a sequence.

Python Identity Operator

Let us proceed to Python Operator identity.

These operators test whether both operators share an identity. We've got two identity operators - 'is' and 'is not.'

a. is

If two operands have the same name, True will be returned. It returns False otherwise. Here, 2 isn't the same as 20, but False comes back. '2' and '2' are the same, too. The gap in quotations does not differentiate them. So, it's Real back.

b. is not

2 is a number, and the string is '2.' Yeah, it's a reality to that.

Bitwise operator Python

- Binary AND(&)
- Binary One's Complement(~)
- Binary OR()
- Binary Left-Shift(<<)
- Binary XOR(^)
- Binary Right-Shift(>>)

Let's now look at the Python Operator from Bitwise.

a. Binary AND (&)

It performs AND the two values bit by bit.

b. Binary OR(|)

It operates on the two values bit by bit OR.

c. Binary XOR(^)

It executes the two values bit by bit XOR (exclusive-OR).

d. Binary One Complement (~)

It returns the one complement of a binary number. It transforms the pieces.

e. Binary Left-Shift (< <)

The value of the left operand transfers the number of places to the left defined by the right operand.

f. Binary Right-Shift (> >)

The value of the left operand transfers the number of places to the right of the operand.

Conclusion – User of Python

Finally, we examined seven different Python operator classes in this tutorial. We did it in the Python Shell(IDLE) to find out how it operates. We may use this operator further under conditions and combine them. Go ahead and do some combinations.

Hope you like DataFlair's Python Operator tutorial.

PYTHON DATA TYPES

Enabled Data Types

Data type is an essential topic in programming.

Data of different types can be protected by variables and various varieties can do different things.

In these groups, Python does have the following data types developed-in by default:

Type of text: str

Types of numeric: int, float, complex.

Type of sequence: tuple, list, range

Type of mapping: dict

Set Types: Frozenset, set

Boolean Type: Bool

Type of Binary: Bytearray, bytes, memory view

Though for Python variables we don't have to declare a type, a value does have a type. For the translator, this knowledge is important. The following Python data types are provided by Python.

1. Numbers of Python

Four numerical Python data types are available.

1). int

Int represents an integer. This form of Python data contains a signed integer. We may use the type) (function to find the class to which it belongs.

2. float

This Python Data Form includes true floating points.

3. long

This form of Python data has an infinite long integer. But in Python 3.x, this build does not exist.

4. Complex

This type of Python data contains a complex number. This is a complex number: a+bj Here, a and b are the real parts, and j is imaginary.

PYTHON STRING FORMATTING

Remember Python's Zen and how "an obvious way in Python to do something?" If you know that there are four main ways to format strings in Python, you might scratch your head.

In this tutorial, you Learn a four main ways and their powers and limitations to string formatting in Python. You will also have a clear thumb rule for choosing the best-standardized string formatting method in your programs.

Let's just hop in because we have a lot to cover. Let's assume that you have the following variables (or constants) to have a simple experimental toy example.

We address the Python string and its examples. Besides, we can learn how the string is declared in a python and divided into the functions of the Python String and Python String. Finally, in Python, we cover escape sequences. As we have seen before, you don't have to consider the type of data when defining a string.

So, let's begin the Tutorial on Python String.

2. What is the Python string?

A Python string is a character set. There is a built-in class 'str' for Python string handling. This can be illustrated by the type) (feature.

3. SHow to declare the Python String?

You can use single or double quotes to declare a Python string.

You can not, however, use a single quote to start a string and a double quote, and vice versa.

4. How can I use quotes in the Python string?

Since we describe strings with quotes, you have to look after certain stuff while using them inside a string.

If double-quotes are needed in a string of Python, define the string with single quotes.

5. A string of cross lines

You can use three quotes if you want to extend a Python string over several lines.

6. How to access the Python string?

A string is unchanging; it can not be modified.

a. Displaying a single character

Put its index in square brackets to show a single character of a string. Indexing starts at 0.

b. Slice a string

Often you only want a section of a string to be shown. Using the slicing operator] [to do this.

7. Concatenation of Python string

Concatenation is a mixture of objects. Using the concatenation operator +, Python strings can join.

8. Formatting Python String

You will want to print variables with a string often. Either you can use commas, or you can use string formatting for it.

i. F-strings

The letter 'f' is preceding the string, and the variables are indicated in curly braces.

ii.   format () Method

The format) (method can be used to do the same. It follows the string and has the variables as comma-separated arguments. Using curly braces in the string to position the variables. You can either put 0,1, within the curly braces. Or variables. Or variables. You must allocate values to them in the format process when you do the above.

1 "Old Style" String Formatting (%Operator)

Strings in Python have a unique built-in process that the percent operator can control. This lets you do basic positional formatting very quickly. You can know how it functions instantly if you have ever worked with a printf-style feature in C.

This makes it easier to maintain and modify your format strings in the future. You don't need to make sure that the command you pass in the values matches the order in which the values are referenced in the format string. The downside is, of course, that this strategy requires a little more typing.

I'm sure that you wondered why this formatting in printf-style is called string formatting "old style." It was theoretically replaced by "modern style" formatting in Python 3, about which we will talk next.

2 "New Style" String Formatting (str.format)

Python 3 has been tried to introduce a new way of formatting strings that were also restored to Python 2.7 later. This new style string formatting eliminates the special syntax of the percent operator and makes the string formatting syntax more natural.

c. % Operator

The percent operator is where the variables are put in a series. For set, percent s is. The string is accompanied by the operator and parenthesis variables.

9. Python Escape Sequences

You may want to put a tab, a line feed, or other stuff into a Python string. Sequences of escape allow us to do this. An escape sequence is a backslash with a character, which depends on what you want to do. Python supports the sequences below.

10. Python String Functions

Python offers us a variety of functions that we can use for string or object formation.

a. len()

The len) (function returns the string length.

b. str()

This function transforms any form of data into a string.

c. upper) (and lower)

These methods return the string in case and case. In case.

d. strip()

It excludes whitespaces from the string start and end.

e. Isdigit ()

Returns True if all string characters are numbers.

f. Isalpha ()

Returns valid if all characters in a series are alphabet characters.

g. isspace()

Returns true if all characters are spaces in a string.

h. Startwith()

It takes a string as an argument and returns True as the string on which the string is applied starts in the argument.

i. Endwith()

It takes a string as an argument and returns True if the string to be added at the ends of the argument is the string.

j. find ()

It needs an argument and looks for it in the string it is applied to. It then returns the substring index.

k. Replace ()

Two reasons are required. The first is to replace the substring. The second is to fix the substring.

l. Split) ()

It needs one argument. The string is then divided around each argument in the string.

m. Join) ()

It takes a list as an argument and combines the elements of the list with the string to which it is applied.

11. Python Operations String

a. Comparison:

Using relational operators, Python Strings can compare.

b. Arithmetic

Strings can be used for certain arithmetic operations.

c. Membership

Python's membership operators can be used to verify if a string is a substring.

d. Identification

The 'is' and 'is not' identity operators of Python can be used for strings.

e. Logical

Pythons can be added and, or not operators, too. An empty string has a False boolean value.

12. A string of Python

We learned about Python string with string functions and operators and how to define and navigate it in this Python string tutorial. Then we heard about concatenation of the python string and python formatters. We have also heard about the features of Python strings. Finally, we looked at operations on strings that we could conduct. Hope you enjoyed the lesson today. Leave your input on Python strings in the comments.

CHAPTER THREE- COMMON PYTHON DATA STRUCTURES (GUIDE)

Data structures are the fundamental frameworks around which the programs are designed. A specific method of organizing data is given by each data structure so that it can be accessed effectively, depending on the case of usage. Python ships in its standard library with a wide range of data structures.

However, the name convention of Python does not provide the same clarification as in other languages. A list is not just a list in Java – it's either a LinkedList or an ArrayList. In Python, not so. Often even seasoned Python developers wonder whether the built-in list form is implemented as a linked list or dynamic array.

You will learn in this guide:

- Can **abstract types of data** are incorporated into the Python standard library

- How Python's most popular abstract data types map

- How to use abstract data types of different algorithms of practice

Dictionaries, Hash Tables and Maps

Dictionaries (or short **dicts**) are a core data structure in Python. Dicts store an arbitrary number of objects, each of which has a single dictionary key.

Dictionaries are often sometimes referred to as **maps, hashmaps, search tables, or related lists**. You can search, insert, and uninstall any object associated with a certain key efficiently.

Phone books make a good analog to dictionary artifacts in the real world. You can quickly get the details (telephone number) associated with a particular key (name of a person). You can leap more or less directly to a name and look up the related detail, instead of trying to scan the phone book front back to find someone's number.

This analogy starts to break down a little in terms of arranging the information to allow quick searches. But the basic characteristics of success remain. Dictionaries help you to find the information related to a specific key easily.

Dictionaries are one of computer science's most significant and widely used data structures. How is Python dealing with dictionaries, then? Take a tour of the dictionary implementations in the Python standard library and heart.

Dict: Go-to Dictionary

Since dictionaries were so essential, Python has robust implementation of dictionary that is embedded straightforwardly as in core language: the form of a dictionary.

Python also contains some useful syntactic sugar for your application dictionaries. For example, the curly-brace}) ({dictionary expression syntax and dictionary comprehensions allow you to set new dictionary objects conveniently.

There are also limits on the use of objects as legitimate keys.

The dictionaries of Python are indexed by keys of any hazardous kind. A hashable object has a value that never changes during a lifetime, (see hash)which can be compared to other objects (see eq). This value can be compared to other objects. Hashable objects which match must have the same hash value.

Immutable types such as strings and numbers can be hashed, and dictionary keys can operate. Tuple objects may also be used as soon as they include only hashable types, dictionary keys.

In most instances, the built-in dictionary implementation of Python can do whatever you need. Dictionaries are highly structured and many parts of the vocabulary are underlying. For instance, the class attributes as well as variables are all stored in a stack framein dictionaries internally.

Python Dictionaries were based on a well-tested and sophisticated implementation of a table that provides the desired performance characteristics: $O(1)$ time complexity for scanning, adding, updating, and deleting operations in the average case.

There is no excuse not to use Python's basic dict program. However, there are different dictionary implementations for third parties such as skip lists or dictionaries based on the B-tree.

In addition to basic dictionary objects, the standard library of Python also contains a variety of specialized dictionary implementations. All these specialized dictionaries are based on the integrated dictionary class (and share its output characteristics).

Let's look at them.

collections.OrderedDict: Recall the Keys Insertion Order

Python contains a specialized dict subclass that recalls the order of key insertions added: collections. OrderedDict.

Although standard dictionaries maintain the order for the insertion of keys in CPython 3.6 and above, the CPython implementation was a side effect but was not specified in the spec until Python 3.7. If it is necessary to work with your algorithm, then it is best to communicate this by using OrderedDict explicitly:

Until Python 3.8, you couldn't iterate reversed) (through dictionary objects. Only OrderedDict instances offered this feature. Dict and OrderedDict objects are still not the same in Python 3.8. OrderedDict cases include a.move to end) (method that can not be used on a single dict instance and a .popitem) (method that is more flexible than that of a single dict instance.

Collections.defaultdict: Missing Keys default return values

The standard dictionary class is another class of dictionaries that accepts a callable in its builder, the return value of which is used if the key is not found.

This can save you some typing and explain your intentions concerning getting() or catching a KeyError exemption in standard dictionaries:

Collections.ChainMap: Single Mapping Multiple Dictionaries Quest

The data structure collections. ChainMap group several dictionaries into a single mapping. Lookups look up the mappings one by one until a key is found. Inserts, updates, and deletions affect the first chain mapping only:

Types.mappingProxyType: *A read-only dictionary wrapper*

MappingProxyType is a wrapper that provides a read-only view of the data in the wrapped dictionary. This class has been added to Python 3.3 and can be used to create immutable dictionary proxy versions.

MappingProxyType can be helpful if, for example, a dictionary with an internal state from a class or module will be returned while discouraging written access to the object. Using MappingProxyType you can implement these limitations without creating a complete copy of the dictionary first:

Python dictionaries: summary

All the implementation of the Python dictionary mentioned in this tutorial is valid implementations built into the Python standard library.

If you want a general recommendation on the mapping type to use in your programs, then I will point you to the built-in dict data type. It is a robust and streamlined implementation of the hash table that is integrated into the central language directly.

If you have specific requirements that go beyond dictation, I would suggest using one of the other data types listed here only.

All implementations were valid options, but if they most of the time depend on standard Python dictionaries the code is simpler and easier to maintain.

ARRAY DATA STRUCTURES

An array is a simple data structure used in most programming languages and has a broad variety of applications across various algorithms.

In this section, you'll look at Python array implementations that only use the core language features or features included in the Python Standard Library. You can see each approach's strengths and weaknesses to assess which implementation is correct for your situation.

But first, let's cover some of the basics before we move in. How do arrays work, and what is their purpose? Arrays consist of fixed data records which allow the efficient positioning of each element based on its index:

Since arrays store data in neighboring memory blocks, the data structures (in contrast to linked data structures such as linked lists, for example) are called neighboring.

A parking lot is a real-world example of an array of data structures. The car park as a whole can be perceived and regarded as a single object; however, there are car parks within the lot indexed by a unique number. Parking lots are vehicle containers — each car park can be either empty or have a car, motorcycle, or other vehicle parked there.

However, not every parking lot is the same. Some parking lots can only be open to one vehicle category. For example, a car park does not allow bikes to be parked in the car park. A small parking lot refers to the a typed data array structure which only allows elements of a certain type of data.

Performance-wise, looking up an element in an array with the index of the element is very simple. A proper array implementation ensures that this case has constant O(1) access time.

In its standard library, Python contains many data structures- like Array each with slightly characteristics differently Let's take a look.

List: *Dynamic Mutable Arrays*

Lists are part of the central language of Python. Despite its name, Python's lists are implemented behind the scenes as dynamic arrays.

This means that a list allows adding or deleting elements and that list automatically modifies the backup store that stores those elements by allocating or freeing the memory.

Python lists can contain arbitrary elements — everything in Python is an entity, including functions. Therefore, you can mix, match, and store various types of data in one file.

This can be a powerful function, but the downside is that many data types are supported at the same time, which typically means less tightly packed data. The entire structure, therefore, takes up more space:

Tuple: *Immutable containers*

Tuples are, like lists, part of the core Python vocabulary. Yet Python's tuple objects are eternal, as opposed to lists. This means that elements can not be dynamically added or removed — all elements in a tuple must be specified when they are formed.

Tuples are another data structure that can contain arbitrary data type elements. With this versatility, it's strong, but again, it means that data are less tightly packed than in a typed array:

Array.array: Basic *Simple array typing*

Python's array module stores simple C-style data types space-effectively, such as floating-point numbers, 32-bit integers, bytes, etc.

Arrays generated with the array.array are mutable and identical to lists except for one important difference: arrays that are limited to a single data type are typed.

Due to this restriction, array. array objects are more efficient in space than lists and tuples with many elements. The elements contained therein are tightly wrapped, and this can be helpful if several elements of the same kind need to be contained.

Additionally, arrays support many of the same methods as standard lists and can be used as a drop-in substitute without any modifications to the application code.

Str: Unicode Character of Immutable Arrays

Str objects is used by Python 3.x to store textual data as unchanging Unicode character sequences. Str is an infinite sequence of characters. It is also a recursive data structure, the string character itself is a string object of length 1.

String objects are space-efficient since they are packed tightly and specialize in one data form. You can use a string if you store Unicode text.

Since strings in Python are unchangeable, modifying a string requires a new copy. The closest equivalent of a mutable string is to store single characters in a list

Bytes: Immutable Arrays single-byte arrays

Bytes objects are immutable single-byte sequences or integral objects in the field 0 to x x to 255. Conceptually, bytes objects are similar to str objects and can also be considered as immutable byte arrays.

Like strings, bytes have their logical syntax and they're effective in space. bytes objects seem to be immutable, but unlike strings, the bytearray type a dedicated mutable byte array will unpack into is:

Bytearray: *Mutable Single-Byte Arrays*

The bytearray sort is a mutable integer sequence ranging from 0 to x to 255. The bytearray object is similarly similar to the byte object, the key distinction of which is that you can freely alter a bytearray, overwrite elements, delete existing elements, or add new ones. The bytearray object increases and decreases accordingly.

A bytearray can be translated back into immovable bytes, but the data stored must be copied in full – a slow operation that takes O(n) time:

Python Arrays: *Summary*

You can use a variety of built-in data structures when implementing arrays in Python. You have concentrated in this section on central language features and data structures in the standard library.

If you're prepared to go further than the Python standard library, third-party packages such as NumPy and Pandas provide a variety of fast-paced implementations for computational computing and data science.

If you want to confine yourself to Python's array data structures, here are a few instructions:

- If you need to store arbitrary objects with mixed data types, use a list or a tuple, whichever you want an immutable data structure.
- If numeric (integer or floating-point) data are necessary and tight packaging and performance are key, try array.array.
- If you have unicode textual info, then use the built-in str of Python. If you might need a mutable data structure of string like, use a character list.
- When you choose to store the contiguous byte block, use the form of bytes or bytearray if you need the data structure to be changed.

I like to start with a simple list in most cases. Only if output or storage space becomes a concern can I specialize later. Using a general array of data structure like lists, you usually get the fastest creation speed and the most ease for programming.

In the beginning, I realized that this is always far more relevant than trying to pull out every last output right from the beginning.

STRUCTS, RECORDS, AND Data Transfer Objects#

List data structures have a fixed number of fields compared to arrays. -- field can have a name and a different form.

In this section, you can find out how records, structures, and plain old data objects in Python can be implemented in the standard library using only built-in data types and classes.

Python provides many types of data you can use for the implementation of documents, structures, and objects for data transfer. In this section, each implementation and its specific features will be examined quickly. Finally, you will find a summary and decision-making guide to help you make a selection of your own.

Dict: *Data Objects Simple*

As previously stated, the Python dictionaries store an infinite number of objects, each of which has a single key. Dictionaries are often referred to as associative, or maps arrays so that any object that associate with a given key can be looked at inserted at removed efficiently.

It is possible to use dictionaries as a record data form or data object in Python. Dictionaries are easy to create in Python because they are dictionary literals that have their syntactic sugar built into the language. The dictionary syntax is brief and easy to read.

Data objects generated using dictionaries are mutable and security from mispelling field names is poor as fields can always be added and deleted freely. Both of these properties can introduce unexpected bugs and a balance between convenience and fault resilience is often necessary:

Tuple: *Immutable Object Groups #*

Tuples of Python are a basic arbitrary object grouping data structure. Tuples were immutable — they cannot be changed once formed.

Performance- Specific, tuples take up much less memory than lists in CPython and are quicker to construct.

As you can see in the disassembly bytecode below, building a tuple constant takes one LOAD CONST opcode while building a list object with the same contents requires several additional operations:

However, these variations should not be stressed too much. In practice, the difference in performance sometimes becomes meaningless, and the effort to pull additional output out of a program by converting lists to tuples is possibly the wrong approach.

A possible drawback of single tuples is that the data you store in them can only be retrieved through integer indexes. You can not assign names to certain properties that are stored in a tuple. This can affect the readability of code.

A tuple is often an ad hoc structure: two tuples have the same number of fields and the same properties stored in them, which are difficult to guarantee.

This facilitates the introduction of float-of-the-mind niggles like field order mixing. I would also recommend which you hold as little as possible the amount of fields contained in a tuple:

Write a customized class: more effort, more tracking

Classes allow you to set reusable data object designs to ensure that each object provides the same set of fields.

It is possible to use standard Python classes as log data types, but it also requires manual work to obtain the flexibility of other implementations. The addition of new fields to the constructor init is verbose and takes time, for example.

Furthermore, the default string representation is not helpful for artifacts from custom classes. You will have to use your repr system to fix this, which is sometimes very verbose, and which needs to be modified anytime you add a new area.

class fields are mutable as well as new fields are created that you may or may not like can be added freely. More access control and reading fields can be generated using the @property decorator, but again, more glue code is needed.

Writing a customized class is an excellent choice if you want to apply business logic and actions to your record objects using methods. This implies, however, that these objects are no longer simply data objects:

Dataclasses.dataclass: *data classes + Python 3.7*

Data classes in Python 3.7 and above are open. They offer an excellent alternative to scratch your own data storage courses.

If you write a data class rather than a simple Python package, you will obtain a few useful features from the box that will save you some typing and manual execution:

- The instance variables specification syntax is shorter since the. init) (the form is not to be enforced.
- Data class instances automatically obtain a nice-looking string representation through the automatically created. repr) (process.
- Instance variables allow annotations that auto-document your data class to a degree. Please be aware that annotations of type are only hints that are not applied without a separate tool for style checks.

Usually, data classes are generated using the @dataclass decorator, as seen in the following code example:

Collections.namedtuple: *Data Objects Convenient*

In Python 2.6 +, the called double class offers an extension of the built-in tuple data form.

Similar to the custom class, *Namedtuple* enables you to set reusable designs and make sure the right field names are used with your information.

Namedtuple objects, like normal tuples, are immutable. This means that after the *Namedtuple* instance is formed, you can not add new fields or alter the existing fields.

Besides, there are *Namedtuple* artifacts, well. Called tuples. Called tuples. Could object stored in it can be accessed through a single identifier. This saves you from recalling integer indexes or using workarounds like identifying integer constants as index mnemonics.

Namedtuple objects are built internally as standard Python classes. In memory usage, they were often better than ordinary classes and as effective memory as normal duplicates:

Namedtuple objects can be an easy way to clean up and make code more readable by enhancing the data structure.

I find that moving from ad hoc data types like fixed format dictionaries to named objects allows me to more clearly express my code's intent. Mostly, I find a better solution to the dilemma I face when I implement this refactoring.

Using named multiple objects through normal (unstructured) duplicates and dictation can also make your colleagues' lives easier by at least somewhat making the data that are passed on self-documentary:

Type.NamedTuple: Enhanced Namedtuples

Typing. NamedTuple is the younger sibling from the namedtuple class in the module sets, introduced in Python 3.6. The key difference is an improved syntax for defining new record types and added support for types of hints. It is very similar to nametuples.

Please be aware that notations of type are not implemented without a separate type-checking method such as mypy. However, even without tool help, they can give useful advice (or be frustrating when the tips get out of date) for other programmers:

Struct.Struct: *Structures Serialized C*

The struct. Struct class translates objects from Python values to serialized C structs to Python bytes. It can be used, for example, to manage binary data saved in files or from network links.

Structures are defined in a small format string language that allows you to define the arrangement of different C data types such as char, int, and long as their unsigned variants.

Serialized structures are rarely used to represent strictly Python code data objects. They are intended mainly as a format for data sharing rather than as a way to retain data in memory that is used by Python code only.

In certain instances, basic data may be packed into systems using less memory than other data types. In most cases, though, this would be an advanced (and potentially unnecessary) optimization:

types.SimpleNamespace *Fancy Access Attribute Types.*

Here's another slightly obscure option for implementing Python data objects: types. SimpleNamespace. This class has been added to Python 3.3 and gives access to its namespace attributes.

This means that instances with SimpleNamespace display all their keys as class attributes. Instead of a square bracket indexing syntax used by regular dicts, you can use the obj.key and dotted attribute access. All instances include by default a meaningful __repr__

As its name says, SimpleNamespace is straightforward! It is essentially a dictionary that allows easy access to and prints of attributes. Add, modify, and delete attributes freely:

Python records, structs and Data objects: summary

As you have seen, many different options are available for implementing records or data objects. Which type will you use in Python for data objects? Generally, your decision would then depend on your use case:

- If just a few fields are available, then it might be all right to use a simple tuple object if the field order is easy to remember or the field names are unnecessary. Think of a point (x, y, z) in three-dimensional space, for example.
- When you need immutable fields, plain tuples,namedtuple collections, and. namedtuple typing are all good options.
- If you must lock field names to avoid typos, collections.namedtuple and. namedtuple are friends for you.
- If you want things to be simple, a simple dictionary object could be a good choice because of the convenient syntax, which closely resembles JSON.
- If your data structure needs full control then it is opportunity to write the custom @property setters as well as getters class.
- You should then write custom class from scratch, or expand collections.namedtuple or type. namedtuple if you need the adding behavior (methods) to the object.

• If you need to tightly pack data to serialize or send it over the network, it is time to read on struct.struct, as this is a great example of how it works!

If you're looking for a safe default choice, I recommend using collections.namedtuple in its younger sibling and Python 2.x, typing NamedTuple in Python, to implement the plain record, struct, or data object in Python.

This section presents how to use built-in data types and classes from the standard library to implement mutable and immutable database and multi-set (bag) data structures in Python.

A set is an unordered object collection that does not allow duplicate elements. Sets are usually used to quickly test a member value in the set, insert or delete new values in the set, and calculate the synchronization or cross-section of two sets.

In a correct set-up, membership tests should run quickly in O(1) time. On average, O(n) time should take Union, intersection, difference, and sub-set operations. These performance features are followed by the set implementations in the Python standard library.

Sets receive special treatment in Python just like dictionaries and have a few syntactic sugars that make them easy to create. For instance, the curly brace setting expression syntax and setting understandings allow you to define new set cases conveniently:

But be careful: you must call the set) (constructor to create an empty set. It's ambiguous to use empty curly-braces}) ({and instead creates an empty dictionary.

Python provides several set implementations with its standard library. Let's look at them.

Set: Your Go-To Set

The set type is the built-in Python set execution. It is mutable and allows elements to be dynamically inserted and deleted.

The sets of Python are supported by the dict data type and have the same performance properties. Any hazardous object can be saved in a set:

frozenset: Sets unchanged

The frozenset class implements an unchanging version of the set which can not be changed after it has been built.

frozenset objects are static and allow query operations, not inserts or deletions only on their elements. Because objects from frozenset are static and hashable, they can also be used as dictionary keys or as components of another set.

Multi-sets collections. Counter:

In the Python standard library, Collections. Counter class implements a multiset, or bag, type that allows elements in the set to occur in many ways.

This is useful for tracking not only if an element is part of a set, but also how often this is included in the set:

One precaution for Counter class is that when counting the number of components for a Counter object, you want to be careful. Calling len) (returns the number of single items in the multiset and with sum) (you can find the total number of elements:

Python Sets and Multisets: Summary

Sets are another valuable and commonly used Python and its standard library data structures. Some guidelines for deciding which one to use are as follows:

- Use the built-in set type if you need a mutable set.
- If you need hazardous objects to use as a dictionary or set keys, you should use a frozenset.
- Use collections.counter when you need a multiset or bag, data structure.

Stacks (LIFO) Stacks

A stack is a collection of objects supporting fast last-in / first-out semantics (LIFO) for inserts and deletes. In contrast to lists or arrays, stacks do not normally allow random access to the objects they contain. Insert and delete operations are often referred to as push and pop.

A useful real-world analogy is a stack of plates for a stack data structure. New plates are added to the top of the stack and only the top of the plate can be moved since the plates are precious and heavy. In other words, the first (LIFO) plate on the stack must be removed. The top plates must be removed one by one to reach the plates that are lower down in the stack.

Performance is expected to take O(1) time to insert and delete operations to properly implement the stack.

Stacks have a wide variety of algorithm applications. They are used, for example, in runtime memory management and language parsing, based on a call stack. A short and beautiful stacked algorithm is the first depth search (DFS) of graph data, or a tree, structure.

Python ships with various stack implementations with slightly different features. Let's take a look at them and compare their characteristics.

List: *Built-in Stacks, Simple*

The built-in list form of Python allows a good stack data structure, as it supports O(1) time-amortized O push and pop operations.

Python's lists are implemented internally as dynamic arrays, which means that they often need to change the storage space for the elements contained in them while adding or removing them. The list over-allocates its backup so that not every push or pop needs to be resized. As a result, for these operations, you get an amortized O(1) time complexity.

The downside was that its output decreases from the stable O(1) stable inserts as well as deletes supported by a list-based linked implementation (as you can see from collections.deque below). Lists, on the other hand, give quick O(1) time random access to stack elements, and this can be an additional advantage.

There is an important performance precaution to be noted when using lists as stacks: To get the depreciated value O(1) for inserts and deletes, the append) (method needs to add new items to the end of the list and remove them from the end through pop). Stacks based on Python lists should expand to higher indexes and decrease to lower ones for optimum performance.

It is much slower to add and to remove from the front, taking O(n) time, since existing elements need to be rotated to make room for the new element. This is an antipattern of success which you should avoid:

Collections.deque: *stacks fast and robust*

The deque class implements a dual-end queue that supports the addition and removal of elements at both ends in O(1) time. Because deques allow the addition and removal of elements from either end, they can function both as stacks, and as queues.

The deck objects are implemented as doubly-linked lists that give them excellent and consistent performance in insertion and deletion elements, but bad O(n) performance in the middle of a stack for random access to elements.

Overall, collections.deque is a great option when you are looking for a Python standard library stack data structure which features the performance properties of implementation in the linked list:

queue.LifoQueue: *Concurrent computation locking semantics*

LifoQueue stack implementation is synchronized and offers locking semantics for multiple concurrent producers and consumers in the Python Standard Library.

In addition to LifoQueue, the queue module includes several classes that are used for parallel processing, multi-producers, multi-consumer queues.

The locking semanticizes may be helpful or they may only require needless overhead, depending on your situation. In this case, the use of a list or deque as a general stack will be better:

Python Stack Implementations: Summary

As you have seen, Python ships for a stack data structure with many implementations. They all have slightly different features, efficiency, and consumption variations.

If you do not want parallel processing support (or if you do not want to manually lock and unlock), then you have to select the built-in list form or collections.deque. The distinction lies in the data structure and general ease of use used behind the scenes.

The list is provided by a dynamic array that makes it great with easy random access but sometimes needs redimensioning when adding or removing components.

The list over-allocates its backup storage to prevent any push or pop requiring redimensioning, and the O(1) time complexity for these operations is amortized. But only insert and delete items with append) (and pop) (must be alert. If not, output slows to O(n).

Collections.deque is provided by the doubly-linked list, that optimizes all add-ons and deletes and ensures consistent O(1) operation efficiency. The deck class is not just more secure but you don't have to think about adding or removing things from the wrong end.

In short, collections.deque is a good option for implementing a Python stack (LIFO queue).

Tailings (FIFOs)

In this section, you can see how the first-in / first-out (FIFO) queue data structure is implemented using only built-in Python library data types and classes.

A queue is a set of objects which allows quick insert and delete FIFO semanticities. Often insert and remove operations are called dequeue and dequeue. In comparison to lists or arrays, queues do not usually allow arbitrary access to the items they contain.

Here is a real-world FIFO queue analogy:

Imagine a line of Pythonists waiting the first day of PyCon registration to receive their conference badges. When new people enter the venue and queue for their badges, they join the line (enqueue) behind the queue. Developers collect their badges and conference swag bags and clear the line at the front of the queue afterward.

Another way to memorize the features of a queue data structure is to see it like a wire. You connect ping pong balls to one end and they go to the other end to take them off. You can't get to them because the ball is in a queue (The solid metal pipe). The only way to deal with balls in the queue is by inserting new ones at the rear of the pipe (line) or eliminating them at the top.

Stacks are identical to queues. The distinction lies in the way objects are separated. For a queue, you delete the newest item (FIFO), but you select the oldest item (LIFO) with a stack.

The proper implementation of the queue will take O(1) time to insert and remove operations in terms of output. These are the two key operations performed in a queue and they should be easy to execute correctly.

Queues provide a broad variety of algorithm implementations and also help to solve planning and parallel programming problems. A quick and beautiful algorithm with a queue is a first-ever search (BFS) on the structure of the tree or the graph.

Scheduling algorithms commonly use internal priority queues. There are tails of specialization. Instead of retrieving the next element by adding time, the highest priority element is located in a priority queue. The priority of each element is calculated by the queue based on the order applied to its keys.

However, a standard queue would not reorder the things it contains. You get what you put in, just like in the pipe example, and in exactly that order.

Python ships with multiple queue implementations, each of which has slightly different features. Let's check them. Let's review them.

List: *Slooooo Terrible Queues*

A standard list can be used as a queue, but it is not ideal from a performance point of view. Lists are very slow since adding or removing an element at the beginning requires all the other elements to be moved one by one which takes O(n) time.

I would therefore not recommend that you use a list in Python as a precautionary queue unless you only have a limited number of elements:

Collections.deque: *Fast and sturdy queues*

The deque class uses a double end queue which allows elements to be added and removed from each end in O(1) time (not amortized). As deques support the addition and removal of elements, they can serve both as queues and as stacks.

Double-linked lists are implemented with the deque artifacts of Python. This gives them excellent and consistent performance in adding and removing elements, but low O(n) performance in the center of the stack for random access to elements.

As a consequence, *collections.deque* is a fantastic default option if you're searching for the Python Standard Library queue data structure:

Queue.Queue: *Concurrent Computation Locking Semantics*

The Python standard library is compatible with the queue. Queue implementations that provide locking semantics for multiple competitors and consumers.

There are several other classes in the queue module which implement multi-producer multi-consumer queues that are useful for parallel computing.

Depending on the using case, semi-locking may be helpful or incur an overhead that is unneeded. In this instance, it would be easier to use *collections.deque* as a general queue:

Multiprocessing.Queue: *Mutual job queues*

Multiprocessing.Queue is a cooperative job queue implementation that allows multiple competitors to parallel process queued objects. The global interpreter lock (GIL) prevents some forms of parallel execution in a single interpreter process is popular for CPython.

Multiprocessing. Queue is a specialist queue implementation designed for data sharing between processes, making it easy to distribute work over various processes to work around GIL limitations. Such a queue will store and pass any pickleable item through process limits:

Python queues: summary

As part of the core language and its standard library, Python provides numerous queue implementations.

List objects are typically not recommended because of slow performance, but it can be used as queues.

If you don't want parallel processing support, then collections.deque implementation is a great default option to implement a Python FIFO queue data structure. It gives you the output features you would expect from a good queue implementation and can be used as a stack (LIFO queue).

Priority Queues

A priority queue is a container data structure that handles many records with strictly organized keys to quickly access the record with the smallest or biggest key.

A prior queue may be viewed as an updated queue. It retrieves a highest priority element instead of the next factor by time of insertion. The priority of each element is determined by the order applied to its keys.

Priority queues are often used for timing problems. For example, you can use them to prioritize more urgent tasks.

Think of the role of an operating system planner:

Ideally, more priority device tasks (e.g. playing a real-time game) can take precedence over lower priority tasks (e.g. context uploading). With the arrangement of pending prior queue tasks that use task urgency as the base, the task manager will pick a highest priority tasks fast and allow them to run first.

This section includes a few options for implementing priority queues in Python using built-in data structures or data structures provided in the standard library of Python. -- application has its upsides and downsides, but for most popular scenarios I think that there is a simple winner. Let's find out what it's.

List: *Sorted Queues manually*

You can easily identify and delete the smallest or largest element through a sorted list. The downside is that it is a slow O(n) procedure to insert new elements in the list.

Since in the O(log n) time the insertion point can be found by using bisect.insort in the standard library, the slow insertion stage still dominates.

It also takes at least O (n log n) time to preserve the order by adding to the list and re-sorting it. Another drawback is that when new elements are added you must manually re-sort the list. Bugs can easily be introduced by missing this step, and your developer always has a burden.

This means that sorted lists can only be used as priority queues when few insertions are made:

Heapq: *Binary Heaps List-Based*

Heapq is a binary heap implementation commonly provided by a single list and supports the smallest element insertion and extraction during O(log n) time.

This module was a good alternative for Python priority queues. Since heapq theoretically only provides a minute cheap implementation, further measures must be taken to ensure the reliability of sorting and other features normally anticipated from a realistic priority queue:

PriorityQueue: *Perfect Priority queues Queueue.*

Queue. PriorityQueue uses heapq but also shares the same internallycomplexity of time and space. The difference was that PriorityQueue is unified and supplies semantics for locking multiple rivals and customers.

This could be beneficial or slow down your program slightly depending on your use case. In any case, the class interface supplied by PriorityQueueue may be superior to the feature interface supplied by heapq:

Python priority queues: description

Python provides multiple implementations of priority queue ready for use.

Queue. PriorityQueue stands out with a good object-oriented interface and a name with a simple target. It should be your favorite choice.

If you want the queue. PriorityQueue to prevent locking overhead, the use of the heapq module is also a reasonable choice.

Conclusion: Structures of Python data

This concludes your tour of Python's popular data structures. You are ready to implement efficient data structures with the knowledge you have acquired, that are just right for your particular Algorithm or case use.

You learned in this tutorial:

- The types of abstract data are incorporated into the standard Python library?
- How to map Python's name scheme by the most popular abstract data types
- How to use abstract data types in different algorithms

PYTHON CONDITION SETTLEMENT

All you saw so far consisted of the **sequential execution** in which declarations are always rendered in precisely the order specified one by one.

However, the world is often more complicated. Often, a program must skip over certain statements, repeatedly perform many statements, or select alternate sets of statements to perform.

This is where systems of **control structure** come in. A **control structure** defines the execution order for the statements in a program (known as the control flow of the program). Here's what you will learn from this tutorial: your first control structure by Python, the if statement, will be found.

In the real world, we often have to evaluate the information about us and then choose one way or another based on what we observe:

The if statement in a Python program is how you make this type of decision. It enables the **conditional** execution of an expression value-based statement or collection of statements.

The following is the outline of this guide:

- First, a quick overview of whether declaration in its simplest form is provided.
- Next, you'll see why control structures need some mechanism to group statements into **compound statements** or **blocks**, with the if statement as a guide. In Python, you'll learn how this is done.
- Finally, you will connect everything and learn how to write complex code for decision making.

Presentation of the if statement

We will begin by looking at the most basic type of statement if. It looks like it in its simplest form

In the above form:

- *< expr >* is a boolean as discussed in the section on logical operators and python beginner guide expressions.

- *< statement >* is indeed a valid Python statement to be indented. (You're going to see why soon.)

If *< expr >* is true (evaluates a "truthful" value), then < statement > is executed. If < expr > is false, then *< statement >* is skipped and not run.

Note that after < expr > colon (:) is required. Some programming languages require the use of < expr >, but Python doesn't.

Grouping statements: Blocks and indentation

So far, so good.

But let's say that you want to assess a condition and do more than one thing if it's true:

If the weather is good, I'll:

- Take the dog for a walk
- Weed the garden
- Mow the lawn

   (If the weather isn't nice, I won't do all this stuff.)

In all examples above, only one < statement > was followed by every $< expr >:$. There must be a way of saying "If < expr > is true, do all the following."

The most frequent approach is to define a syntactic device grouping multiple statements into one **compound declaration** or **block**. A block is syntactically considered to be a single entity. If the objective of if statement is true and then < expr > is true, and then all statements in this block are carried out. If < expr > is wrong, none of it is wrong.

Virtually all programming languages can define blocks, but not all of them offer them in the same way. Let's see how it's done by Python.

Python: This is everything about indentation

Python is following a convention recognized as the off-side rule, a term coined by Peter J. Landin, a British computer scientist. (The term is taken from the off-sided law of football associations.) Languages which adhere to the off-sided rule define blocks of indentation. Python is among a relatively small set of rules.

Remember from the previous Python tutorial that indentation in a Python program is particularly important. Now you know why: indentation is being used to define the statements or blocks of compounds. Contiguous statements indented to the same level are supposed to be a part of the same block in a Python program.

All indentation level statements (lines 2 to 5) are considered to be part of the same block. The whole blocks are executed if < expr > is true, or if < expr > is wrong. Either way, < following statement > (line 6) is executed subsequently.

Notice no token indicating the end of the block. Rather, a line that is less than the lines of the block itself indicates the end of the block.

Consider this *foo.py* script file:

On lines 2 to 5, the four print) (statements are indented to a similar level. They are the block to be carried out if the condition were true. But it's wrong, so all the statements are missed in the block. Once the compound has ended (whether the declaration in the block is executed inline 2 to 5 or not), execution proceeds to the first statement with a lower level of indentation: print) (on line 6.

Blocks may be arbitrarily nested. Each indent defines a new block, and the previous block ends with every outdent. The resulting structure is simple, uniform, and intuitive.

A more complicated file called blocks.py is here:

The output generated by running this script is shown below:

What are other languages doing?

You might be curious about the alternatives. How are blocks defined in languages which do not comply with the off-side rule?

The tactic used in most programming languages is to specify special tokens marking the beginning and end of a block. In Perl blocks, for example, such as this, pairs of curly braces}) ({are defined:

Other languages, like Pascal and Algol, use keywords to start and end blocks.

What's Better?

Better is in the beholder's eye. In general, programmers tend to feel pretty strong about how they do things. Discussions on the merits of the off-side rule can be hot.

On the surface:

- Clean, concise, and consistent use of indentation by Python.
- Code indents are completely independent of the block definition and code function in programming languages that do not use the off-side rule. Code can be written in a way that does not correspond to the execution of the code, creating an erroneous impression when a person just looks at it. In Python, this kind of error is virtually impossible to make.
- The use of indenting to define blocks forces that you are likely to use anyway to maintain code formatting standards.

On the downside:

- Many programmers don't like to have to do things somehow. They tend to have strong opinions about what looks good and what doesn't look good and does not like to get into a particular choice.
- A mix of the space and table characters is inserted in some editors to the left of the indented lines, making it difficult for a Python interpreter for indentation level determination. On the other hand, editors can often be configured not to do so. In general, a combination of tabs and spaces in the source code is not considered desirable, regardless of language.

Like it or not, you're stuck with the off-side rule if you program in Python. As you will see in several future tutorials, all control structures in Python use it.

For what it is worth, a lot of the programmers who used more conventional block description languages initially came back to Python's direction, but we're happy with it and even became more preferable.

The else and Elif Clauses

You now know how to use an if statement to execute one or more statements conditionally. It's time to learn what else you can do.

Often you want to verify a condition and take a path if it is valid, but you want to suggest an alternate path if not. This is achieved with another clause:

If < expr > is true, the first suite and the second one are omitted. If < expr > is wrong, the first suite will be skipped and the second one will be executed. Sooner or later, execution resumes after that second suite. Both suites were defined as mentioned above by indentation.

In this example, x is below 50, so that the first suite (lines 4 to 5) is executed and the second suite (lines 7 to 8) is overwritten:

Here, on the other hand, x is larger than 50, so that the first suite is exceeded and the second suite is implemented:

There is also a branching syntax based on many alternatives. Use one or more *elif* (short if) clauses for this purpose. -- < expr > is evaluated by Python and the set corresponds to the first which is valid. If none of the expressions is valid and another clause is defined, the suite is implemented:

There may be an infinite number of *elif* clauses. The other element is optional. There can be only one if it is present and last must be specified:

Up to one of the specified code blocks will be executed. If there is no other clause and all words are false, no block will be executed.

If an *elif* clause argument uses a short-circuit calculation, similar to what you saw with and or with the operators. If one of the phrases is valid and its block is executed, none of the other phrases shall be checked. This is seen below:

The second term includes a zero division and the third is an unknown element. Any would cause an error, but the first condition stated is not valid, neither is evaluated.

One-line if statements#

It is normal to write if < expr > is written on one line and < statement > is written on this line:

The latter interpretation is provided by Python. The semicolon that distinguishes the < statements > is above the colon after < expr > — in lingo computers, it is said that the demicolon connects tighter than the colon. The < statements > are then regarded as a set, and both are implemented.

Although all these works and the interpreter allows, it is generally discouraged because it leads to poor readability, particularly if complex sentences.

As normal, it's a bit of a taste. Most people will find the following at first glance more visually enticing and easier to understand than the example above:

If a sentence is clear enough, however, it can be fair to place anything on a single line. Something like this would probably not raise hackles of anyone too much:

Conditional Expressions (Ternary Operator of Python)

Python supports another decision-making entity known as a conditional word. (The Python Literature also refers to it as a conditional operator or ternary operator in different places.) Conditional expressions were also proposed for language inclusion in PEP 308 and Guido in green-lighting in 2005.

The syntax of the conditional expression in its simplest form is as follows:

This is different from the if statement types mentioned above since it is not a control system that governs the execution of the program. It functions more like an operator describing an expression. In the example above, < conditional expr > is first evaluated. If valid, the phrase will be < expr1 >. If the expression is false, it evaluates to < expr2 >.

Note the non-obvious order: the middle expression is first tested and one of the end expressions is returned based on the result. Here are some examples to explain, I hope:

The variable assignment is a typical use of the conditional expression. For instance, suppose you want to find two numbers larger. Naturally, there is a built-in max) (function which just does the (and more) you can use. But suppose you want your scratch code to be written.

You can use a norm if you have a sentence with another clause:

But a conditional expression is even shorter and more legible:

Note that the conditional expression is syntactically like a noun. It can be used for a longer time. Conditional expression is less common than almost all other operators, so it has to be classified in parentheses.

The + operator attaches tighter than the conditional expression so that $1 + x$ and $y + 2$ are evaluated first, followed by the conditional expression. In the second case the parentheses are needless and do not affect the outcome:

If you use a conditional expression in a wider language, it is usually a good idea to use grouping parenthesis even if it is not necessary.

Conditional expressions like composite logical expressions often use short circuit evaluation. Conditional speech parts are not checked if they don't have to be.

If < conditional expr > then < expr2 >: In < expr1 >:

- If < conditional expr > is valid, the value of < expr1 > is returned.
- If < conditional expr > is false, it returns < expr2 > and does not check < expr1 >.

As before, you can check this with words that cause an error:

In both cases, the 1/0 words are not measured, so there is no difference.

Conditional sentences can also be mixed, as a kind of if / elif / else option, as seen here:

It is not clear that this has a substantial benefit over the corresponding if / elif / else argument, but Python is syntactically accurate.

The Python Declaration

Often you might notice that you want to write a code stub: a placeholder where you can eventually put a code block that you haven't implemented yet.

In languages where token boundaries, like the curly braces in Perl and C, define lines, empty boundaries can also be used to define code stub. For example, Perl or C code is legitimate:

An empty block is defined by the empty curly braces. Perl or C will test the x expression and then quietly do nothing even though it is valid.

Since Python uses indentation instead of boundaries, an empty block can not be defined. If you enter an if statement with if < expr >:, something must follow, on the same line or in the indentation.

The declaration of the Python Pass solves this problem. It doesn't affect the actions of the software at all. It is used as a placeholder to appease the interpreter if a sentence is syntactically appropriate, but you want to do nothing:

Finalization

After this tutorial is completed, you start writing Python code which goes beyond simple the sequential execution:

- The idea of control systems was presented to you. These are compound statements that modify program control flow — the order in which program statements are executed.
- You have learned how to combine individual statements into a block or suite together.
- You encountered the first control structure, if declaration, which allows a statement or a block dependent on program data evaluation to be carried out conditionally.

All these principles are important to the creation of a more complex Python code.

Two new control mechanisms will appear in the next two tutorials: the While statement and the Fact fact. These frameworks promote repeated repetition, declaration execution, or blocking of statements.

PYTHON FUNCTIONS

Many programming languages have such a special function which is performed automatically while a program is running on an operating system. This function is typically called *main( )* (and must have a particular return form and language default arguments. On the other hand, the Python interpreter executes scripts from the top of the file, and Python does not automatically perform any particular operation.

However, it is important to understand how a program operates to have a certain starting point for the execution of a program. Python programmers have built many conventions to describe this point of departure.

You will understand by the end of this course:

- What is the special __name__ variable and how Python describes it?
- Why in Python would you like to use main( )
- What conventions exist in Python to define main( )
- What are the best practices for which code your main( ) can enter?

A function is a block of reusable, structured code used to perform a single *action.functions* offer the application more modularity and a high degree of code reuse.

As you know, Python provides several integrated functions such as *print( )*, (etc. but you can also build your own functions. These functions are called functions specified by the user.

Defining a function

Functions can be specified to provide the necessary functionality. Here are basic rules for defining a Python function.

- Function blocks start with **def**, followed by parentheses (( )) and the name of the method.
- Any input parameters or arguments inside these parentheses should be marked. In these parentheses, you can also specify parameters.
- An optional declaration-the function documentation string or **docstring**-may be the first declaration of the function.
- The code block begins with a *colon (:)* in each feature and is indented.
- The *return* statement *[expression]* exits a function, and the caller options to return an object. A return assertion without arguments is equivalent to a return declaration None.

Calling a function

The function description only names a function, defines the parameters to be used in the function, and structures the code blocks.

If the basic structure of a function is done, you can execute it directly from the Python prompt by calling another function.

value vs Pass by reference.

In the Python language, all parameters (arguments) are passed by reference. This implies that if you modify the parameter within a function, the adjustment is also reflected in the calling function.

Function Arguments

You may use the following types of formal arguments to call a function

- Required Arguments
- keywords Arguments
- Default Arguments
- Variable-length Arguments

Required Arguments

The argument needed is the argument passed in the correct positional order to a function. Here, the number of arguments should fit the function description exactly in the function call.

To call the printme), (one argument must be transmitted, otherwise a syntax error occurs.

Keyword Argument

Keyword Arguments relate to calls to work. If you are using keyword arguments in a function call, the caller uses the parameter name to define the arguments.

This helps you to skip or set out arguments since the Python interpreter can use keywords to fit parameters for the values. The printme) (function can also be named by keywords.

default Arguments

A default argument is indeed a default value argument, if the function call does not contain a value.

Variable-length Arguments

For more arguments than you defined, you may need to process a feature when defining the feature. These arguments, in contrast to necessary and default arguments, are called variable-length arguments and are not specified in the function specification.

The variable name with the values of all nonkeyword variable arguments is marked with an asterisk (*). This tuple remains empty if during the call function no additional arguments are defined.

The Anonymous Function

These functions are called anonymous since they are not defined by def keyword in the traditional way. To build small anonymous functions, use the lambda keyword.

- Lambda forms can take a number of arguments but return only one expression value. It is not possible to include commands or multiple phrases.
- A direct print call cannot be an anonymous function, because lambda needs an expression
- The Lambda functions have a local namespace of their own and can not access variables other than in the parameter list and in the global namespace.
- Even if Lambda appears to be a one-line version of a method, it is not the same as inline statements in either C or C++, the object of which is to transfer stack allocation during invocation for reasons of performance.

The lambda functions syntax includes only one assertion

The declaration of return

The return statement [expression] leaves a function and optionally transfers a caller expression. A return declaration without arguments is the same as return None.

All of the above examples return no value. You can return a function value.

Variables

Not all program variables will be available at all locations in the program. This depends on where a variable has been identified.

The scope of a variable specifies the section of the program where a specific identifier can be accessed. Python has two simple sets of variables −

- General variables
- Local variables

Local Variables vs Global

Variables specified within a function body have the variables and local scope, defined outside have the global scope.

This means that local variables could only be accessed inside the declared function, while global variables in the program community are available across all functions. When you call a method, it brings into scope the variables defined inside it.

PYTHON MODULES

A module helps you to arrange your Python code logically. Grouping the relevant code into a module simplifies the interpretation and use of the code. A module is a Python object with attributes that you can connect and reference arbitrarily.

Simply put, a module is a Python code file. Functions, classes, and variables can be described in a module. Executable code can also be used in a module.

Import Statement

By executing an import statement in another Python source file, you can use any Python source file as a module.

If an interpreter reaches an import requirement, the module is imported if the module is present in the search path. A search path is a list of directories to look for before the interpreter imports a file.

A module is only loaded once, irrespective of how many times it is imported. This prevents the execution of the module from occurring again and again if any imports occur.

The from ... import statement

Python's statement allows you to import unique attributes to the current namespace from a module.

The from ... import * statement

All names from a module can also be imported into the current namespace by using the following import statement.

This is a simple way to import all the things from a module into a current namespace, but it must be used sparingly.

Locating Modules

In the following sequences, the Python interpreter looks for the module when importing a file.

- The current directory.
- If it is not found in the module, Python searches each directory in the PYTHONPATH shell variable.
- When anything else fails, the default route is verified by Python. Typically this default route is /usr / local / lib / python/ on UNIX.

The search path of the module is stored as the api.path variable in the api module. The sys.path variable includes PYTHONPATH, the current directory, and the default system-dependent.

The variable PYTHONPATH

The PYTHONPATH is a directory list environment variable. The PYTHONPATH syntax is the same as the PATH shell.

Scoping and namespaces

Variables are names that map to objects. A namespace is a dictionary containing variable names (keys) and their respective properties (values).

In a local namespace and global namespace, a Python statement may access the variables. If both a local variable and a global one have the same name, the local variable shades the global variable.

There is a local namespace for and function. Class methods obey the same rule of scope as general functions.

Python makes well-informed assessments of whether variables are local or global. It implies that value in a function is local in any context.

To assign a value to a global variable within a function, you must use the global statement first.

The global VarName statement says VarName is a global variable for Python. Python avoids checking the local variable namespace.

The dir( ) function

The built-in dir ( ) (function returns a sorted list of strings with module names.

The list includes the names of all modules, variables, and functions specified in one module.

The functions globals( ) and locals( )

The functions global( ) and local( ) can be used to return names in global and local namespaces, depending on where they are called.

If localals( ) (is called from inside a function, all names accessed locally from this function will be returned.

If globals ( ) is called from inside a function, all the names accessible globally from that function will be returned.

The form of return of these two functions is a dictionary. Names can then be extracted with the key( ) function.

The reload ( ) function

The code in the top-level section of a module is executed only once when the module is inserted into a document.

Therefore, you can use the reload) (function if you want to reexecute the top-level module code. The reload) (function again imports a module already imported. The reload ( ) (function is this —

Python Packages

A package is a hierarchical folder structure that defines a single Python application environment consisting of modules, subpacks, subpacks, etc.

Take a Pots.py file in your phone directory. This file has a source code line —

In order to make all of your functions accessible when importing a machine, you must put the following specific import statements in init .py.

You have all these classes available when you import the Phone package after you have attached those lines to init .py.

INHERITANCE IN PYTHON

Inheritance is the right of a class to acquire or inherit other class properties. The advantages of heritage are:

1. It well reflects relationships in the real world.
2. It provides code **reusability**. We don't have to constantly write the same code. It also allows us to add additional features without altering a class.
3. It is transitive in nature, and if class B is inherited from other class A, then all subclass B would be inherited from class A automatically.

What is the object class?

Like the *Java Object class,* the object is the root of all classes in Python (version 3.x).

"Class Test(Object)" and "Class Test" are the same in Python 3.x.

'class test(object)' creates an object class In Python 2.x as parent (so-called new-style class), and 'class test' creates an old-style class (without parent object). See this for more stats.

Subclassing (Calling parent class constructor)

A child class must decide which class is its parent class. This can be achieved by defining the parent class name in the child class specification.

The variables specified in __init__() are named as variables or objects of the case. Therefore, 'name' and 'idnumber' are class person objects. The 'salary' and 'post' are likewise members of the employee class. Since that the class Employee inherits from the class Worker, the class Employee also has 'name' and 'idnumber.'

If you fail to invoke the __init__() of the parent class, the child class does not have access to its instance variables.

Various types of inheritance:

1. Single inheritance: When only one parent class belongs to a kid's family, it is considered a single heritage. We have given an example above.

2. Multiple inheritance: when a child family heritage from many parent groups, it is considered a multiple heritage.

Python supports multiple heritages, as opposed to Java and C++. All parent classes are listed as a comma-separated bracket list.

4. Hierarchical inheritance   Upwards of one derived classes are produced from a single basis.

4.Hybrid inheritance: this form incorporates more than one heritage form. It is basically a mixture of more than one heritage type.

Private parent class members

We may not always want the parent class instance variables to be inherited by the child class, that is, we can build certain parent class instance variables personally, which are not available to the child class.

CHAPTER FOUR - PYTHON PROJECTS FOR BEGINNERS

Python can be difficult to learn. You could spend time watching videos, or reading a textbook, but then you can fight to actually put into practice what you have learned. Or you could spend a ton of time syntax learning and get bored or lose motivation.

How can your chances of success be increased? By building projects for Python. That's how you learn by doing what you want to do!

Project-based learning is also the philosophy behind Dataquest's teaching method, where we teach Python information science. Why? Why? Because we've seen it work again and again!

But building Python projects for beginners can be difficult. Where do you start? Where do you begin? What makes the project a good one? When you get stuck, what do you do? We will talk in this chapter about:

- What to do before you construct your first project.
- What makes the project successful?
- Use strategies when stuck.
- Examples of perfect project selection.

Why the best way to learn is to build projects?

Let us first consider why a project-based approach to learning is so effective.

Motivation: Have the momentum to continue

First, Python's building helps you learn more efficiently because you can choose an interesting project or topic.

It helps you to remain motivated, which is important to avoid giving up when things get hard.

Efficiency: Learn only what you need

The second reason why a project-based approach works are that there is no difference between learning the skill and implementing it. You won't spend time learning things that are irrelevant, because you're going to actively try to learn what your project needs.

You will also get where you want to go much faster. For example, if you try to learn Python for data science by developing projects in data science, you will not waste time learning Python concepts which may be important for the programming of robotics, but which do not correspond to your data science goals.

Problem resolution: Learn the skills of key programming

Problem-solving is a key skill when working with Python (or any other language of programming). When building a project, you will have to come up with ways to solve problems and use code.

Building projects, therefore, forces you to practice what may be the most important programming skills. And the more practical you can practice in resolving code problems, the faster you develop your skills.

Portfolio: Use your projects to support you in getting a job

The fourth and final reason that Python projects are working for beginners is that you can get your first job started (if that's your aim).

When employers want to employ entrant candidates, they want to see that they have the main skills they need. An excellent way to do this is to have a portfolio of relevant projects that show your skills.

If you are looking for your first job in the field, employers would like tangible evidence of Python's skills. In other words, they'll want to see what projects you've constructed.

You can read more on creating a portfolio in the Data Science Career Guide if you are interested (which, while specifically aiming at individuals interested in entering data, is equally valuable if your goal is another application from Python!).

Before you build your first Python project

You might be able to immerse yourself in building a project if you have some programming experience. However, for most people, you will need to take some time to first learn some of Python's basics. The idea is to spend a little time learning these basics so you have what you need to immerse yourself in projects.

At this stage, you can use a few resources:

- *Dataquest – Python Fundamental Programming. At* Dataquest, we teaches Python in the field of data science learning. This is the first course on our curriculum and you can register and start free of charge. Try it! Give it a try!

It's normal to feel a bit overwhelmed after learning some of the basics. After all, you are learning something totally new. Even if you may not be prepared to start a project, you probably are.

You may want to try and build a structured or guided project as a first step. Structured projects are important since they allow you to build something, which can be difficult if you are a beginner, without starting from scratch.

At Dataquest, we included a guided project in each course, which help bridge that gap between learning from the course and building your own project. An alternative path to Python's blog posts could be found on either the Dataquest site or on thousands of other sites online.

What makes for beginners a Great Python Project?

Now it is time to construct your Python project, you must decide what to construct! It is very important to choose what to build – whether or not your project will succeed. So what makes a great project for beginners in Python?

Choose a Topic in which you are interested

The first and foremost factor is the choice of a subject you want. You will have more motivation if you are interested in what you are building. Motivation is important because when you hit roadblocks it is the momentum that leads you through.

Some may be motivated by sports, others by social good projects. Others could be motivated by finance or the stock market. You may be obsessed with movies or a favorite television series. Whatever that "thing" is for you, this should be your project.

Think about your Goal

The second factor to consider is what your overall objective is to learn Python. If you want to develop web, a project that builds a small web application is ideal. If you are interested in data science, A evaluating a dataset project is a good choice. Align your business with your targets, you will get closer to your ultimate goal, rather than "detour."

Start Small

The final factor is not too ambitious. Naturally, a big plan can be drawn up, e.g. "I'm looking to build a website that allows people to create a custom NBA data shot chart," sounds like it's based on a topic that motivates people (presuming you like basketball) and crosses a goal (learning to create websites).

The challenge with this choice of project is that it is too large. To do so, beginners need to learn the basics of building an online application, how to store and retrieve any data, how to produce graphic views, and how to show them on demand to a user.

It's much better to start with a very small and simple version of your project and then add more features afterward. If you don't, it takes a very long time before you get a sense of achievement and even give up. You are much more likely to succeed by starting small and expanding.

A better version of the project could be a simple web application that shows a single NBA for a small selection of players. Once you've built this, you can expand it by adding more players, more statistics, or any extra complexity that may appeal to you.

Python project building: roadblocks and difficulties

You must have learned the basics of Python, you've completed a guided project and you've selected the perfect subject for your first solo project. You have a problem after about half an hour: something you don't know how to do!

It's going to happen, I promise you, and it isn't a nice feeling. Nobody likes to get stuck. That said, what is presented to you is a chance. These moments — roadblocks — are where the learning takes place. The key is to know how to research and continue working to get around the roadblock.

The good news is that most of the time there was somebody — with the same roadblock — in the same situation as now. What you need to do is find the resources that these people have left behind. Enter: Google (or your favorite search engine).

How to Search for help

The key to finding help is to find information about a general version of what you want to do.

Say you have a Python dictionary in which the dictionary keys are the names of the NBA player and the values are the number of games they played. You're trying to find out who's got the most games.

However, it is probably not helpful to search for "how to find out which NBA players have the most games in the Python dictionary." You must create a general form for your question, which may be: "See which key is of the highest value in a Python dictionary."

Indeed, that precise search of Google seems to take us to a Stack Overflow question with helpful answers!

Finding these basic questions can be difficult at first, but it's an important ability that almost every programmer uses every day. Don't be afraid to dive in and practice. If you still can not find assistance, you might have to divide your problem into smaller chunks and search individually for each chunk.

You will find that the majority of your help searches end in one of the three locations:

- An online tutorial explaining what you want to do.
- Stack overflow (Q&A site for online programming) threads of someone in similar circumstances.
- The Python or Python library documentation you are using.

You must post your question in an area like Dataquest community, or Stack Overflow if you still can't find the answers, where others could answer your question. You may be surprised how fast other programmers jump into to help a beginner!

Examples of Project

Let's now take a look at some fictional examples of people with interests and goals and see how they can pick a Python project that fits their needs.

Danielle Data-Focused

Danielle wants to break into the area of data science and she has discovered that a data entry-level task will be an analyst type role.

She likes Star Trek, so it is decided that some data concerning Star Trek episodes should be analyzed as an ideal project.

To start little and build-up, she will find a data set to summarize episode data (she will probably use this list of places to find free data sets to launch projects).

She plans to expand her project by creating visualizations once she has done so.

Fun Python project ideas for data development:

- Find out how much money you spent on Amazon — Dig into your own expenses with this tutorial!
- Analysis of Survey Data — This step will show how Python can be configured and how survey data from any dataset you can find are filtered.

- Guided Projects Dataquest — These guided projects will help you build real-world, complexity data projects with suggestions on how to expand each project.
- Analyze everything — take free data and start poking around! • Analyze everything. If you are stuck or don't know where to start, our Python courses are here to help you and free to try!

Gamer Greg

Greg wants to learn Python to make fun of games and love puzzles.

Greg has decided that by building games in the Pygame library he is going to learn Python. Starting with a structured project using some Pygame tutorials, he creates a simple version of Rock–paper–scissors then gradually increases his projects' complexity.

Fun Python game dev projects:

- Rock, Paper, Scissors — Look at the start of your Python path with a simple but fun game everyone knows about.
- Construct a Text Adventure Game — It's a classic Python startup project that will teach you many basic concepts for advanced games that will be useful in the future, as well.
- Guessing Game — This is another project at the beginner level that will help you to learn and practice the basics.
- Mad Libs — Get to know how to make Python Mad Libs interactive!
- Hangman — Another classic childhood that you can do to extend your skills in Python.
- Snake — It's a little more difficult, but it's a classic (and surprisingly fun) game.

Wanda website

Wanda wants to use Python to create worksites, and she likes fitness and exercise. She will start by following a web framework tutorial on the Python flask and then try to build a very basic website that she can use to log on every time she practices.

She plans to expand and add new features one by one once this simple version has been built.

Fun Python projects for web devs beginners:

• URL shortener — This free video course will show you how to shorten your own URLs with Python and Django, such as Bit.ly.

Building a Simple Website with Django-a very detailed tutorial to build a website with Python and Django which has even drawings.

• Build a simple website with Django.

Dev Aaron App

Aaron wants to learn Python in order to build mobile and web apps.

For aspiring developers, Fun Python projects:

- Password Generator — Create a secure Python password generator.
- Use Tweepy to create a Twitter bot — it's a bit more advanced because it's definitely a fun Twitter API to use.
- Build an Address Book — this could begin with a simple Python dictionary or get as advanced as this!
- Create a Crypto App with Python — This free video course will help you to create applications using cryptocurrency data using some APIs and Python.

The following steps

Each of the examples in the previous section followed the advice for beginners when choosing a great Python project:

- Think about what you are interested in and choose a project that overlaps with motivation.
- Think about your Python objectives and ensure that your project moves you to those aims.
- Small start. You can either expand or build one after you have built a small project.

PYTHON PROGRAMMING LANGUAGE IS CONSIDERED BETTER THAN OTHER LANGUAGES

Python is a high-level language for scripting. Because of its dynamic character and simple syntax which allow small lines of code it is easy to learn and powerful than other languages. The indentation and object-oriented functional programming included making it easy. Python's advantages vary from other languages, which is why Python is primarily used for production in businesses. Machine learning with python has become popular in the industry. It has regular collections used in science and numerical calculations. Even Linux, Windows, Mac OS, and UNIX can be included. Students in Python are taking online video training and python programming tutorials.

Python features: Why is Python machine learning superior to other languages? Python has many capabilities in comparison to other programming languages. Here are some fundamental features that render Python better than other languages:

- High-level language is Python. It means that the meaning of Python is not machine language but user-friendly.

- Python's collaborative nature makes it simple and user-friendly. Users can check the output for each statement in interactive mode.
- It allows the reuse and recycling of programs as an object-oriented programming language.
- Python's syntax can be expanded by several libraries.

Python applications: Python has many benefits making it distinct from other applications. Its applications made it a requested language for the development of apps, web creation, graphic design, and other applications. Its basic libraries support web protocols, such as HTML, JSON, XML, IMAP, FTP, etc. Libraries can support many operations such as Data Mining, NLP, and other machine learning applications. Because of these benefits and uses, students prefer tutorials to Python programming instead of other languages. There are also various online video training courses available for users or any interested applicant. You don't have to worry about the location, you can learn from your house.

How to learn Python: Python's immense uses and cases have been illustrated. It is mainly used as a simple programming language in machine learning and artificial intelligence companies. Python should be understood by students who wish to begin their career in AI and in machine learning. There are several online video training courses and tutorials for Python programming. Furthermore, it is easy to learn as a beginner. The beginners will take Python online courses or tutorials. It is easy to understand and the user can think like a programmer because of his understandable and comprehensible syntax. Python helps one to build something by computer programs; it just takes time to understand Python and his regular libraries. PyCharm is its IDE that makes interface during learning so simple and relaxed. By using PyCharm's debugging function, we can easily analyze the performance of each line and detect the error.

Python is being used in many major companies, such as Instagram, Google, Reddit, Dropbox, and many more. Because of the increasing demand for Python programmers, Python is selected as its core programming language by students and beginners in the industry. Python's features also make learning very easy. Python is the best language for beginners and a powerful language for development. It can be concluded. It is good for scientific and numerical work. Thus many students opt for python programming tutorial online video training courses. They can thus learn from anywhere and do their programming career in Python.

Learn Python to code and shine your future. Go for Online Python Video Course for better results, which is a good beginning for beginners who want to step up programming. You will have confidence in programming and can work on your own projects after online video training courses. As most companies use Python as a basic programming language, Python offers many jobs. So the online tutorial for python programming is very helpful for your industry growth. You only have to choose the right path from the right place.

IS PYTHON MORE POPULAR THAN RUBY?

Python and Ruby are two of the most common, dynamically-typed, new-generation programming languages that support object-oriented programming and whose implementation varies greatly from those of the prevailing programming languages such as Java and C. None of the modern languages have the most robust syntax or hierarchy, instead of concentrating on allowing developers to "do things quickly." Then both Python and Ruby have an integrated shell and library collections that improve the respective languages. They are also commonly used with their respective frameworks Ruby on Rails and , Django (Python) for web creation. So, while Python and Ruby are close in many respects, they are rival languages and have some significant differences. But let's first take a quick look at the two languages.

Application

In 1995 the Japanese computer scientist Yukihiro "Matz" Matsumoto developed Ruby as a dynamic, analytical, objectively oriented programming language of general use. Ruby's philosophy revolves around the idea that it should be user-friendly instead of designed to work best on computers in a programming language. In other words, the programming language should not allow the programmer to determine the best way to do a task while programming, rather than what the machine can do. Ruby's Least Astonishment Theory (POLA) reflects the ethos of existing code causing developers less frustration because of its elegant prose.

Ruby is highly object-oriented and all values are treated as objects, including classes, type instances, and even methods. Methods identified at the highest level become members of the Object class, which is the ancestor of all other classes and as such is accessible in all fields and acts as a global approach. As it supports both procedural and functional programming, Ruby was described as a multi-paradigm programming language. Ruby's syntax is somewhat like Perl and Python but with a strong object-oriented architecture influence. Ruby also has a developer community that follows its developments closely and helps develop "gems," Ruby's term for libraries, and in some cases, applications and IDE. Ruby is an open-source and Ruby's greatest strength is the Ruby on Rails framework, which made the language very popular after its release in 2005 and was used to create popular websites like Twitter and Groupon.

The Python

Python is a high programming language for general purposes, which is also known as a multi-paradigm programming language in support of object-oriented programming, structured programming, functional program, and aspect-oriented programming. It was first implemented by Guido Van Rossum in 1989, but in the 2000s became very popular. Contrary to the philosophy of Perl and Ruby as to 'many ways of doing something,' Python's motto 'There should be only one, and preferably only one, obvious way of doing that.' is a direct challenge to Perl and Ruby, and is largely influenced by the competition between the two languages of the new generation.

Python About Ruby Success

While Python and Ruby have always been around for a period, Ruby gained popularity with the arrival of Ruby on Rails in 2005. At that point, Python has already become a programmer-friendly and efficient language and established a niche for himself. Even if Ruby on Rails remains more popular with Python's Django now, it also means that Ruby remains restricted.

One of Python's main reasons for success is its language architecture, which makes writing and reading code easier. Since it is easy to understand, many beginners follow it, and schools and colleges include it in their curriculum. Since code readability is a strong advantage of Python, experienced programmers can use it to cut down on the maintenance and updating of code. Moreover, Python works very well with most platforms. It is used as a basic component with the most Linux, FreeBSD, NetBSD, OpenBSD, OS X, and AmigaOS4 operating systems and is completely supporting other OSes such as Windows, making it easy for programmers to access the language and enabling beginners to explore the language. A quick web search reveals that Python emerges from two new-generation programming languages as the most common language.

PYTHON LANGUAGE: WHY ONE SHOULD LEARN IT AND HOW IT CAN HELP

Many languages of programming are used today, some are used and others are outdated. In recent years, the programming situation has radically changed, with developers and programmers looking for more common and open languages. This is why the Python language has recently become so popular. The Python community is rising day by day as many programmers now see it as one of the most user-friendly languages.

Python's language is so popular that every sector and field is now a user of it. While the other programming languages don't lose followers, Python's fan base is-. More and more people now seek to learn Python. Some of the reasons for Python certification are discussed below:

Machine learning

Today, almost all of the algorithms run through whether they are a search engine, social media, chatbots, automated personal assistants, etc. These machine learning products are sophisticated algorithms, and the whole technological scenario has been modified. For machine learning, Python is the main programming language used, and you can find several libraries devoted exclusively to machine learning.

Big data

Python is the most widely used in the field of data science and professionals in this area need to know the language of programming. Although there are numerous other languages including Java, R and so on which data science is based, Python is still the favorite. This is due to its variety in automation technology along with the different platforms and libraries available such as NumPy, PyBrain, etc.

web Development

Many websites are currently created using Python language, such as Reddit. The key explanation for Python programming is its speed and efficiency in web creation. It can take hours for PHP to create a website and just a few minutes to use Python. In addition, frameworks and libraries such as Django and Flask simplify the work.

Community;

One of the fields programmers are currently looking for is the communities. In those groups, developers and programmers will interact and share their experiences and technology with others from all over the world. This helps them learn new things about Python and how to solve different problems during coding.

Libraries

Libraries are also helpful in the creation of websites and applications. Any form of code can be found. Python has many frameworks and modules such as Django, Flask, Scipy, NumPy, Keras, Pandas, etc. One must focus on logic and purpose and libraries can easily access codes.

Simple

Finally, the key reason why programmers use Python is that it is a basic language of programming. It is a user-friendly beginner language, as many complex codes and syntaxes that are not understandable are not required. Python has clear and readable syntax and code, making it much easier to set up and use.

WHAT IS NEW IN PYTHON PROGRAMMING?

Python programming is an increasingly important aspect of a programmer's education in today's workplace. As a dynamic language, whose philosophy of design revolves around reading and conciseness, Python is a common option for use as a language of writing. It is more versatile than compiled languages like other interpretive languages and can be used to bind various structures together. Indeed, Python has many applications in-fields as a flexible language.

For instance, Python is a popular software programming language. Raspberry Pi, a one-board student computer programming project, uses Python as its primary programming language. Moreover, much of the One Laptop program by Child XO is written in Python. At the other end of the educational continuum, Python is also a very powerful language for theoretical numerical, and scientific computing applications. As the production of educational software continues to expand, Python is becoming increasingly important to know.

Python is also a favorite language for AI tasks in addition to educational applications. Since Python is the scripting language with comprehensive module architecture, text processing tools, and simple syntax, Python is a natural option for natural language processing applications. Programms such as Wolfram Alpha and Siri have just started to enter the end-user market, and all of these programs will be written in Python.

In addition, Python is also used as a web application scripting language. In its Google App Engine, for example, Google has introduced Python is among of the languages available for creating and hosting web applications. Python is also used as a platform for software communication for web applications such as Dropbox between computers. Since the creation of web applications is an increasingly growing field, programmers will do well to receive Python training to improve their skills.

Python is also very useful as a modern Perl-like scripting language, which can be used to bind various systems together. Due to Python being a basic component for many operating systems in Linux and Unix, and since Python is widely used in the information security industry, Python is a valuable tool for system administrators and programmers to learn.

Python training is becoming an increasingly important language for programming. Python has a wide range of applications in many rising fields due to its flexibility. Both programmers and system managers will do well to take some knowledge of Python to upgrade their skills.

What Is Python Web Programming?

The Python programming language was originally created by Guido van Rossum in the 1980s and is a modern web programming language. Since then, Python has developed into a modular and extensible high-performance programming language. Some of the world's biggest websites use Python-like Twitter, Disqus, and Reddit. Python provides a variety of features, including simplicity, portability, object-oriented development, a strong standard library, and a set of third-party modules or paquets.

Stability

Since the late 1980s Python has been continuously evolving and is considered a mature programming language. The Python language developers perform comprehensive functionality and regression tests to ensure that the language remains bug-free and stable with each update.

Portability

Python programming provides many features that make it an appealing choice for creating web applications. Python programs are portable since Python interpreters for all modern operating systems and embedded computing systems are available.

Object-oriented Development

The object-oriented nature of Python makes the programmers suitable as a first language and easy to learn from other object-oriented languages for programmers who move to Python. The programming of Python is intuitive and enhances strong software structure and object-oriented methodologies.

Standard Library

The basic Python library provides developers a wide range of features that are comparable to more complicated languages, such as C++. Comprehensive file-based I / O, interactivity with the database, advanced exception handling, and a host of built-in data types make Python suitable for both web and general use programming. This makes python web programming a simple job for software developers looking to create web apps.

Third-Party Modules

Python is considered to be a complex language with comprehensive features in the standard library. However, the increasing popularity of python programming has led to a wide variety of third-party packages or modules that expand the functionality of Python and allow the language to solve specific programming challenges. Modules for managing non-standard database interactions and advanced cryptography features are for example available. Modules for the handling of basic tasks are also available such as reading file metadata, rendering diagrams, and compiling Python applications into structured executables. Due to the availability of a large number of web-centered modules, web programming in Python is made simpler for tasks such as e-mail, HTTP maintenance, JavaScript interaction, and other basic web development tasks.

CONCLUSION

Despite what assembly code and C coding may tell us, high-level languages can play a part in any toolbox of the programmer, and some of them are much more than computer science. Python seems to be the most fascinating of the many more high-level languages we could choose from today for those who want to research something different and do real work. His innovative implementation and his simple and easy-to-understand syntax of object-oriented programming make it a language that is enjoyable to learn and use. This is not a matter in most other languages.

Python is a popular language of web programming used to build some of the world's largest websites. It is very versatile, compact, and stable which enhances programmers' appeal to learn. Python's future is promising as more programmers engage in the community.

Python is recognized as one of today's best programming languages. Guido van Rossum invented it as a powerful time-saver. Python uses a collection of philosophical rules that make it very popular. This leads to increased extensibility, seamless integration of modules, better software quality, and consistent cross-platform support and therefore an increase in the efficiency of the developer.

CODING IN PYTHON

50 step by step Programming Projects in Games, art and More

Mark Slatkin

INTRODUCTION

Python is a high-level language for scripting. The dynamic nature and the simple syntax allowing small lines of code is easy to learn and powerful than other languages. This is made simple by including object-oriented and indentation functional programming. Python's advantages differ from other languages and that is why Python is preferred mainly for company development.

Machine learning with python has become popular in the industry. It has standard libraries used in scientific and numerical calculations. It is also available on Mac OS, Windows, Linux, and UNIX. Students who want to build a future in Python participate in online video and python programming courses. In many large companies like Dropbox, Google, Reddit, Instagram, and many others Python is used to achieve more jobs. Python is being chosen by students and beginners in the industry because of the growing demand of Python programmers as their main programming language. Python's features also make learning very easy.

It can be concluded that Python is the best starting language as well as a powerful development language. It is good for scientific and numerical work. Thus many students choose online python programming training courses. They are therefore able to learn from anywhere and make their Python programming career.

Learn Python to code and shine your future. Read this book, which is a good start for beginners who wish to increase programming, for better results. Since most companies use Python as a basic programming language, Python offers many jobs. The only thing is to choose the right course.

CHAPTER ONE

WHAT IS CODING?

Coding means code, as the word itself suggests. If a concept had been so simple, people wouldn't need expert help to understand it. The story doesn't end. It raises many other questions for the user about what's coded and, more importantly, who is coded for?

Here are the replies. People and organizations code their data so that any external party cannot easily access them. For various types of information, there are different coding languages. Another purpose is to compact data or information. There are a lot of large organizational files. Organizations code them to manage them in a smaller way. This is where coding assistance can be useful.

A third interpretation is the writing, assembly, and compilation of computer codes. HTML, for instance, is the code people use to create their own websites using the software.

Now that you know the purposes of code a file, data, or other information for various contexts, the question remains how to code a file. More than one answer to this question is also available.

It is also important to know that codes are generally in the form of digits before we get to that answer. If the codes are in alphabets instead of numbers, there is no common reason behind these words. That is why everybody calls codes and needs coding assistance before they can be used by anyone.

There are many stages in the development of a code for your interface or data. You will have to begin by defining the computer you are going to use in simpler terms. You'll have to script your desktop once you decide the language. Now that you have completed the first step, you will continue to develop the web and add the language to it.

JavaScript is a key component throughout this process. Once you can layout your page with web help, i.e. HTML, continue scripting on the server-side. You did scripting on your own system first. You will now perform a similar type of online scripting at the end of your server.

You've done most of the major tasks now. You just need to define your application programming interface and write your commands. The rest is up to you how you make it easier for the end-user and more attractive.

WHAT IS PYTHON PROGRAMMING?

The python language was originally designed and developed in the 1980s by Guido van Rossum and is a modern web programming language. Since then, Python has evolved into a modular and extendable high-performance programming language. Some of the world's largest websites use Python, such as Disqus, YouTube, and Reddit. Python provides several features that make it an attractive programming platform that includes stability, object-oriented development, portability, a powerful standard library, and a wealth of modules or packages from outside parties.

Stability

Since the late 1980s, Python has been actively developing and is regarded as a mature programming language. The Python language developers conduct comprehensive functionality and regression tests in order to ensure that every new release remains bug-free and stable.

Portability

Python programming offers several features that make web application development an attractive option. The fact is that interpreters of python are available to all modern operating systems (OS) and some of embedded computer systems means that Python applications are portable.

Object-oriented implementation

Python's object-oriented nature makes it an ideal first language for new programmers as well as easy to learn from other object-oriented languages for programs migrating to Python. The programming of Python is intuitive and strengthens good program structure and object-oriented methods.

Standard Library

Standard Python library gives developers a host of features similar to more complex languages like as C++ while keeping the language syntax simple and accessible. Comprehensive I/O file-based, database interactivity, advanced exceptional management, and a host of built-in data types that make Python right for web applications as well as for general programming. This makes python web programming an easy challenge for application developers looking to develop web applications.

Modules for third parties

Python is known as a complete language with extensive functionality in the standard library. However, Python's growing popularity has led to a wide range of packages or modules that enhance the functionality of Python and enable language to address unique programming challenges. For example, modules for the handling of non-standard database interactions and advanced encryption functionality are available. Modules are available for handling common tasks, such as file metadata reading, rendering charts, and Python applications for standardized executable applications. Due to the availability of many web-centered modules, Python Web programming is simplified to handle tasks such as e-mail, interaction with JavaScript, HTTP maintenance, and other typical web development tasks.

EVOLUTION OF PYTHON OVER THE YEARS

Python is among the most popular 2015 coding languages. In addition to being a general programming and high level language, Python is open source and object-oriented. Many developers worldwide use Python to build GUI applications, mobile applications, and websites. Python's differentiating factor is that it allows programmers to develop concepts through less readable code. Developers can use several Python frameworks to further mitigate the time and effort needed to build modern software applications.

A number of highly frequented websites such as Google, Yahoo Groups, Linux Weekly News, Yahoo Maps, Shopzilla, and Web Therapy are currently using the programming language. Python is also very useful for creating gaming, scientific, financial, and educational applications. Developers also use different language versions. According to the statistical usage of W3techs and market share data from Python, 99.4% of websites currently use Python 2, whereas Python 3 is only used by 0.6% of websites. This is why every programmer needs to understand Python's various versions and their development over many years.

How has Python evolved over the years?

Designed as a programming hobby project

In December 1989, Python was originally designed by Guido van Rossum as a hobby project, although it was one of the most popular coding languages of 2015. As the office of Van Rossum was closed during Christmas, he was looking for a hobby project, which would keep him busy during the holidays. He planned to create a new scripting language interpreter and called the project Python. Python was therefore originally designed as an ABC programming language successor. After the interpreter had written, Van Rossum published the code in February 1991. However, the Python Software Foundation currently manages the open-source programming language.

Python version 1

In January 1994, Python 1.0 was released. The major release included several new features and features such as lambda, map, filter, and reduction. Version 1.4 was released with several new features such as keyword arguments, comprehensive number support, and a basic form of data hiding. Two minor releases, version 1.5 in December 1997 and version 1.6 in September 2000 were followed. Version 1 of Python lacked the features that popular languages of the time offered. However, the initial versions formed a solid basis for developing a powerful and futuristic language of programming.

Python version 2

Python 2.0 was released in October 2000 with a new list understanding and waste collection system. The list-understanding syntax was inspired by other functional programming languages such as Haskell. But Python 2.0 preferred alphabetical keywords over punctuation characters, unlike Haskell. The waste collection system also collected reference cycles. Several minor releases followed the main release. These releases added a number of programming language functionalities such as support for nesting scopes and the combination of classes and types in Python into one hierarchy. The Python Software Foundation has announced that no Python 2.8 will exist. However, the Foundation will support the programming language version 2.7 by 2020.

Python version 3

In December 2008, Python 3.0 was released. It featured several new features and improvements, together with several deprecated features. Deprecated characteristics and backward incompatibility make Python version 3 completely different from previous versions. So many developers are still using the latest Python 2.6 or 2.7 features. But Python 3's new features made it more modern and popular. Many developers have even switched to version 3.0 to use these awesome features.

With the built-in print) (function, Python 3.0 replaced the printer statement, allowing programmers to use custom separators between rows. Likewise, the rules of order comparison were simplified. In case the operators are not organized in natural and meaningful order, orders can now raise an exception to TypeError. In addition to Unicode and 8-bit strings, version 3 of the programming language uses text and data. It represents binary data as encoded Unicode while treating all codes as Unicode by default.

Because the backward incompatibility of Python 3 means that programmers cannot access functions like string exceptions, old-style classes, and relatively implicit imports. Developers must also be familiar with syntax and API changes. You can use a tool called "2to3" to move your application smoothly from Python 2 to 3. The tool emphasizes incompatibility and concerns with observations and warnings. The comments help programmers to change the code and upgrade their existing applications to the latest programming language version.

Latest Python versions

Currently, programmers can choose either Python version 3.4.3 or 2.7.10. Python 2.7 allows developers to improve numerical handling and improvements for standard library applications. The version also facilitates the migration of developers to Python 3. Python 3.4, on the other hand, includes several new features and library modules, security improvements, and improvements to Python's implementation. However, several features in both the Python API and programming languages are deprecated. Developers can still use Python 3.4 for longer-term support.

Python version 4

Python 4.0 is expected to be released by Python 3.9 in 2023. It is going to come with features which will assist programmers to control from version three to four seamlessly. Likewise, as they gain understanding, the master Python designers can exploit various in reverse viable highlights to modernize their current applications without investing any additional time and energy. However, the developers still have to wait many years to get a clear picture of Python 4.0. However, the latest releases must be monitored to easily migrate to the popular code language version 4.0.

Python version 2 and version 3 are completely different. Therefore, each programmer needs to understand and compare the features of these different versions based on the specific needs of the project. He must also check the Python version that every framework supports. Likewise, the latest version of Python must be used by every developer to utilize new features and long-term support.

WHY PYTHON BECOME AN INDUSTRY FAVORITE AMONG PROGRAMMERS

With the world entering into a new era of technological development, it's not difficult to imagine a future full of screens. And, if so, there will definitely increase demand for people with strong programming skills, with more people needed to develop and support applications. For these wishes to be part of this constantly developing industry, Python Training is always a good idea. Python language is not only easy to understand, but it emphasizes less syntax, so a few errors here, and there are not as many difficulties as some other languages.

What makes Python among programmers a preferred choice?

Python is an easy programming language that supports various types of applications, from training to scientific computing to web development. Tech giants such as Google and Instagram have also taken advantage of Python and continue to increase their popularity. Below are some of the advantages that Python offers:

First steps in the programming world

Python can be used by aspiring programmers to enter the programming world. Like many others, such as Perl, Ruby, JavaScript, C++, C#, etc. Python is also a language of object-oriented programming. Those who know Python thoroughly can easily adapt to other environments. Working knowledge is always recommended so as to be aware of the methodologies used in various applications.

Easy to understand and code

Many people agree that learning and understanding a program, compared to a tense baseball game, is not so exciting. But Python, on the other hand, was developed with newcomers in mind. It'll seem meaningful and easy to understand even to a layman's eye. Curious brackets and tiring variable statements do not form part of this programming language, so language learning is much easier.

Making Innovative

Python has helped bring Raspberry Pi closer to the real world and computing. This cheap, card-sized microcomputer helps technology enthusiasts build various brickwork items such as video game consoles, remote-controlled cars, and robots. Python is the programming language this microcomputer can use. Aspirants may select and improve their skills and motivations from various DIY projects online.

Python supports web development as well

Python is also a favorite among web developers to build various types of web applications with its huge capabilities. Django has been developed using Python to provide the basis for popular websites such as 'The Guardian,' 'Pinterest,' 'The NY Times,' and more.

Python is a solid foundation for aspiring programmers to connect to different fields. Python programming training ensures that students can use this highly possible language of programming in an exciting and fun way to the best of their ability. Those who want to make a big career as software programmers will definitely find that Python meets their expectations.

REASONS TO LEARN THE PYTHON LANGUAGE?

Python is a high-level open-source programming language for use in a variety of operating systems. Due to the dynamic and diverse nature, it is called the most important programming language. Python is simple to use with a simple syntax and it is very easy for people who learn to grasp the concepts for the first time. With pioneering websites like DropBox, YouTube, Python has strong market demand. Register for Python Training if you want to benefit from Python.

Python is one of today's most flexible and efficient programming languages. It emphasizes a lot about the readability of the code and programmers have to write fewer codes compared to C++ and Java due to its syntax and implementation. Python memory management is automatically performed, and several standard libraries for the programmer are available here. A programmer can gain expertise in multiple top IT companies after completing a certificate program in Python training.

Python programming supports a variety of styles, for example imperative, functional, and object-oriented programming. Here are the top five reasons why a Python language programmer has to learn:

Easy to learn – Python was developed with the newbie in mind. Completion of fundamental tasks in Python requires less code than other languages. The codes are usually three to five times smaller than Java and five to ten times smaller than C++. Python codes are easy to read and new developers can learn a lot from looking at the code with some knowledge.

Most preferred for web growth and development Python contains a range of frameworks that are useful for web design. Django is one of the most popular frameworks for python development. Because of these frameworks, Python's web design is extremely flexible. There are now nearly 1 billion online websites, and with the growing scope for more, this is natural that programming from Python will continue to be an important component for web developers.

The ideal time and budget for start-ups are essential constraints for any new product or service, and more so if this is a start-up. You can create a product in any language that differentiates from the rest. However, Python is the ideal language for quick development, lower code, and lower costs. Python can easily extend any complex application to a small team. You are not only saving resources but also developing applications with Python in the right direction.

Unlimited resource availability and testing framework- Several resources are now available for Python and are constantly updated. As a result, a Python developer is very rare. The large standard library offers built-in features. Its built-in test framework allows fast workflows and fewer debugging times.

Today, Python is used by top IT companies like Google, IBM, Yahoo, and Nokia. It has grown incredibly among all programming languages in the last few years.

Python is clear to web-based programmers as a vital language. More can be learned at a well-known Python training center.

Let's now learn the key reasons why Python is used in a broader range of people.

• Programming oriented object

One of Python's powerful tools is object-oriented programming that creates and reuses data structures. Due to this reusability, work is carried out efficiently and time is reduced. Object-oriented programming has concerned classes and so many interactive objects in recent years. Object-oriented techniques of programming can be utilized in one software and implemented in some of the programming languages.

• Readability

The python programming language is very simple to understand with simple syntax. Therefore, after testing the code, Python can be used as a prototype and implemented in another language of programming.

• Python is free of charge

Since Python is an open-source programming language, it is free of charge and permits unlimited use. It can be altered, redistributed, and commercially used with this open-source license. The license is available free of charge even for the entire source code. CPython, the most frequently used Python implementation, can be used in all operating systems. Well designed, scalable, robust, and portable software has become a widely used language for programming.

• Faster programming.

Python is indeed a high-level language and programming in this language is faster than running the other low-level languages.

• Operating capacity for cross-platform operations

All major operating systems like Mac OS, Microsoft Windows, Linus, and Unix can be run on Python. This language provides the best experience to work with any of the operating systems.

Capabilities for integration

The following are also the notable integration skills of Python:

- Control of processes is powerful
- The ability to be integrated as the language of programming
- Easy web service development
- Helps implement many protocols for the Internet

If you would like to work with Python, please register at the Python Training Institute, where you can benefit more from your training. See Python Training for information. The training courses for the aspirants will be well understood by highly talented and professional faculties. Aspirants can check their level of understanding by using online mock tests. Exact test results in the form of analytical reports will be provided. Aspirants can also choose other training solutions such as boot camp training, corporate education, training in classrooms, etc.

CHAPTER TWO

PYTHON FUNCTIONS

The function is a block of reusable organized code used to perform a single related action. Functions offer better modularity and a high level of code reuse for your application.

As you know, Python gives you many integrated functions such as print), (etc. but you can also create functions yourself. These functions are called functions defined by the user. A Python function is used to use the code in a program in more than one location. It is also known as procedures or methods.

Defining a function

Functions to provide the required functionality can be defined. Here are simple rules for defining a Python function.

- The function blocks start with the def keyword followed by the name and parentheses of the function(( )).

- Any input parameters or arguments within these parentheses should be placed. In these parentheses, you can also define parameters.

- An optional statement can be the first statement of a function-the function documentation string or the docstring.

- The code block starts with a colon (:) in each function and is indented.

- The return statement [expression] exits a function and optionally transfers a caller expression. An unargued return statement is the same as return None.

Why use the Python function?

As I mentioned above, a function is a code block that carries out a certain mission. Let us explore what we can do in Python using our code functions:

1. Code re-usability: Let's say that we write an application in Python, where we have a certain task to perform in many locations, assume we have 10 lines of code to perform that same task. It is easier to write these 10 lines of code into a feature and call the feature only when it is appropriate because writing these 10 lines every time you do this task is repetitive, makes the code long, less readable, and increases the possibility of human errors.

2. Improves readability: You render the code organized and readable by using functions for regular tasks. It is easier for anyone to look at the code and understand the structure and intent of the code.

3. Avoid redundancy: if you no longer duplicate the same code lines and use functions in their place, you avoid redundancies which you may have generated by not using features.

Default arguments in Function

Now that we can declare and call a function, we can see how the default arguments can be used. We may prevent errors that occur when calling a function with default arguments without passing all the parameters. Take an example to understand:

Types of functions

There are two types of functions in Python:

1. Built-in functions: This predefined in Python and we don't need to announce them before calling. We may invoke them freely when and when appropriate.

2. User defined functions: this are the functions that we build in our code. The add) (function we have generated is a user-defined function in these examples.

Calling a Function

Defining the function only names it, defines the parameters to be used in the structures and function code blocks.

When the general premise of a function is done, you can execute this function directly from a Python prompt or from another application.

Variable-length arguments

You might have to process the function for more reasons than you defined when defining the functionality. These arguments are called arguments of variable length and are not named unlike the usual and the default arguments in the function description.

An asterisk (*) is placed in front of the variable name which contains all non-keyword variable arguments. If no additional arguments are defined during function call, this tuple remains empty.

Pass by value vs. comparison

All parameters (arguments) are transferred by reference in the Python language. If you change the parameter a function refers to, the change will also be reflected in the calling function.

Arguments Function

The following forms of formal arguments can be used to call a function
- Arguments needed
- Arguments needed
- Arguments for keywords
- Arguments of variable length
- Arguments default

The arguments needed are the arguments passed in the correct positional order to a function. The number of arguments in the call function should match the function description exactly.

You must definitely pass one argument to call the function printme(), otherwise it gives a syntax error.

Arguments for keywords

Keyword statements refer to calls to work. When you use keyword arguments in a function call, the caller uses the parameter name to define the arguments.

This enables you to skip or disorder arguments because the Python interpreter will use the keywords given to fit parameters with the values. You may also use the printme() function to make keyword calls.

Arguments default

Default is an argument which assumes the default value if the function call for that argument does not have a value.

Anonymous functions

These functions are called anonymous since they are not defined by def keyword in the traditional way. You can construct small anonymous functions with the lambda keyword.

• Lambda forms can take all sorts of arguments, but only return one value as an expression. The commands or multiple expressions are not included.

• An anonymous function cannot be a direct printing call, as lambda needs an expression

• Lambda functions have a local namespace of their own and cannot access other than the parameters in their list and the global namespace variables.

• While lambda appears to be a One-line version of a function, it does not equate to inline statements in C or C++ which, for performance reasons, are allocated bypassing stack function at the time of invocation.

The declaration of return

The return statement [expression] exits a function, which optionally returns a caller's expression. An unargued return argument is the same as the None return.

Variables set

Not all program variables can be accessed at all locations in the program. This changes depending on where a variable has been identified.
The scope of a variable determines the part of the program where a specific identifier can be accessed. In Python there are two simple sets of variables:

• Global variables
• Local variables

Local vs. Global variables

Variables defined within the feature body are local and externally defined have a global scope.

This means that the local variables could be accessed in the function they are declared, while global variables can be accessed by all features in the entire program body. If you call a function, the declared variables are put in the scope.

Python modules

A module helps you to arrange your Python code logically. Grouping the code into a module makes it easier to understand and use the code. A module is a Python object with attributes that can be linked and referenced arbitrarily.

Simply put, a module is a Python code file. A module can set attributes, classes, and variables. An operating code may also be included in a module.

Import Declaration

Any Python source file may be used as a module if an import statement is executed in a separate Python source file.

When the interpreter detects an import expression, the module is imported if the search path module is present. A search path is a directory list searched by the interpreter before importing a file.

Scoping and namespaces

Variables are names that correspond to objects (identifiers). A namespace is a dictionary of the names (keys) of the attribute and their related objects (values).

In a local namespace and a global namespace, a Python statement may access variables. If the variable local and global have the same name, the local variable is the global variable's shadow.

The function has a separate local namespace. Class methods adopt the same pattern as regular functions.

Python makes well-informed assessments of whether local or global variables are present. It assumes that any variable that a function assigns a value is local.

Therefore, to assign the value to the global variable within a function, the global statement must first be used.

The global VarName statement informs Python that VarName is a global variable. Python avoids checking the local variable namespace.

PYTHON COMPILERS

The compiler is called a computer program that translates code in one programming language into another. Python leads the group of programming languages that are growing fast. There is also no lack of Python compilers to satisfy various project needs.

Compilers are mainly programs that translate source code for producing an executable program written in a high-level programming language to a low-level programming language, such as machine code.

Best compilers for Python

While the de-facto Python compiler is a CPython compiler (-cum-interpreter), it is part of the standard Python implementation. CPython, a range of other Python compilers are available to developers. The 7 best ones are described as follows:

1. Brython

Supports – 3 to 3.7 Python
This is a popular Python compiler that converts Python code to JavaScript code and is classified as a "Python 3 web programming implementation for client-side programming." Evolved to the HTML5, Brython is fitted with a DOM object and event GUI.

Brython is a Web Python contraction. It provides a wide range of features, from basic document elements to drag and drop to 3D navigation. In Firefox, the compiler of Python is much better than in the Google Chrome.

Brython supports all desktop browsers and browsers of mobile web. The Python compiler has a JavaScript console that can be used to test the execution time of a certain JS program in contrast with its Python counterpart in the editor.

Brython's founder and lead developer, Pierre Quentel's official site, says Brython is much quicker than Pypy.js and Skulpt. In certain instances, the compiler Python is much faster than the reference implementation Python. CPython. CPython.

Brython supports much of Python 3 's syntax, such as understandings, generators, and imports. It also supports several CPython deployment modules and includes libraries to communicate with DOM elements and events.

The latest specifications for HTML5 / CSS3 can also be provided in Brython, and common CSS frameworks such as BootStrap3 and LESS can be used in the Python compiler.

2. Nuitka

Supports Python of 2.6, 2.7, 3.3, and 3.7.
A Python converter from source to source, Nuitka uses Python code and compiles it to C / C++ source or executables. Nuitka can be used to build standalone programs even if you don't run Python on your computer.

Written entirely in Python, Nuitka enables different libraries and extension modules to be used. The Python compiler is available on the Apache license version 2.0 for FreeBSD, macOS X, NetBSD, Linux, and Windows platforms.

Nuitka is also provided with Anaconda for those who use it to build data science and machine learning projects.

2. PyJS

Supports – Python 2.7 up to
PyJS is one of the choices for people who are interested in writing and executing Python code in web browsers. PyJS converts Python code to JavaScript counterpart to allow it to run inside a web browser.

A significant feature of PyJS is the AJAX frame that fills the gaps between JS and DOM support for different web browsers. PyJS uses the abstract syntax tree of Python to create equivalent JS code.

You may use the PyJS Desktop module to execute a Python Web Application source code as a standalone desktop application (running under Python). Interestingly, many Unix systems have PyJS and PyJS server versions pre-installed.

While Python and JavaScript vary, most data types are the same among the two common programming languages. Some types of Python data are transformed into custom objects, including lists while using PyJS.

PyJS is an application that is lightweight. It can also be accessed directly from the Web browser and enables programs to be run from a JS web browser console.

The PyJS compiler also provides runtime support for runtime errors. Since Python code can be incorporated into the JS developers, JS code can design and build apps using PyJS in a pure object paradigm.

3. Shed Skin

Python 2.4 – 2.6 supports
Shed Skin is another common Python compiler. It transforms a Python program statically typed into an analogous pure C++ program. Statically defined means that the variables in use can only be based on a single form of data.

Shed Skin does not accept such common features, including the use of nest functions and functions to describe a variety of arguments. Shed Skin can only use some of the standard Python library features.

Shed Skin offers to convert statically typed Python programs into C++-optimized code with some limitations as an experimental compiler software. Also, Shed Skin cannot scale much beyond a few thousand lines of code.

If you have an incompatible Shed Skin module, you need to uninstall it and add plain code to replicate your desired features.

Shed Skin can build standalone programming or extension modules that can be imported and used in larger Python programs, despite its experimental status.

The greatest advantage of using Shed Skin is that it makes a substantial improvement inefficiency. This is partly due to the fact that the Python compiler has implemented the incorporated Python data types in its own collection of classes in an efficient C++ code.

4. Skulpt

Supports – Python 3.3 up to
Written in javascript, Skulpt provides a genuine environment where the compiled code is executed in JS format and is accessible under the MIT license.

Since Skulpt is a browser-based implementation of Python, no further processing, plug-ins, or server-side support required for Python to run in a web browser is required. Any code of Python written in Skulpt is executed directly in the web browser.

Skulpt is a good choice for developers to create a web application that allows users to run Python programs within a web browser while retaining the protected background servers. The famous Python compiler can also be easily incorporated into an existing blog or website.

Skulpt code can be added to the HTML for custom integration. You can also teach Skulpt how to import your own individual modules for more power. Although Skulpt converts Python code into JS code, it doesn't make it simple for the latter to function.

5. Transcrypt

Supports – 3 to 3.7 Python
Transcrypt is another common Python compiler. It allows a reasonably large subset of Python to be compiled into a JavaScript code that is lightweight, readable, and easy to debug. The Python compiler follows a simple and efficient syntax without any further extensions.

Transcrypt pre-compiles to quick Javascript code readable that can be debugged using source maps from Python source code. The lightweight Python compiler supports I j: k] matrix-slicing operations and +,*, -, and / operators vector operations.

The Transcrypt is combined with a linter, miniature, and a static form validator. The Python compiler increases team cohesion in full-scale projects. Transcrypt also has the ability to run on Node.js as well as easy access to any Javascript library.

Transcrypt has a versatile and robust overall structure by support for hierarchical modules, local classes, and multiple heritage.

6. WinPython

Supports – Python 3.7 up to
WinPython is a Python distribution created for the operating system in Windows. The previous versions of CPython were not well built for Windows and thus had some bugs. As a solution to the problem, WinPython was incubated.

Although the latest CPython versions are highly stable on Windows, WinPython provides many unique features. Since WinPython is a Python distribution, you only have to download and unpack it to start.

WinPython also comes pre-packed with some of the most common Python libraries, such as NumPy, SciPy, and Pandas. Therefore, you will instantly work with these Python libraries.

WinPython comes with many bundled features that are usually not necessary, as the C++ and C compilers. This can be a serious restriction since only certain features that are appropriate can be selected and downloaded.

However, WinPython is available in a zero package option that contains only the Python compiler and nothing else.

That completes our list of the best Python compilers. All each of them is designed to meet unique requirements, you can use them for a particular set of needs. The more a programmer learns, the better it is in programming. So start today!

CODE EDITORS AND PYTHON IDES

Writing Python with IDLE and Python Shell is wonderful for simple things, but those tools quickly transform larger programs into frustrating despair boxes. To use an IDE, or a good code editor, does coding fun, but what's best for you?

Don't be afraid, Gentle Reader! We are here to help you understand and demystify the various options. We cannot choose what works best for you and your method but we can clarify the advantages and drawbacks of each of them and help you make an educated decision.

To make it simpler, we will divide list to two broad categories of tools: those developed specifically for the development of Python and those designed for general development, which can be used by Python. For each of us, we'll point out some Why s and Why Points. Finally, none of these options are mutually unique, so you can try them with a very little penalty on your own.

What are IDEs and editors of code?

An IDE (or Integrated Development Environment) is a software development program. As the name suggests, IDEs incorporate many software development tools. In general, these methods include:

• A code-controlled editor (such as syntax highlighting and self-finishing)

• Tools for building, executing and debugging

• Some sort of control of the source

Most IDEs support a wide range of different languages and have many more features. So you can be huge and take time to download and update. You will also need specialized knowledge to properly use them.

In comparison, a dedicated code editor can be as quick as a text editor with the ability to highlight syntax and format code. The best code editors will execute code and search a debugger. The best work with source control systems. Compared to an IDE, a good code editor is usually smaller and simpler, but also less rich in functionality.

Healthy Python development environment requirements

So what stuff in a coding world do we really need? Configuration lists differ from application to app, but a core collection of features enables coding:

• **Save files and restore them.**
If an IDE or editor doesn't let you save your work and reopen it later, it was not much of an IDE in the same state you entered.

• **Run code within the system**
Likewise, if you have to remove your Python code from the file, then this is not much more than a basic text editor.

• **Support for debugging**
The ability to transfer the code as it works is the main feature in all IDEs and best editors in code.

• **Highlighting syntax**
Being able to identify variables, keywords, and symbols in your code easily make it much easier for you to read and understand code.

• **Automated formatting of code**
At the end of a while, every editor or IDE worth salt recognizes the colon or declaration and knows that the next line should be indented.

There are of course several other features you would like, such as source code management, extension model, tools for building and testing, language support, and so on. However, the above list is what I would see as "essential features" that should support a good editing environment.

Let's look at some general-purpose tools we can use for Python development with these features in mind.

Python Help General Editors and IDEs

PyDev + Eclipse

If you spent a lot of time in the open-source environment, you heard of Eclipse. Eclipse is a de-facto, open-source IDE for Java development, for Linux, Windows, and OS X. It has a wealth of extensions and supplements on the market, making Eclipse useful for a variety of development projects.

One extension is PyDev, which allows Python to debug, complete code, and have the Python interactive console. It's easy to install PyDev into Eclipse: from Eclipse, select Help, search for PyDev, then PyDev. If necessary, click Install and restart Eclipse.

Pros: Adding PyDev will be faster and easier if you already have Eclipse mounted. For the experienced Eclipse developer, PyDev is very accessible.
Con: Eclipse can handle a lot when you're just starting with Python or with software development generally. Recall when I said that IDEs are larger and need more knowledge to be properly used? Eclipse is anything and a (micro)chip.

Supreme Text

Written by a Google engineer dreaming of a better word editor, Sublime Text is a very popular code editor. Sublime Text supports Python code editing and a wide range of plugins (called packages) that expand syntax and edit functionality on all platforms.

Pros: It has great community support. As the code editor, Sublime Text alone is simple, small, and also well supported.

Con: Sublime It is not secure, even though the evaluation version can be used indefinitely. Installing extensions can be difficult and the execution or debugging of code from the editor does not have direct support.

Atom

Accessible on all platforms, Atom is described as the "Hackable 21st Century Text Editor." A sleek GUI, file system explorer and marketplace extension are used for developing open-source Atom, Electron, a web framework for HTML, JavaScript, and CSS applications. Python's language support is an enhancement that can be added as Atom runs.

Pros: Thanks to Electron, it has wide support on all platforms. Atom is thin, so it easily downloads and loads.
Con: Support for building and debugging is not built-in but community add-ons are given. Since Atom is based on Electron, it always runs in JavaScript and does not run as a native program.

GNU Emacs

Prior to the Android vs iPhone War, before Windows vs. Linux war, the editor war, and before the Mac vs. PC war, with a GNU Emacs as the warriors. GNU Emacs has been known to be "the extensible, customizable, self-documenting, and real-time view editor" almost as long as UNIX and has a good follow-up.

GNU Emacs uses a type of powerful Lisp computer program for customization, and numerous customization scripts exist for Python development on any platform (in one type or another).

Pros: You know Emacs, you use Emacs, you love Emacs, you know Emacs. Lisp is a second language, and you know the strength it gives you can do something.

Customization means to write (or to copy/paste) Lisp code to different script files. If it's not already provided, you may have to learn Lisp to find out how to do it.

Moreover, if Emacs just had a decent text editor, you know that it would be a perfect operating system.

Vi / Vim

The VI (aka VIM) stands on the other side of the Text Editor Battle. VI has an equally fervent follow on almost every UNIX system and Mac OS X by design.

VI and VIM are modal editors that distinguish a file from a file editing. VIM provides several enhancements to the original VI, including the extensibility model and the in-place code creation. For various Python development tasks, VIMScripts are open.

Pros: You know VI, you use VI, you love VI, you love VI. VIMScripts don't frighten you, because you know that you can bend it.
Cos: Like Emacs, you don't find or write your own scripts for the development of Python and don't know how a modal editor works.

Moreover, you know that if only it had a good operating system VI would be a perfect text editor.

Visual Studio

Designed by Microsoft, Visual Studio is a complete IDE, comparable in several ways to Eclipse. Designed for Windows and Mac OS alone, VS is available in both free (Community) and paid (Professional) versions. Visual Studio allows a range of channels to be established and has its own growth market.

Python Tools for Visual Studio (aka PTVS) allow Visual Studio Python, as well as Python Intelligence, debugging, and other resources.

Pros: If you have Visual Studio already installed for other creative tasks, it is faster and simpler to add PTVS.

Con: Visual Studio is a major Python download. Plus, if you're on Linux, you are out of luck: no installation on that platform is in Visual Studio.

Visual Studio Code

Visual Studio Code (along with VS Code) is a robust code editor for Linux, Mac OS X, and Windows platforms that cannot be confused with full Visual Studio edition. VS Code is lightweight, small, but fully-functional and open source, extendable and configurable for virtually any mission. Like Atom, the Electron VS Code has the same advantages and disadvantages.

It's very accessible to install Python support in VS code: the marketplace is easy to click away. Click Install, check for Python, and restart when necessary. VS Code is going to automatically recognize the Python libraries and installation.

Pros: VS Code is available on all platforms, which is remarkably complete, considering a limited footprint and an open-source.

Con: Electron implies that VS Code is not a native version. Furthermore, some people may have key reasons not to use Microsoft tools.

Be sure to review our tutorial on the use of Visual Studio Code and the complementary video course for the production of Python.

Editors and IDEs Python-specific

PyCharm

PyCharm is one of the best (and only) dedicated IDEs for Python. PyCharm can be installed easily and rapidly on the Windows, Mac OS X, and Linux platforms in both payable (Professional) and free open-source (Community) versions.

PyCharm explicitly supports Python creation from the package. You can only open a new file and begin writing code. You can directly run and debug Python in PyCharm and have source control and project support.

Pros: This is de-facto Python IDE environment, and loads of support. It will edit, run, and debug Python.

Contrary: PyCharm can be loaded slowly, and default settings for existing projects may need tweaking.

Spyder

Spyder is a Python IDE open-source designed for workflows in the area of data science. Spyder comes with the Anaconda package manager delivery so you can get it installed on your computer depending on your setup.

What's interesting about Spyder is that data scientists using Python are the target audience. You're going to see this all over. Spyder integrates well with popular Python data science libraries such as SciPy, NumPy, and Matplotlib, for example.

Spyder features most "simple IDE features," such as a powerful syntax highlighting code editor, Python code completion, and even integrated plugin documentation.

Spyder's "variable explorer" is a special function that I haven't seen in other Python editing environments that enables you to show data right inside the IDE using a table-based layout. Personally, I don't really need it, but it looks good. If you use Python on a regular basis, you may be in love with this unique function. The integration of IPython / Jupyter is also cool.

Overall, I'd say Spyder feels more fundamental than other IDEs. I prefer to see it rather than as something I use every day as my primary editing environment as a special-purpose tool. What's good about this Python IDE is that it's free on macOS, Windows, and Linux and is fully open-source.

Pros: You are an Anaconda Python distribution data scientist.
Con: More experienced Python developers can find Spyder too simple to work with every day and choose a more complex IDE or custom editor solution instead.

Thonny

Thonny is a recent addition to the Python IDE family and is known for beginners as an IDE. The Institute of Computer Science at the University of Tartu, Estonia, has been written and maintained. Thonny can be installed on-site for all main platforms with instructions.

Thonny installs by default with its own Python bundled version, so you don't have to install something new. More experienced users may have to adjust this configuration so that already configured libraries are found and used.

Pros: You are an early user of Python and you want a roll-ready IDE.
Con: More seasoned Python developers find Thonny too simple for most applications, and the built-in interpreter isn't about it. Plus, with a new method, problems can be discovered that cannot be solved immediately.

What is the IDE of Python correct for you?

You can only decide, but here are some simple recommendations:
• New developers of Python should try as few customizations as possible for solutions. The less it gets, the better.

• If you have other projects using text editors (such as web pages or documentation), take a glance for code editor solutions.

• You can find it easier to add Python functionality to your existing toolset if you are already developing other tools.

INSTALL PYTHON (ANACONDA) ON WINDOWS

Anaconda is an environment manager, a package manager, and distribution for Python which includes a number of open-source packages (numbersome, scikit-learning, scipy, pandas). You can use a package manager, conda, or pip from Anaconda to install these packages if you need additional packages after you install Anaconda. This is very beneficial because you do not have to handle the dependencies between different packages. It's also simple for Conda to turn between Python 2 and 3 (you can read more here).

This tutorial contains:

- Way to download Anaconda on Windows and install it?
- How to test the device
- How to resolve common installation problems
- What to do after Anaconda has been installed.

Let's start with that!

Anaconda Download and Update

1.) Go on to the Anaconda Website and pick either the graphical (A) Python 3.x installer or the graphical (B) Python 2.x installer. If you don't know which version of Python you want to install, choose Python 3. Do not want both

2. Find your file. Find your email.

Ideally, you open/run the admin tab.

3. Tap on I Accept and read the License Agreement.

4. Can choose Only Me (recommended) or All Users.

5. Please note your location (1) and then press Next (2).

6. This is an essential aspect of the process of implementation. The recommendation is not to check the box (1) to add Anaconda to your route. This means that if you want to use the Anaconda (you can still add Anaconda to the Route later when you don't check the box), you must use the Anaconda or the command prompt of Anaconda (located at start menu under the "Anaconda"). Please use the alternative method and check the box if you want anaconda to be included in your command prompt. Click Update (2). Update.

7. Select next. Next press.

8. If you like, you can install PyCharm, but it's optional. Select Next. Select next.

9. Click Stop.

How to test your system?

Opening a Jupyter Notebook is a good way to review your installation. Either Anaconda Request or Anaconda Navigator will do this.

Navigator Anaconda

- Locate Navigator Anaconda and click on Navigator Anaconda.
- Click on Start under Jupyter Notebook.

Prompt Anaconda

- Anaconda Prompt Find.
- Type the command for a Jupyter (IPython) Notebook to start.

Path Add Anaconda (optional)

It's an optional move. This is the case wherein step 6 you did not check the box and now would like to add Anaconda to your Route. The advantage is that you can use Anaconda in your Prompt Command.

1. Open the Prompt Button.

2. Check that you have added Anaconda to your route already. Enter the commands in your Prompt file. This checks if Anaconda has already been added to the route. If you do not receive an order, proceed to phase

3. If you do not understand where your python or conda are, open the Anaconda Prompt and type the commands below. This tells you where conda and python are on your machine.

4. Attach your Route conda and python. You can do this by incorporating the performance of phase 3 into your Direction by going to your device or environmental variables. Please see the video during this phase (this can vary depending on your Windows).

5. Open a new Prompt Button. Try typing the conda version and python version into the Prompt Command to verify that all went well. You should also try to open a Jupyter Notebook.

Other Important Questions

Jupyter is not approved

If you don't recognize a jupyter, if python is not recognized or similar, then you probably have a trajectory problem. Please refer to the section Adding Anaconda to Path (optional).

EnvironmentNotWritableError: There are no written permissions for the current user in the target environment. Location of the environment:

C:\ProgramData\ProgramDatabase3

While the image error occurs after downloading a library, it should be remembered that this kind of error can occur while downloading anaconda (especially if you clicked All Users for step 4 in Download and Install Anaconda). Please open the prompt / anaconda browser or anaconda prompt to install your packages, if you have an error and want to update libraries.

DLL load failed: Unable to locate the required module

This is because the path environment variable does not add anything. You probably haven't added bin to your course, I suppose.

This tutorial offered a fast guide on how to install Anaconda on Windows and how common installation problems can be treated.

PYTHON REQUESTS

What is the Module of Requests?
Requests is a Python module you can use to submit HTTP requests of all kinds. It's a user-friendly library with several features ranging from passing URL parameters to sending custom SSL and headers verification.

You can submit requests HTTP/1.1 with requests. Also, you can add headers, multipart files, parameters, and form data in the same way with easy Python dictionaries.

- Enable application Requests
- Simply to install requests:
- Installation of $pip requests

Or, if you have to:
$Requests easy install

Having a GET application

It is very quick to submit an HTTP request with requests. You first import the module and then request the package.

So, all the information is somewhere stored, right?
Yes, it is stored as req in a response variable.

For instance, you want a web-page encoding, so you can search or use it elsewhere. This can be done using the property req.encoding.

Another advantage is that you can also extract many features such as the status code (in the request). This can be done with the property req.status code.

We can also access the cookies sent back by the server. This is done with req.cookies as simple as that! You can also get the response headers. This is achieved by using req.headers.

Please note that the property req.headers returns a case-insensitive dictionary of the response headers. So, what does that mean?

This means that req.headers, req.headers['content-length'] and req.headers['CONTENT-LENGTH'] all return the value of the response header 'Contents-Length.'

We may also verify that the received answer is a well-forming HTTP redirect (or not) that could automatically be processed using the req.is redirect property. This returns True or False on the basis of the reply.

You can also get the time between sending the request and returning a reply using another property. Do you guess? Yeah, it's the property req.elapsed.

Remember the URL you transferred to the get) (function initially? Well, for several purposes it can be different from the final URL of the answer, and redirects are also included.
And you can use the req.url property to display the actual answer URL.

Do you not think it is nice to get all this webpage information? But, it's most likely you want to access the actual content, right?

If the content is text, you can still access the req.txt address. Remember that the material is then only checked as Unicode. You can use the req.encoding property that we discussed before to decode this file.

For non-text answers, you can easily access them. Currently, when you use req.content, it is done in binary format. This module decodes the gzip and deflate

transfer encodes for us automatically. This can be very helpful if you manage media files directly. You can also access the content JSON-encoded of the reply, if accessible, use req.json().
Quite simple and very flexible, right?

Also, if needed, you can get the raw answer from the server just by using req.raw. Note that you must pass stream = True on your request to get the raw answer as desired.
But, some of the files that you download via the Requests module from the Internet may be massive, correct? Well, in such situations, the whole answer or file will not be loaded in the memory at once. But you should convert a file into chunks or chunks by the method of iter content (chunk size = 1, decode Unicode = False).

This method then iterates the response data in chunk size bytes at a time. And if the stream = True is set, this method will prevent the entire file from being read into memory for the large answers at once.

Note that either an integer or None can be the chunk size parameter. But chunk size specifies the number of bytes that can be read in the memory at once when setting to an integer.

When chunk size is set to None and the stream is set to Valid, the data is read as it comes in any piece size as it is obtained. However, when the chunk size is set to None and the stream is set to False, all data is only returned as one single piece of data.

CHAPTER THREE

PANDAS PYTHON LIBRARY

Pandas is quite a game-changer when it comes to analyzing Python data and is one of the most common and used tools for mung/wrangling data if not THE most used. Pandas is an open, free (under a BSD license) source and was initially intended by Wes McKinney.

The cool thing about Pandas is that it uses data (such as a CSV or TSV or a SQL database) and creates a Python object with rows and columns known as a data frame which looks very much like a table in statistical software (such as Excel or SPSS, for instance. This is much easier to deal with compared to dealing with lists and/or dictionaries for loops or list understanding.

Installation and starting up

You need to update it to "play" Pandas. You will need Python 3.5.3 and higher. It is also based on other libraries as well as optional dependencies (like Matplotlib for plotting), as a pre-requirement for installation (when operating with Python 3.6, 3.7, or 3.8). Therefore, I believe that the most convenient way to set up Pandas is to install it through a package such as the Anaconda distribution, "a cross-platform distribution for data analysis and scientific computing." If you want to update otherwise, these are complete installation instructions.

To use Pandas in Python IDEs such as Jupyter Notebook or Spyder (both with Anaconda by default), you first have to import the Pandas library. Importing a library means loading this into the memory and then working with it. To import Pandas, simply execute the following code:
• import pandas as pd
• import NumPy as np

Normally, the second element ('as the pd') is added so that you can access Pandas by 'pd.command' rather than writing 'pandas.command' each time you need to use it. You'd also import NumPy because it's a very useful library for scientific Python programming. Pandas is now ready to use! Remember, each time you begin a fresh Jupyter Notebook, spyder file, etc., you should do this.

Pandas works with

Loading and saving Pandas data
You will normally use Pandas for data processing in three different ways:
• Convert a list, dictionary or Numpy array from Python to the Pandas dataset
• Use Pandas to open a local file, usually the CSV but may also be text file delimited like Excel, TSV, etc.
• Open the remote database or file, such as a CSV or JSON, from a website via URL or from SQL table/database.
There are different commands for each of these options, but they will look like this when you open a file:

pd.read_filetype()

As I said before, Pandas will operate with various file types, so that you can substitute "filetype" for the actual file type (similar to CSV). In the parenthesis, you would offer the path, filename, etc. You may also transfer various claims inside the parenthesis concerning how to open the file. There are several reasons, and you can read the documentation to know all of them (for example, for pd.read csv) (documentation will contain all the reasons that can be passed into this Pandas command).

The basic command for translating a certain object from Python (dictionary, lists, etc.) is: pd.DataFrame()

In the parenthesis, the object(s) from which the data frame is generated will be defined. There are also different reasons for this command (clickable link).
You can also save a data frame for various types of files (such as CSV, Excel, JSON, and SQL tables). The general code is as follows: df.to_filetype(filename)

Data presentation and review

It's time to look now that you've loaded your files. What does the picture look like? The data frame name will give you entire table, but the first rows N with the df.head(n) or even the final n rows and df.tail(n) can be obtained as well. Df.shape is going to give you number of columns and rows. Df.info) (will send you information about the index, datatype and memory. The s.value counts(dropna = False) command will allow you to display single values and series counts (such as a column or a few columns). A really useful command is df.describe) (which provides numerical column overview statistics. Statistics on the entire data frame or sequence (column, etc) can also be obtained:

- df.mean()Returns all columns' mean
- df.corr()Returns the correlation among data frame columns
- df.count()Returns the non-zero values in each column of the data frame
- df.max()Returns the highest column value
- df.min()Returns the lowest column value
- df.median()Returns each column's median
- df.std()Returns the default column deviation

Data collection

One of the things in Pandas so much simpler than choosing a value from a list or dictionary is to pick the data you want. You can pick (df[col]) column and return columns with Series mark columns or columns (df[[col1, col2]]). Place (s.iloc[0]) or index (s.loc['index one']) are accessible. You can use df.iloc[0,:] to select the first row, and you can select the first element of the first column from df.iloc[0,0]. They can also be used in various combinations, so I hope it gives you an idea of the variety and indexing you can do in Pandas.

Sort and Groupby Filters
You may use various conditions for filtering columns. For instance, df[df[year] > 1985] will only give you more than the 1984 column year. You can apply different conditions to your filtering using & (and) or (or). This is often referred to as boolean filtering.

The values can be sorted by using df.sort values(col1) in an ascending order and by means of df.sort values(col2,ascending = False) also in a descending order. In addition, col1 values can be sorted in an ascending order then col2 in descending order, using df.sort values([col1,col2],ascending=[True, False]).

Groupby is the last command in this portion. It involves dividing the data into groups on the basis of certain parameters, separately using one function for each group, and integrating results into the data structure. df.groupby(col) returns the object of groupby for a single column value, while the df.groupby([col1,col2]) returns the object of groupby for multi-column values.

Cleaning of data

The cleaning of data is an extremely essential step in the analysis of data. For instance, we often search for values missing in a data with pd.isnull), (checking for missing values, and returning boolean array (the array of missing values for true and missing values for false). Run pd.isnull().sum) (to get the sum of missing/null values. The opposite of pd.isnull) (is pd.notnull). You can either delete or drop them by using df.dropna) (to drop a rows, and df.dropna (axis=1) to drop the columns after you have a missing list of values. Another solution will be substitute null values and other values using df.fillna(x) to fill out the missing values by x (the mean is almost any function in the statistics section), or s.fillna(s.mean()) to substitute all null values by the average.

Values must sometimes be replaced with different values. For example, s.replace(1,'one') will substitute 'one' for all the values equal to 1. It can be done for several values: s.replace will replace all 1 by 'one' and 3 by 'three.' You may also rename those columns by running: df.rename(columns={'old name': 'new name'}) or by running df.set index('column one') to adjust the dataset index.

Combine / Enter

The last set of Pandas basic commands are used to mount or combine data frames or columns / rows.

These are the most basic commands for Pandas but you could see the way strong Pandas could be to analyze data. Hope this post made you feel like using Pandas to take a dataset!

BEAUTIFULSOUP

You haven't written this horrible book. You just want to get some details out of it. Lovely Soup's here to help.

Beautiful Soup is a library of Python that offers knowledge from XML, HTML, and other bookmark languages. Say you've found some web pages which show data relevant to your studies, such as address or date information, but which do not directly download the data. Beautiful Soup can help you remove certain content from a site, remove the HTML markup, and save information. It is a web scraping tool that allows you to clean and analyze documents that you have retrieved from the web.

The documents of Beautiful Soup will give you a sense of several aspects that the Beautiful Soup library will allow you to isolate titles and links, remove all the text from the HTML tags, and modify the Code in your paper.

Beautiful Soup Installation

It is easiest to install Beautiful Soup if you have a pip or other Python installer. If you don't have pip, run a short tutorial on the installation of python modules. If you have a pip mounted, run the command Beautiful Soup in the terminal: pip install beautifulsoup4

You will have to preface this line to "sudo," which allows your machine to write to your root directories and requires that you enter your password again. This is the same logic behind you when you install a new application that asks you to enter your password.
The command with sudo is: sudo pip install beautifulsoup4

Where do we go?

Since I like to see how the finish would be before the start, I will commence with a perspective of what we try to build.

Beautiful Soup is a Python library for rapid reversal tasks such as screen scraping. Three characteristics make it powerful:

1. Beautiful Soup gives you some basic methods and pythonic idioms to navigate, scan, and change the parsing tree: a toolkit to pick a document and extract what you need.

2. Beautiful Soup converts the incoming documents to the Unicode and the outgoing documents to the UTF-8 automatically. You don't have to worry about encoding unless you mention an encoding in the text and Beautiful Soup cannot detect any. The original encoding must then be specified.

3. Beautiful Soup is on top of common Python parsers like html5lib and lxml that allows for versatility in testing different strategies parsing or commercial pace.

Beautiful Soup scrutinizes everything you offer and does things for you through the flower. You can say, 'Find all of the links,' 'Find all external Links,' or 'Find the bold text table,' give me this text.'

Valuable data that once we're locked up on maliciously designed websites are now open to you. Projects that only took hours of Beautiful Soup.

OPENCV PYTHON

You will have to learn OpenCV along the way, no matter whether you are interested in learning how to apply visual recognition to video streams, build a complete deep learning pipeline to classify images, or simply tinker with your Raspberry Pi and attach image recognition to a hobby project.

The reality is that OpenCV was previously very difficult to understand. It was difficult to navigate the files. The tutorials were difficult to follow and unfinished.

The good news is that OpenCV is not as complicated as it used to be. And I will go so far as to suggest that learning OpenCV has become much easier.

And to prove this (and to help you learn OpenCV), I have built this complete guide to learning the basics of the OpenCV library with the Python programming language.

OpenCV is used for all kinds of image and video processing, such as face recognition and identification, photo editing, robot advanced vision, optical character recognition, and many more.

Here we will work through several examples from Python. It is actually much simpler to start with OpenCV's Python bindings than many people first. Two major libraries are required with a third option: python-OpenCV, Numpy, and Matplotlib.

Matplotlib is an alternative for viewing video or image frames. Here are a few examples we can demonstrate. Numpy is used for everything, "numbers and Python." We primarily use the array features of Numpy. In the end, we use the python bindings called python-OpenCV for OpenCV.

Some OpenCV operations are not possible without a complete OpenCV installation (about 3 GB in size), but the limited installation of python-OpenCV is a good thing. We will complete the installation of OpenCV so you will be free to have it when you want to, but these three modules will make us busy for some time!

First, in the field of image and video processing, we must grasp some basic concepts and paradigms. Like any video camera record today, videos are simply frames that are viewed 30-60 times a second, one after another. At the heart, however, are static frames, like pictures. The bulk of image recognition and video processing also use the same approaches. Some items, like direction tracking, may involve the sequence of photo (frames), but almost the same code on pictures and videos can be used for anything like object recognition or facial detection.

Next, a lot of picture and video processing is performed as much as possible to simplify the source. This almost always starts with a grayscale conversion, but it can also be a color filter, a gradient, or a mixture of them. From here we can carry out all kinds of analyzes and source transformations. In general, the transformation is completed, then the analysis is done and any overlays we may like to add are added back to the original source. Thus, sometimes you can see the "finished product" of a potential object or face recognition on a full-color image or video. However, the data are rarely stored in raw form.

The black is the pixel values of (0.0,0) in the case of edge detection, while white lines are (255,255, 255). As with the edge detection, we can deduce where the edges of each image and image from a video are based on where the white pixels correspond to the black. If we want to see the original image marked with edges, we find all-white pixel coordinate positions then mark these positions on the original image or video feed source image.

At the end of this tutorial, you can do the above and train your computer in order to recognize any object you want. The first step is typically to turn into gray. We must load the image before that. Yeah, let's do it! I encourage you to use your own data to play within this whole tutorial. If you've got a camera, use it certainly, or you'll find a picture you think is fun to use.

First of all, we import a few things, those 3 modules that I had all of you mounted. Then we specify that img is cv2.read(image file, parms). The default is IMREAD COLOR, which has no alpha channel color. Alpha is the degree of obscurity (the opposite of transparency) if you're not established. You can also use IMREAD UNCHANGED if you need to keep the alpha switch. You will always read in the color version and convert it to gray later. If you don't have a webcam, this is the main method you will use to load a file.

You may also use simple numbers instead of using IMREAD COLOR ... etc. You should know all choices so that you understand what the individual does. You may use -1, 0, or 1. for the second parameter. Color is 1, 0 is grayscale and -1 is unchanged.

Computer vision is among the most thrilling computer science types. For decades a lot of research has been conducted in this area. Cloud technology and powerful GPUs and TPUs allow image processing quicker and more effective. Cars, robots, and drones begin to see in pictures and videos what we see. In the next few years, the "computer vision" interface between machines and humans will become even more relevant.

119

Computer vision in the age of artificial intelligence is considered to be the hottest field. For newbies, it can be hectic and most people face certain obstacles when making a transition into a computer vision.

- File Preprocessing -Image Server Cleaning?

- Is the paradigm of computer vision trainable without GPU & TPU?

- Can we collect more pictures before our computer vision model is built?

- Why do we use profound learning for computer vision instead of machine learning?

I faced these problems too, so you came up with this guide to help you with computer vision.

Computer vision is a field of profound learning which enables the machine to recognize and process images as do people. When it comes to machines detecting objects, people perform exceptionally well, but they require many complicated steps, including feature removal (detection of shapes, edges, etc.), function classification, etc.

"OpenCV is published under a BSD license and is thus suitable for commercial and academic use. It supports frameworks C, C++, Python, and Java and supports Windows, Mac OS, Linux, iOS, and Android. OpenCV has been developed with a strong emphasis on real-time applications and computational performance. Written in optimized C / C++, multi-core processing can be used in the library. OpenCL allows it to benefit from hardware enhancement of the heterogeneous computing architecture underlying it.

OpenCV includes more than 2500 algorithm implementations! It is available free for both commercial and academic purposes. The library has multi-language frameworks, including Python, Java, and C++.

OpenCV setup

It should be noted here that several tutorials for installing Opencv can be found on your ubuntu or windows machines. Follow this connection which helps me to set everything on the fly.

Photos read, write and show

A multidimensional array can represent an image. Since a computer can show it as numbers and NumPy can represent it in python, while it can be shown in Mat format in C-programming language.

A generic term called pixel values is typically used for images. We have three channels colored for color images. Color images also have several single-pixel values. These arrays can differ in size depending on the resolution and color depth. The color values differ between 0 and 255. These color channels are usually represented, for example, Red Green Blue (RGB).

The reading of the image in Opencv is simple, so it should be noted that the imread function reads images by default as BGR (Blue-Green-Red). In the imread function, we can read images in various formats using extra flags:
• cv2.IMREAD COLOR: Default color picture load flag.
• cv2.IMREAD GRAYSCALE: Loads grayscale files.

OpenCV correctly loaded the image as a NumPy array, but every pixel color was sorted as BGR. Matplotlib 's plot expects an RGB image, so it is important to switch these channels to view the image properly. This process can be achieved either by using the cv2.cvtColor) (OpenCV conversion functions or by using the NumPy array directly.

Many computer vision models typically work with defined input types. True pain happens when we scrap picture data sets on the web. Redimensioning is very effective in teaching profound learning models. However, the interpolation and downsampling functions are also part of OpenCV with the following parameters.

• Linear
• Intrea
• Inter Cubique.
• Inter Lamation

Rotation / Flipping Picture
Data increase enables us to produce more samples for our profound learning model. -- data uses the data samples available to generate new ones by applying image operations such as scaling, rotation, translation, etc.

It also allows our model to be stable and widespread. Rotation or flip plays an important role during the data augmentation technique. It rotates the image at a certain angle with the same labels.

Blending photos

With the magic of OpenCV, with the help of the cv2.addWeighted) (the method we can add or mix two images. AddWeighted) (returns the NumPy array of the corresponding image pixel values.

Blending is nothing but two picture matrix addition. Then if we want to add two images, that means that we have to add two matrices. The size of the two images should be the same for the combination of two matrices.

Establishment of an Area of Interest
We can construct ROI in OpenCV The fundamental concept behind ROI is that it maps each object's location in the image to a new position in the final output image. ROI also adds model change invariance. Changing the object location model can help to learn trends that contribute to the generalizable use of the model. ROI in the image preprocessing stage.

Thresholding of the picture

Thresholding is a process in which our pixel values are shifted to the threshold value. The threshold is essentially compared to the threshold value for each pixel. If the pixel value is less than the threshold, the maximum value, i.e. 255 is set to 0. It helps to separate an object from its context. It is rotated by two values below or above the threshold.

Regardless of the simple threshold, we have adaptive thresholds, the threshold value for smaller regions is estimated and, thus, the threshold values for larger regions would be larger.

Smoothing and Blurring
One of the most popular and common techniques for reducing image noise. It eliminates high-frequency material such as edges from the image and the image processing procedure that is widely used to minimize image noise. The method eliminates high-frequency material from the input image such as edges.

In general, blurring is accomplished when the input image is convoluted by a low pass filter kernel. Basically, there are two forms of blurring

• Medium blowing ring.
• Gaussian Blowing Ring
• Median Ringing Ratio
The picture is complicated with a box filter in Normal Blurring. The image's central feature is replaced by an average of all kernel pixels.

In addition, in the picture of Gaussian Blur, a Gaussian filter is added. This filter is nothing other than a low-pass filter that removes high-frequency image data.

Detection of the edge
The edges are the points where the luminosity varies significantly and where there are various discontinuities including

• Profound discontinuities
• Discontinuities in orientation
Edge detection has been very useful for capturing image characteristics for various imaging applications such as object recognition.

Contours Image
A contour is a closed curve with points or line parts representing the borders of the image set. Contours are primarily the features of an image object.

Contours are called a set of points or lines that represent an object's shape in a picture overall.

Detection of the face
OpenCV is perfect for detecting faces using an object detection algorithm based on a hair-cascade. Haar cascades are essentially a qualified classifier model that calculates various features such as lines, contours, boundaries, etc.

These training ML models, which detect the face, eyes, etc, are open-sourced at OpenCV GitHub rests. We can also prepare for any purpose your own hair cascade.

So OpenCV really is a beautiful and strong library for vision tasks of computer. Run the sample code on your computer since the best way to learn is to try it yourself.
In addition, several other methods and techniques for image manipulation are available at OpenCV. I recommend you to search the GitHub repository and their official documentation for its implementation.

FLASK PYTHON WEB APP FRAMEWORK

If you build a web app in Python, you can probably leverage a system. A framework "is a code library that facilitates developer lives by providing reusable code or extensions to common operations for scalable, secure, and maintainable web applications." Python has a range of modules, including Flask, Pyramid, Tornado, and Django. New developers in Python sometimes ask: What should I use?

This series allows developers to address this question by contrasting those four frameworks. To compare its functionality and operations, I will use each of them to create an API for a simple To-Do List web application. The API itself is fairly simple:

- New site users should be in a position to register new accounts.
- Registered users can log in, log out, view profile information, and edit information.
- Registered users can create new tasks, display their current tasks, and delete current tasks.

All these are compact API endpoints which must be implemented in and backend along with the authorized HTTP methods.

Start and configuration of flasks
Like most commonly used Python libraries, the Python Package Index (PPI) installs the Flask package. First, you create a directory (a fine directory name is somehow like flask todo), then install the package flask. You will also install Flask-sqlalchemy so you can speak easily to a SQL database in your Flask application.

This is a great place to run git init if you want to turn it into a Git repository. It will be the origin of the project and it will help you get all necessary setup files if you want to export a codebase to another machine.
One good way to move is to turn the codebase into a Python installable distribution. Create directory called todo and also the setup.py to hold the source code at the root of the project.

This way you will have all the required packages in the required list whenever you want to install or implement your project. In site-packages, you will also have everything you need to configure and install the package.

Create your app.py file and a blank init .py file in the whole directory actually contains your source code. The file init .py lets you import from everything as if the package were installed. The app.py file will be the root of the application. Here is where all the goodness of the Flask app goes and you will create an environment variable pointing to that file. You can locate your virtual environment with pipenv_venv and configure the environment variable in the active script of your environment if you use pipenv (like I am).

It is the basic Flask application. The app is a Flask instance that takes the name file of the script. This allows Python to know how to import files related to it. The app.route decorator adorns the first perspective function; one route to the application can be specified.

Any of your view you specify should be decorated to be the application functional part by app.route. You can get many functions as you wish across the application, but you must decorate and specify a route to get to view for this functionality from anything outside the application.

Connecting the Flask database
While the example of code above represents a full Flask application, it does no good. One interesting aspect of a web application is persistent user data, but it needs assistance and connection to a database.

Flask is a web framework "do it yourself." This means that no integrated database interaction is possible, but a SQL database is connected by a flask-sqlalchemy package to a Flask application. The package of flask-sqlalchemy only needs one connection to a SQL database: the URL for a database.

Note that flask-sqlalchemy is capable of using a wide range of SQL database management systems as long as the DBMS is an intermediary following the DBAPI-2 standard. I will use PostgreSQL (mainly because I used it a lot), so psycopg2 is the intermediary to talk to the Postgres database. Make sure that psycopg2 is installed and includes it in the list of packages required for setup.py. You don't have to do anything else. Postgres from the URL database will be recognized by flask-sqlalchemy.

Flask requires a database URL to be a key part of its SQLALCHEMY DATABASE URI configuration. The hardcode of a database URL in the application is a quick and dirty solution.

This is not, however, a sustainable solution. You need to take extra steps to ensure that your information is environmentally friendly when you change databases but doesn't want the database URL visible in the source control.

You can simplify things by using environmental variables. They ensure that whatever the machine on which the code runs, it always points to the right thing if it is configured throughout running environment. This ensures that although you need the data to operate the application and it never appears as a hardcoded source control value.

Declares the DATABASE URL pointing to the place of your Postgres database at the same place you declared FLASK APP. Development works locally, so point to your local database.

Defining Flask Items

It is a good first step to have a database to talk to. It is now time to identify those objects to fill in that database.

A "model" refers to application development to the data representation of a real or conceptual entity. For example, if you create a car dealership application, you can define a car model that includes all the characteristics and behaviors of a vehicle.

In this case, a To-Do list with tasks is created and each task belongs to one person. Start by identifying objects for tasks and users until you think too much about how they are connected.

The package flask-sqlalchemy uses SQLAlchemy to set up and notify the database structure. You define a model that is inherited from the db. Model object and describe its attributes as db. Column instances in the database. You must define a data type for each column so that you can transfer the data type into db. Column as the first argument.

As the description of the model takes on a different conceptual space than the application configuration, render models.py separate from app.py to carry model definitions. The task model should be designed with the following attributes:

• ID: an attribute that is a specific database identifier
• title: the title or title of the task to be shown by the user on the list of tasks
• Note: any additional comments a person would like to leave with his mission
• Creation_date: day and time of the assignment
• Due_date: the date and time of completion of the task (if any)
• Done: a way to tell whether the mission has been accomplished or not

Please notice the extension of the building class form. In the end, any model you create is still a Python object and therefore needs to be designed to be instantiated. It is necessary to ensure that the instance's creation date represents its actual creation date. This relationship can be clearly defined by saying effectively, "When a model instance is created, record its date and time and set it as its creation date."

Relationships with model
You may want to be capable of expressing relationships among objects in a given web application. In the to-do list example, users have many tasks, and only one user is responsible for each task. This is an example of a partnership "many to one," also known as a primary external partnership, in which the tasks are the "various" and the person who owns certain tasks is the "one."

In Flask the db.relationship function may be used to define a many-to-one relationship. Create the User object first.

It looks very much like a task object; most objects have the same basic format as the table columns. Every time you go to something new, including the magic of many heritages, but that's the norm.

Now that the user model has been developed, the main foreign relationship can be defined. Set fields for the "many" of the user id who owns this feature and the user object with that Name. Make sure you have a keyword (back populates) statement that changes the user model when the user is an owner of the job.

Set a field for the tasks the consumer owns for the "one." Set a keyword argument for the user relation field, similar to maintaining a two-way relationship on the task objective, to change the task when it is allocated to a user.

Memory initialization

Now that the model relationships and configurations have been created, start creating your database. Flask doesn't have its own database management functionality, so you must write your own (to some extent). You don't have to be fancy; you just need to know the tables are to be created and code to build them (or just delete them if necessary). If you need something complicated, such as managing database tables changes (such as database migration), you are going to look at a Flask-Alembic or Flask-Migrate tool.

Build an initializedb.py script next to the setup.py for database management. (Of course, this does not actually have to be named, but why not have names that file function is appropriate?) Import a database object from application.py within initializedb.py and use it to build or drop tables.

Views and setup of URL

The views and routes are the last bits required to link the entire application. In web development, a "vision" (in concept) is functionality that works if the application has a specific access point ("route"). These access points appear as URLs: functionality paths in an application that returns certain data or processes certain given data. The views are logical structures that manage certain HTTP requests from a particular client and return a certain HTTP response.

With Flask, a feature is labelled as an app.route view. In turn, the app.route adds a map from the specified route to the feature that works when the path is accessed to the central application configuration. You can start building the rest of the API with this.

Begin with a view that manages only GET requests and address all usable routes and the approaches that can be used with the JSON.

Since you want your view to handle one particular form of the HTTP request, use the app.route to add that cap. The keyword methods argument takes a string list as a reference, with each string a potential HTTP method. In practice, you can confine app.route to one or more forms of HTTP requests or accept them by simply leaving the keyword argument methods.

Either a string or an entity that Flask transforms into a string when creating a properly formatted HTTP answer must be whatever you wish from your view function. The exceptions to that rule are when you want to control the application's redirects and exceptions. For you, the developer this means that you must be able to encapsulate the reaction you are trying to return to the customer in something that can be represented as a string.

A Python dictionary is a good framework that includes complexity but can still be streamlined. Therefore, whenever you want to send data to a customer, I suggest that you select a Python dictum whatever key-value pair you need to convey information. To transform this dictionary into a correctly formatted JSON response, headers, and all of it, pass it to the Jsonification function of Flask (from jsonify flask import).

The above view function lists any route which this API want to sends and handle it to client whenever it accesses the Http:/domainname / API / v1 path. Notice that Flask itself supports routing for matching URIs exactly, so it will generate 404 errors if you accessed the same path by trailing.

An interesting case is that if the given route had an overpass and a customer demanded the route without the overpass, the decorators would not have to be doubled. Flask will better redirect the client's order. It's weird that it doesn't work in both directions.

Flask software and the DB

The web interface is focused on the processing of incoming HTTP requests and the return of HTTP answers. The previously written view has nothing to do with HTTP requests apart from the accessed URI. It processes no data. Let's see how Flask acts when data needs to be processed.

The first thing to be aware of is that Flask does not provide each view feature with a separate request object. It has one global request object that can be used by each view feature and is easily called request and can be imported from the Flask kit.

Next, the route patterns for Flask may have a little more complexity. One scenario is a hardcoded route to trigger the view feature perfectly. Another example is a path pattern that can accommodate a variety of routes. Any path mapping to one view makes a variable part of the route. If the variable of the route in question remains, it would be possible to access the corresponding value from the same-named variable in the list of parameters.

To interact with the database in the view, the db object to the top of the script must be used. Your session attribute is your client link if you want to make changes. If you want only to search for objects, db. Model objects have their own interaction layer by the query attribute.

Finally, you must intentionally construct some answers from a view that is more complex than a string. Earlier, you generated an answer with a "jsonified," but some assumptions have been made (e.g. 200 status code, "OK" status message, "Text / plain" content-type). Any special sauce you want must be intentionally added to your HTTP response.

Knowing these facts about working with Flask views enables you to develop a view that creates new task artifacts.

SELENIUM PYTHON

Python is now more common than other modern languages of programming. The language of object-oriented and interpreted programming is also very common as a strong scripting language of server-side among developers worldwide. Python helps developers, by writing less and readable code, to express ideas, making it easier for programmers to drastically reduce the development time. At the same time, developers also have the option to easily build high-performance and complex Python Web apps using common Web frameworks like Django. However, developers do need to thoroughly analyze the look, sound, and efficiency of the Python web application to improve its profitability and popularity.

The developers have the option to choose from a range of browser automation tools such as PyXPCOM, PAMIE, windmill, Selenium, and SST while checking Internet applications. But many developers like Selenium than other frameworks for efficient testing of their Python applications. In comparison to other web browser software, Selenium enables technical testing experts to write scripts in a variety of languages, including C #, Python, Java, PHP, Python, and Ruby. Therefore, testers can test the web application Python by writing Python test scripts. There are many explanations for why developers worldwide use Selenium to test Python web applications.

Why do QA professionals choose to use Selenium to test web applications for Python?

The key operating systems and web browsers are supported

Selenium currently supports all major web browsers and operating systems. The platform supports Microsoft Windows and Linux at this time. It also supports most common web browsers such as Firefox, Chrome, Safari, Internet Explorer, and Opera. Compatibility allows the testing of Python web application software across multiple platforms and web browsers without the use of specific codes or external test automation tools by QA professionals. Selenium also has the functionality to automatically create and execute test scripts through various web browsers and systems simultaneously.

Allows users to create the full automation test suite

Selenium testers can create a full test automation kit by integrating Selenium WebDriver and Selenium IDE. Selenium WebDriver helps you to build navigation automation suites and tests easily with browser-based regression. In addition, test scripts can be evaluated and spread through multiple environments. The Selenium IDE makes it easier for testers to quickly create error replication files. This allows QA professionals to combine separate sections of Selenium to create a full test automation tool without the need for approved or third party APIs.

Runs check faster

In order to identify all web applications' glitches and performance problems, QA professionals have to conduct tests regularly and frequently. However, the testers must also complete all experiments within a limited time period. Selenium enables cloud-based test grids to be used by research practitioners to enhance the efficiency of their test runs. These tools enable testers to perform parallel tests in addition to optimizing the test infrastructure. It is also easier for the testers to conduct experiments regularly and quickly. The testers may also choose from a range of cloud-based open-source interactive test grids to reduce increased overheads for projects.

Basic HTML Concepts Includes

Selenium supports many modern languages in programming. However, it takes only basic HTML concepts when checking a Python web application. HTML is used to define a web page, while HTML tags represent the contents of a document. HTML tags, therefore, define how content is viewed on web browsers. Selenium divides the elements or attributes of HTML into three distinct groups, i.e., person, community, and entity. It identifies individual items with its name, link, or link text, while the group elements are defined based on combined values or index properties. It is also easier for testers to figure out where the fault or flaw is. The function enables the detection of exact bugs and performance problems easily.

Helps testers fix maintenance problems

In addition to quickly developing and running test scripts, QA professionals often need to keep the test cases functional. Selenium helps testers solve maintenance problems by structuring an automated test code into a pattern called page artifacts. Instead of testing how services are applied, the page artifacts concentrate on the layout of the HTML code for a certain website. Testers can then use page artifacts to quickly find the code, move seamlessly between different web pages, and make adjustments only once. The tester can easily increase the code base without inserting fresh selenium code as most selenium code is placed inside page items.

Provides Python API for Selenium

Python supports many languages like English, as stated earlier. The testers, therefore, have the option of writing Python test scripts. They also can write acceptance and functional tests using the Selenium Python API, using Selenium WebDrivers such as Help, Popular, Firefox, Chrome, i.e. Remote and phantomjs. Multiple versions of Python including 3.2, 3.3, 3.4, and 2.7 are supported in the new API update. Furthermore, the Selenium Python bindings can be easily downloaded and installed. Thus, an enterprise may use the abilities of current Python programmers to effectively conduct acceptance and functional testing.

Works with different test systems

During testing of the Python web application with Selenium, a variety of test frameworks can be used by QA professionals. The mobile web browser automation system currently works with PyUnit, robot frameworks, and Pytest. PyUnit allows testers to easily write tests and run multiple tests in text or GUI mode, as part of the standard library of Python 2.1. Pytest also has a range of features that help testers write better programs. The QA professionals can use the test frameworks to ensure seamless user experience for many web browsers is provided in the Python web application.

Python is an open-source programming language, while Selenium is an open-source automation tool for web browsers. Organizations can therefore incorporate the language of programming and the web testing tool to minimize project costs. The combination will however allow them to further test the application across major web browsers within a specified time frame.

CHAPTER FOUR

WHY USING DJANGO FOR PYTHON?

Django can be described as a high-level Python Model that lets users grow more quickly and cleaner along with practical website design. For some purposes, developers today tend to use Django than Ruby on rails. The following are described:

language

Python is expressed as a script exceptionally well. You can find detailed guidelines along with guidance on how to write or format codes. You can also find in the codes a clean structure, regardless of what you do. In fact, it follows the good old principle: "Codes are more read than written."

Third-party libraries participation

With respect to third-party libraries, it is not easy for the developer to use Python. The libraries are powerful and mature enough to make coding smooth, fast, and hiccup-free.

Resources for Support

This comes with some tools to enable developers to make their lives even easier. These tools help you hold the codes and deploy them.

In other words, because of the benefits it provides, one system is chosen over another. In this respect, Django scores Ruby in a variety of respects.

Django is actually the platform for those who are perfectionists, particularly those who prefer to work with strict deadlines. Django is the dream platform of the developer with a variety of value-added features, such as helpers, working ORMs, a great admin interface, and a few more.

Ensure the site longevity

This is another interesting aspect of Django. The arrangement lets sites experience longevity. This means that the web is not easy to go down. This means a higher life expectancy is one of the key reasons why Django is made up of sites rather than anything else today.

It's fast

Every bit of this system is planned to take the speed factor into account. The Django prototype language is much quicker. The pace is so rapid that even the caching compiled templates seem slower than when each request is re-rendered.

Scales Django

Whatever you do-Django is ultimate in managing all your information effectively from launching and running personal websites running on shared hostings to small band websites and large public information databases to Social Networking sites. The development system of Django, therefore, features some impressive scalability that makes a difference. Above all, the budget involved is manageable and practical.

HOW IS DJANGO BENEFICIAL FOR EXISTING PYTHON DEVELOPERS?

As a popular server-side scripting language, Python simplifies the creation of high-performance websites for developers. Modules and packages are supported by object-oriented programming. This helps developers to split the code into different modules and to reuse these modules in various projects. By using a Python web platform, they can greatly reduce overall development time and effort.

As many surveys have shown, current Python developers worldwide prefer Django to other common Python web frameworks such as web.py, Falcon, web2py, Pyramid, and TurboGears. Django is also scalable and extensible along with high-level web platform features that help developers build personalized internet applications. There are also many reasons why Django is common among beginners and established Python programmers alike.

What makes Django popular with current Python programmers?

Cleaner and Shorter Code

The new Python programmers recognize the long-term advantages of a shorter, cleaner codebase. Since Python helps people with less code to convey common concepts, they can still avoid creating longer code. Django supports the (MVC) model-view-controller design simultaneously. The design promotes programmers' efficiency in organizing their code by separating business logic, user interface, and application details. Python and Django merge seasoned developers to render code shorter, readable, and cleaner.

Online apps design options

Today, every organization wants to provide its website with different and rich people experience. Developers of Python are searching for ways to customize website sections without any additional time and effort. Django allows them to configure various parts of a website as a modular web interface. Instead of utilizing reconstructed web software, programmers must concentrate on customizing website components in accordance with the customer's unique needs. The emphasis helps them to develop applications that provide valuable content or information according to user needs.

Built-in software to carry out basic tasks

Django is constantly updated with new features and integrated resources. It contains a range of integrated resources that help users perform basic web development tasks with no lengthy code writing. These integrated tools help programmers and the time it takes to create large websites.

Various products

The current Python programmers further improve their web application performance with Django packages. Django products provide applications, software, and websites that can be reused. Apps such as Django Rest System, Django Celery, Django Extensions, and the South are widely used among many developers. They also create e-commerce sites using Satchless, Django-oscar, Django Store, Satchmo, or Cartridge. They can also select from a range of interchangeable software, frameworks, and websites depending on the design and specifications of the Web app. These packages promote the output of the website without writing extra code.

Object-relational Mapper (ORM)

It provides a default implementing mechanism that enables developers to write Python class databases and to search Python for the same databases. This means that no one SQL line has to be written manually.

Database options vary from customer to customer. Experienced Python developers tend to write database queries with the object-relation mapper without SQL. Django provides an Object-relational Mapper that allows developers to do manipulate the database without having to write long queries of SQL. The framework executes the Object-relational Mapper by design, allowing programmers to define a Python class in the database layout. At the same time, they can also use a Python API for more powerful data access. Since the API is created on the fly, no other code is needed for the developers. This is why Django is commonly used for data-driven website creation.

Human URLs Readable

The value of human-readable URLs is frequently overlooked by beginners. But current Python developers understand the advantages for the web application of human-readable URLs. Visitors to the website can more readily understand and recall the URL. In addition, the human-readable URLs render web pages higher on the results pages of search engines. Django encourages the development of legible, simple, and easily rememberable URLs for both visitors to the website and search engine bases.

Admin Interactive Interface

To handle the application smoothly, every customer needs easy and dynamic administrative GUI. Django is designed with features to construct an administrative interface ready for development. The dynamic admin interface allows users to authenticate objects. It thus makes editing or modifying the website content simpler for the organization without using a backend GUI. This function is used by established Python programmers to set up and run administrative sites when designing the models.

Whenever it comes to maintaining a given website or client, it is imperative that the entire content is handled in a competent and faulty manner. This does not mean, however, that codes and other texts need to be written to save time. It saves both time and effort. That's just what Django does.

It is also a strong tool and well designed, and at the end of the day, this makes a big difference.

Defense Optimized

Python scores in the security category over other common web programming languages. The current Python developers also use Django's features to optimize web application performance. In comparison to other web frameworks, Django also dynamically creates web pages and sends the content to web browsers via templates. The source code is also secret both from the web browser and from end-users. The internet application requires broad security shielding since the source code is not explicitly available to the end-users. In parallel, the developers can also use Django to stop cross-site scripting, SQL injection, and other security risks.

Exchange of ideas option

Like other open source technologies, a large and active community also supports Django. The current Python web developer also uses community resources to fix new issues. They also share suggestions and best practices frequently with other members of the group. The exchange helps them to keep track of the latest developments in web development as well as understand how these developments can be applied easily.

Current Python programmers are now updating to Django's latest version to include new functionality and upgrades along with a number of bug fixes. They can also use daily security updates to secure the application against new security threats for the latest version of the web framework. Many programmers are also updating their code base to the new Django update.

MySQL Important Features

MySQL allows you to first know the general query language (SQL) that can be used to sort, extract, remove, update, and insert data. You can manipulate data with SQL, when you use RDBMS, including Access, MySQL, PostgresSQL, Ingres Microsoft SQL Server, Oracle, Sybase, etc.

The Standardized Query Language (SQL) has the full support of the ANSI, which has defined some rules for its use. So you can choose one of the above mentioned RDBMS, specific to your usage if you want to build a solid foundation in SQL. As an alert, three key considerations should be taken into consideration before you settle on a database system: the framework on which you are operating, what you want to achieve, and your finances.

As you know, all of these RDBMS support essential and standard SQL statements, but every RDBMS has its own collection of proprietary statements and extensions. A folder maintained or processed your data files (like your friends' names and emails) in layman's words. You can display your information and analyze your data based on the search criteria features of the program by using small programs like Perl for your database.

For beginners, some of the essential features of MySQL are:

- for any application it is very fast and very reliable;

- His command-line tool has the power to run SQL database queries;

- supports and indexing binary objects;

- Makes changes in table layout while the server is running;

- a wide user base with a memory allocation system based on a fast thread;

- the code is evaluated by various compilers;

- written in language and C++ and C;

- It is available in a server/client network environment as a separate program;

- It is available on most platforms of Unix;

- Window OS Windows 95 and 98, and NT Window are available;

- (k) C, PHP, Delphi, Python, Java, etc. programming libraries are available to link to the MySQL database;

- l) Much more.

- In addition to this, the following are some of the benefits using MySQL:

- The source code is available for recompilation;

- supports over 20 different platforms, including Mac OS X, Microsoft Windows, and Unix Linux distribution;

- is considered one of the most common open-source database systems in the world;

- It is highly effective and highly secure RDBMS, in which several gigabytes of data is stored;

- It's a highly efficient and straightforward program that can manage most enterprise database applications.

134

If you are a strong supporter of open-source software all over the world, you can wonder what is 100 percent free of MySQL on Linux and how it can be combined with Linux, Apache, My SQL, and PHP (LAMP).

There are other stuff if you know more about MySQL for beginners, like RDBMS for beginners, but just say a decent registration and online tutorial would serve you better in terms of your actual usage.

IMPORTANT OF PYTHON FRAMEWORKS FOR DEVELOPERS

Python is used by developers worldwide to construct a variety of software applications as a dynamic, general-purpose, and object-oriented programming language. In comparison to other modern programming languages, Python helps programmers to use less legible code to express concepts. Users can also combine Python seamlessly with other popular programming languages and tools. But it cannot be used to write various software types directly.

Python developers also have to use a number of frameworks and tools to build software applications of high quality in a shorter period. Python Frameworks resources help users to reduce the time and effort needed for modern applications. They can also select from a variety of structures depending on the design and specifications of individual projects. However, some of the Python frameworks which will remain popular in the longer run are also important for the programmers.

Structures of Pythons that remain popular

Kivy
As a Python library open-source, Kivy makes multi-touch user interfaces simpler for programmers. It supports a range of popular Windows, Linux, iOS, OS X, and Android platforms. Therefore, the cross-platform architecture helps users to build the software with the same code base for different platforms. It is also designed to utilize native inputs, protocols, and devices. Kivy also has a simple graphics engine, allowing users to choose from more than 20 widgets.

Qt
The Python project open source is written in C++. Qt helps developers to construct linked apps and user interfaces on different operating systems and devices. The developers can also build cross-platform applications and user interfaces without changing the code. With its robust library of APIs and tools, Qt scores higher over other frameworks. The programmers may either use Qt under a community license or under a commercial licence.

PyGUI

PyGUI is considered simpler than other implementations of Python. However, it enables developers to build GUI API using Python's language features. Windows, OS X, and Linux are currently supported by PyGUI. This allows developers to use it to create lightweight GUI APIs on these three platforms. You can fully document the API without referring to any third-party GUI library documentation.

WxPython

The Python GUI toolkit helps programmers create apps with highly functional (GUI) graphical user interfaces. With wxPython support for Linux, Windows, and OS X, it is easier for developers to run the same software without changing code on multiple platforms. Users can write programs in Python using the 2D path drawing engine, standard dialogs, docking windows, and other system features.

Django

Django is Python's most common web application development platform. While open-source, Django offers an easy and quick development environment for the rapid creation of a variety of websites and web applications. It also helps programmers create a web application without writing long code. It also comes with features to avoid some of the developers' famous security mistakes.

CherryPy

CherryPy helps programmers to build web applications and websites like other Python object-oriented programs as a lightweight web platform. It is thus easier for developers to create web applications without having to write a long code. CherryPy has a clean interface and allows developers to choose the best interface and data storage option. While CherryPy is the oldest web application development framework on the market, programmers still use CherryPy to build a range of modern websites.

Flask

This is the Python micro application framework. Its center is simple to use but incredibly extensible. There are also several functions offered by other web frameworks, including the abstraction of the database layer and form validation. It also does not allow users to add popular functionality through third-party libraries to the web application. However, Flask helps programmers to easily build websites using extensions and snippets of code. Other members have provided samples and patterns to help developers perform basic tasks like accessing a database, uploading, caching, and authentication without having to write additional code.

Pyramid

Despite its lightweight and simple Python web platform, Pyramid's high and rapid performance makes it extremely popular with programmers. The platform open source can be used to build a number of applications. If the standard development framework for Python has been set up, developers can use Pyramid to create apps quickly. Furthermore, Pyramid enables users to use an individual Model View Controller (MVC) framework. At the same time, other constructs can be manipulated by combining them with the Pyramid.

Web.py

Web.py allows programmers to quickly create a wide range of modern web applications as a simple yet powerful software platform for Python. The combination of simple architecture and amazing development potential allows users to resolve some of the typical web development constraints and drawbacks. There are also many features that other existing web frameworks have. And developers can simply integrate web.py with some frameworks to use advanced functionality and functions.

TurboGears

As a highly elastic web design and development system for Python, TurboGears allows users to remove technical limitations and constraints. It can be used as a full-stack or micro-framework. It also offers a versatile object connection mapper (ORM), supports multiple databases, various data sharing formats, and the horizontal data partitioning. The developers can further create AJAX-heavy web applications using the new widget framework provided by TurboGears.

All in all, Python developers can select from a wide variety of frames. Some of these frameworks create GUI desktop applications while others help programmers quickly construct modern websites and Web applications. The developers also have the option of writing mobile apps in Python using those frames. That is why it is important for the developer to determine the appropriateness of each framework for its project based on its characteristics and functionality. The user should also suggest combining the application with other frameworks and resources in order to use more advanced functionality and functions.

WILL YOU GO FROM PERL TO PYTHON?

Python and Perl are both mature, open-source, general, high level and interpreted languages of programming. But the statistics on usage published on various websites show that Python is more popular now than Perl. A software developer can therefore improve his career prospects by switching to Python from Perl.

A beginner can continue learning and using Python without putting extra time and effort into it. However, regardless of its success and use, you must not turn to a new programming language. When deciding to migrate from Perl to Python, you must remember the major differences between the two programming languages.

12 points You need to keep in mind as you move from Perl to Python

Design goal

Perl originally was designed to simplify report processing capabilities as a scripting language. This includes built-in text processing capabilities. Python, on the other hand, was initially designed as a hobby programming language. However, it has features designed to help programmers create applications that contain concise, readable, and reusable codes. These two programming languages are different in function and performance categories.

Syntax Rules

Python and Perl syntax laws are inspired by several other languages. For example, Perl uses many languages such as C, shell script, sed, AWK, and Lisp. Python also incorporates Lisp-like functional programming functionality. However, due to its simple syntax rules, Python is extremely popular with modern programming languages. In addition to being simple to use, Python's syntax rules also allow programmers to except many less readable code concepts.

Language Family

Perl is part of a family of high-level languages including Perl 5 and Perl 6. Perl versions 5 and 6 are mutually compatible. A developer can easily switch from Perl 5 to Perl 6 without requiring additional time and effort. The programmers can select Python 2 and Python 2 from two distinct versions. But the two versions of Python are not mutually compatible. A programmer must therefore choose from two different versions of the language of programming.

Achievement of the same results

Python allows programmers to express concepts without writing longer code lines. Yet programmers need to perform tasks or achieve results in a single and specific manner. On the other hand, Perl allows programmers to perform a single task or to achieve the same results in several ways. Many programmers also assume that Perl is more versatile than Python. However, numerous ways to achieve the same result also make it difficult to maintain the code written in Perl.

Language Web Scripting

Perl was designed as a UNIX scripting language originally. Many developers use Perl to use their built-in text processing capabilities as a scripting language. However, most web developers said that Perl is too slower than some commonly used languages. Python is widely used by web application development programmers. But there are no integrated web development capabilities. Developers must also use different frameworks and resources to write Web applications easily and quickly in Python.

Systems for Web Application

Most developers now use the tools and features of various frameworks to create web applications quickly and efficiently. You have the option for Perl web programmers to choose between Dancer, Catalyst, Poet, Mojolicious, Jifty, Interchange, Gantry, and other frameworks. Similarly, web developers can use a range of web frameworks from Python, including Flask, Jango, Bottle, Pyramid, and cherrypy. However, the number of web frames from Python is much higher than that of Perl.

Usage

As already mentioned, both Python and Perl are general languages of programming. Each programming language is therefore used to develop a range of software applications. Perl is widely used for graphics and system management, network programming, and financial and biometric application development. However, Python has a robust standards library which simplifies the development of web applications, scientific computing, the development of large data solution, and artificial intelligence tasks. Developers, therefore, prefer to use Python to develop advanced, mission-critical software applications.

Speed and performance

Several studies have demonstrated that Python is slower than other programming languages such as Java and C++. Therefore, developers often explore ways to improve the speed of execution of Python code. Some developers are even replacing Python's default runtime with their own individual runtime to speed up the Python applications. Many programmers even think that Perl is faster than Python. Many web developers use Perl to speed up web applications and provide an improved user experience.

Analysis of structured data

Big data is currently one of the hottest trends in the development of software. Many companies are currently building custom applications to collect, store, and analyze large amounts of structured and unstructured data. Perl's PDL allows developers to analyze large data. Perl's integrated text processing capability further simplifies and accelerates the analyzes of large quantities of structured data. But Python is widely used by data analysis programmers. Developers take advantage of robust Python libraries, such as Numpy, to quickly and efficiently process and analyze large volumes of information.

JVM Interoperability

Currently, Java is one of the programming languages widely used for desktop, web, and mobile applications development. Compared to Perl, Python interacts seamlessly and efficiently with Java Virtual Machine (JVM). Therefore, developers can write Python code instead of running JVM smoothly while using robust Java APIs and objects. This interoperability helps programmers to develop applications by targeting the popular Java platform while writing Java instead of Python.

Object-Oriented Programming Advanced

Both Python and Perl are programming languages oriented towards objects. But Python is better at implementing advanced object-oriented programming languages than Perl. When writing code in Perl, programmers still have to use packages rather than classes. Python programmers can use classes and objects to write high quality and modular code. Many developers find it hard to keep the code easy and readable while in Perl writing object-oriented code. However, Perl makes it much easier for developers to perform a variety of tasks using a single liner.

Capability for Text Processing

Unlike Python, Perl has been designed to process text. Many programmers, therefore, prefer to use Perl to generate reports. Perl also makes regex and string comparison operations such as replacement, matching, replacement easier for programmers. Furthermore, developers do not need to write additional code for exceptional handling and I / O operations. Many programmers, therefore, prefer Perl to Python while building applications for textual data processing or report generation.

In general, many software developers like Python to Perl. However, there are some programming Languages-C, Java, C #, and C++, -now more popular than both Perl and Python. Like other technologies, Python also has its own weaknesses. For instance, while writing applications in the programming language, you will need to use Python frameworks. You must therefore remember the advantages and disadvantages of both languages before leave Perl to Python.

CHAPTER FIVE

LEARN YOUR PROGRAMMING LANGUAGE

Programming is a very useful and enjoyable hobby. There's no better feeling than when someone sees you using a program to make your life more simple and says it looks very useful. Many people just wanted to be able to do something on their computers or phones at some stage in their lives and couldn't. If you know a programming language, you also have a reasonable chance of writing a program for yourself. Although there are many programming languages, many of them have a lot of similarities, but once you learn a language very well, you can probably find a new language much faster.

Limitations

One thing all new programmers need to achieve is the time it takes to learn a programming language. While you can write many programs quickly when you are an expert, you need to note that many programs have taken years to build entire teams of developers. It is therefore necessary to recognize that it is not sufficient to write any of the more complicated programs you have seen to know a programming language or even many. Do not look at this new hobby as a way to save money, since you will be unable to write your own version of most of the programs that you already have to pay for.

The most important thing for a new programmer to realize is that books like "Learn Software in 24 hours" simply are not real. A more fitting title would be "Take 10,000 hours of programming." You won't build a next Windows or a new state of the art game if you spend 24 hours or a week studying a language. You can learn to write a program in 10 minutes, and you just have to learn a new language, so you will not be a professional. The only way to become an expert is to learn the violin; practice, practice, and practice are the answers.

No, or Yes, IDEs?

Many purists say IDEs are a myth and they are filled with needless resources and menus that require disk time and space to learn. Although that's real, I feel an IDE certainly deserves to be found. Many people give free IDEs for the most common languages such as Netbeans and Eclipse. Visual Studio is also available, which I listed previously; it is very intuitive, strong, and supports several languages, such as Netbeans and Eclipse. I would recommend Netbeans if you decided to use Java, as there is the packaged (JDK) Java Development Kit version of Netbeans. Most languages require an SDK (Software Development Kit), which is always the toughest part of the process when properly configured and connected to the IDE. Visual Studio has already developed development kits, making life simpler, but it can be very hard to set up other languages such as Java and Python properly. That's why I proposed the Netbeans + JDK package to play with Java, as it deals with the complex set up to save hours.

There are three big benefits of using a completely functioning IDE. First of all, it is typically extensible, so many free plug-ins are available which will make your life much simpler as you get a little further. Secondly, and most significantly, an IDE helps you to debug the code with ease. Most IDEs allow you to set interfaces in the code which stop the program at this point and allow you to move it line by line so that you can check the contents of all variables at any time. Nearly no non-trivial software would work for the first time, and I would not want someone to try to discover where the issues lie without the need for a debugger. Finally, an IDE will also advise you about how to correct problems in the code. This could be good for fixing error and saves any other minute on Google.

English Literacy

It's now time to learn the language now that you have a vocabulary and an IDE. This is not complicated, as you may or may not be shocked to hear-it just takes time. There is no better way than experimentation to learn to program for the first time. When you read a book that goes through measures, you cannot know much, so you won't understand the logic behind what they do and sometimes people are disheartened by this tedium.

The secret to learning is to have a target. Think of a job such as a system that monitors where you are on all the different TV shows that you are watching, or a system that lets you look at all the books that you own in a certain category. The advice would be to begin tiny, maybe by creating a sequence of message boxes that annoy the user or a very simple device. When you start, it is crucial that your goals are interesting, entertaining, and challenging. If you make dull programs, you'll get disheartened easily, so try adding some humor into your program. The calculator is a really good introductory program, but it's important to set realistic goals after you get a general idea, because you will never learn anything new if you do basic things. Any of the experiences you have learned from previous work is important to try to integrate. One of the reasons most books don't really teach programming is because they use the small example for anything they add, while what you really need to do is design the task without knowing what you have to do. This means that you can code some of them by using what you know already, but most importantly, you don't know how to code any of them. Learning by doing is the best way to learn. Go for a complete software that does a job you'd want to do in the past and work on it. When you're done, you'll learn a lot and have a useful (at least entertaining) software which's much better than any toy show lists.

I said that by choosing to do projects you can't do those pieces, you need to learn but how do you figure out how to do them? It's fast, and probably the way you find this post. Go to your favorite search engine (like Google) and check for what you want to do-search "Java drop-down list" for example to find examples of dropdowns in Java. Since you need it for another mission, and not simply to do the same thing you did, you must play with the examples you find and try to make them do what you want. Just look at every bit you need, and soon, you find that most of the basics are as normal as waking up in the morning and that you have done everything without spending a little fortune on books, without getting tired, and hopefully while you are having fun. I still break one of my very first programs, which is a list of boxes and the random number generator, if I'm bored to this day. It's up to you to try and fill in all the boxes so that the numbers you send by random numbers are in ascent. When you don't leave space and can't fit a number into a void, you lose and must restart. It is a basic program, but when I did it for the first time, I had a lot of work and learned a lot from it.

You will find that after you have a few good programs under your belt, you know the language well. You would also find it unusual to be able to write a program without Google at least once to verify something, no matter how well you know a language. In this sense, it can be claimed that you mastered the language without ever attempting to learn it. Clearly, there are guidelines and good practices that you cannot discover on your own, but you will easily follow your own principles as you see more examples and read the comments.

Another Language Learning

If you've mastered every language, the most important thing you've discovered is all of the keywords you look for. If you want to do something in a foreign language, you just need to look for what you want to do and the name of the language. But now, you can know the names used for what you want to do so that your searches will be much more productive and provide examples and answers much faster. As programming concepts are often the same, irrespective of the language you are using, you will ideally formulate much more effectively the interpretation of most of the code once you find an example and take up most of the language rather quickly.

If you don't delete something from this post, note that practice, practice, and practice are the best way to learn skills, but do not presume to become an expert overnight. Remember which programming can not be mastered overnight. You will need to spend at least 10,000 hours of programming to become a passable professional, and so you need to find ways to stay motivated. Don't think of it as learning to program- only start programming, and you will be an expert before you know. Programming is a skill and while it's pretty easy, if you feel it, seeing the tiny machine that took you a week can be very overwhelming and then thinking about a modern play like "Batman: Arkham City" and knowing how far you've got to go.

Programming is simple when you know how, but it is not an insignificant thing to do, so you have to set yourself up tasks. These activities should be exciting and even better enjoyable because this is what keeps you organizing and learning more and more before one day you wake up and remember that you know a lot. You are your best tutor and the key is just to jump in and start.

How Python Language Can Help

Many programming languages are still being used, others are being used and others are outdated. In recent years, the programming situation has radically changed as developers and programmers look for more common and open languages. This is why the Python language has recently become so popular. The Python community grows with each day as many programmers now consider among the most user-friendly languages for programming.

Python is so renowned that every area and sector is now a user of this language. Even if other languages don't lose their followers, Python raises its customer base. More people are now striving to learn Python now. Below are some of the reasons why a qualification in Python can be useful:

Machine learning

Almost all now pass through algorithms whether it's a search engine, social media, chatbots, automated personal helpers, etc. These advanced algorithms are the product of machine learning and the whole technical scenario has been transformed. The key programming language used for machine learning is Python and several libraries dedicated only to machine learning can be found.

Big data

Python is most commonly used in data science, and the professionals in this area need to know this programming language. Although several other languages are used for the data science, like R, Java, etc., Python is the favorite. Due to their versatility in automation technology, along with the different frameworks and libraries such as PyBrain, NumPy, etc.

Web development

Many websites, such as Reddit, are now created with the Python language. The key reason why web development is using the Python programming language is its speed and performance. PHP will take hours to create a website when using Python takes just a few minutes. Frameworks and libraries like Django and Flask are also available to promote the work.

Community

A few of the things programmers are looking for in the communities these days. The programmers and developers in these groups will relate to others in any part of the world and share their technologies and experiences. This helps them learn new things regarding Python as well as how to solve some problems during coding.

Bibliothèques

Libraries are very useful in the creation of software and websites. Any form of code can be found. Python has many frameworks, including NumPy, Django, Scipy, Tensorflow, Pandas, Keras, Flask, and so on. You have to rely on logic and purpose and library codes are readily accessible.

Quick

Finally, the main reason why Python is used by programmers is that it is a basic programming language. This is a user-friendly language for beginners since it does not need many complicated syntaxes and codes which are incomprehensible. Python has a simple and readable syntax and code making it much easier to set up and use.

WHY ONE MUST LEARN IT

However, your company may need a complex web-based solution; you may be overwhelmed by the vast range of options available in programming languages. The selection of a language or platform in a start-up is one of the most important decisions. Although there are several developmental languages, and Python is now most preferred, especially for multiple reasons among start-ups. Besides being known for its rapid development, Python can meet changing and growing demands very quickly.

Here is a list of reasons why Python is a favorite startup language:

1. Friendly to the user

Python is a language very popular mainly because it is easy to read. Its uncluttered syntax makes it easy for startups to use this language. Python also has a built-in dictionary structure of data, making it friendly of user. Python are also high-level data typing that minimizes the support code length.

2. Speed and Increased Productivity

When it comes to simple startups, factors such as speedy marketing and new features are very important. Python has an object-oriented design that enables process control and strong integration, contributing to speed and productivity increase. Python is also considered a favored choice for the construction of complex network applications.

3. Helps Uncertainty Tackle

Most web-based startups and social networks and Python is perfect to deal with complexities. By using Python, you can solve many problems such as integrating multiple systems, which would take more time and effort otherwise. Python also offers scalability, which is important to start-ups in the future.

4. A Little Team Sufficiency

Python helps programmers to quickly record proof of the design. A large team of developers and designers is not needed to build a high-quality product by using Python. This certainly helps medium-sized companies and organizations conserve money and continue to focus on new projects.

5. Opportunity to gain money easily

As Python makes you work faster, startups can make bigger profits with a small initial investment. If you develop and maintain your Python project, the returns are quicker. Python thus allows start-ups quickly to raise money, which undoubtedly benefits them.

6. Support promptly

Most startups tend to use Python as they get prompt assistance when severe technical problems arise. It also helps the product to be high quality and less vulnerable to failure.

7. Easier to create prototypes

For big projects, Python is also a simple solution. Anything written in Python is also easier to rewrite. Python is also useful for writing prototypes since it has a working prototype already. This feature certainly allows entrepreneurs to save time and resources and also see if a business idea works.

In this highly competitive business climate, start-ups need to expand rapidly. Python allows newly established enterprises to get a working product at discounted rates at minimum time.

Python does not need small companies to employ a huge team of experts.

WHY IS PYTHON HERE TO STAY?

The key and backward-incompatible programming language version were also published on 3 December 2008. But a number of surveyors have recently considered Python to be the most common coding language in 2015. The broad popularity demonstrates Python's efficiency as a modern language of programming. At the same time, developers around the world are currently using Python 3 to build a range of web, GUI, and mobile desktop apps. There are also a variety of reasons why over a longer time Python's vast popularity and market share remain intact.

8 Reasons Why Will Python's massive popularity remain intact in the future

1) Support several paradigms of programming.

Good developers also use various programming paradigms to reduce the time and effort needed to create detailed and complex applications. Python supports many widely used types of programming, including object-oriented, procedural, process, and imperative, as well as other popular programming languages. It also features automated memory management and a dynamic device sort. Programmers will also use the language to create broad and complex software applications.

2) Allows programmers not to write long code

Python is developed with full coding readability emphasis. The programmers should build a readable code base that members of distributed teams can use. At the same time, the basic syntax of the programming language allows them to communicate ideas without any longer code lines. The function simplifies broad and complex applications for developers within a specified period. As they can easily bypass certain tasks that other programming languages need, maintaining and upgrading their applications becomes simpler for developers.

3) Offers an integrated reference library

Thanks to its comprehensive standard library, Python even scores over other programming languages. These libraries are available to programmers to perform a number of tasks without writing longer lines of code. In addition, the Python standard library is equipped with a wide range of highly-used programming tasks. Thus, it helps programmers perform tasks such as string operations, web site creation and implementation, working on internet protocols, and the management of the operating system interface.

4) Creates a Mobile Application

Python is developed as a general programming language and does not have integrated web development tools. But web developers use a number of add-ons to write modern web apps in Python. When writing Python web apps, programmers can use many high-level web

146

frameworks, including web2py, CubicWeb, TurboGears, Django, and Reahl. These web frameworks help programmers conduct a series of operations with no additional code, such as manipulation of databases, URL routing, session storage and recovery, and output template formatting. The web frames can also be used to defend the web application against cross-site scripting attacks, SQL injection, and forgery on cross-site requests.

5) Promotes high-grade Software, science, and numerical applications development

Python is currently used in big Linux, Mac OS X, Windows, and UNIX operating systems. The desktop GUI applications can therefore be deployed on several platforms in the programming language. The programs can also speed up the development of cross-platform GUI applications using frameworks such as wxPython, Kivy, and PyGtk. Several studies have shown that Python is commonly used to create computational and scientific applications. During the development of scientific and numerical applications in Python, developers may use resources such as Scipy, IPython, Pandas, and the Python Imaging Library.

6) Simplifies device prototyping

The company now wishes to resolve competition by designing applications with distinct and creative features. This is why prototyping has become part of a modern lifecycle of software development. Before writing the code, developers must create the application prototype to show different stakeholders its features and functions. Python enables programmers to develop the final code in a simple and quick way without putting extra time and effort. At the same time, developers can also start developing the system directly from the prototype by simply restoring the code.

7) Can also be used for the creation of mobile apps

Frameworks such as Kivy also render Python accessible for mobile app creation. Kivy can be used as a library to build both desktop and mobile applications. But it allows developers to write the code once on multiple platforms and deploy the same code. Kivy also comes with built-in camera adaptors, rendering, and playback modules, and modules to accept user input through gestures, multi-touches, and interfacing with mobile device hardware. Programmers can also use Kivy to build multiple versions of the same Android, iOS, and Windows Phone applications. The framework also does not demand that developers write longer lines of code during the development of Kivy programs. You can buy the app individually for the individual app store after developing multiple versions of the mobile app. The alternative enables the development of numerous versions of the mobile app without the use of separate developers.

8) Source Available

Python is still available as open-source and free software, although it is listed as the most common programming language of 2015. Startups and freelance software developers can use the programming language together with large IT companies without paying any fees or royalties. Thus, Python makes it easier for enterprises to significantly reduce development costs. The programmers may also benefit from the help of the vast and active community to add out-of-box functionality to the software application.

Python's last major release was in December 2008. Python 3 was released with most of the key features returning to Python 2.6 and 2.7 as a backward version. However, the programming language is regularly updated by the community. On 23 February the group released Python 3.4.3 with different features and patches. The developer should also still use the new Python language version to create different software applications.

PYTHON FILE AND DICT

Chart of Dict Hash

The powerful structure of Python's key/value hash table is called the "rule." The dict contents can be given as key: value pairs into the braces}, {e.g. dict = {key1: value1, key2: value2, etc. }. The "empty dictum" is only an empty, curly pair of braces{}.

If you look up or set the value in the dictionary, you use square brackets. For instance, dict['foo'] glance up avalue under 'foo' key. Lines, tuples, and numbers are keys, and all kind of value can be. Other types may or may not function properly as keys (strings and tuples are clean because they are unchanging). Looking at a value that isn't in dict throws the KeyError-use the "in" to see whether key is in dict or try use dict.get(key), that returns value, and None when the key isn't present (or get(key, not-found).

A loop on a dictionary is iterated by default over its keys. The keys are shown randomly. The dict.keys) (and dict.values) (methods specifically return lists of keys or values. There is also an item) (which returns a list of tuples (key, value), the most effective way of evaluating all the key-value data in the dictionary. You can pass all these lists to the sorted) (function.

These methods called (itervalues), (iterkeys), and (iteritems) are "iter" in the variants, which avoid the expense of creating the whole list-a performance win if the data is big. I typically prefer the simple keys) (and values) (methods with their sensitive names, however. In revision Python 3000, the need for the iterkeys) (variants go away.

Strategy note: The dictionary is one of the best tools in terms of its efficiency and should be used as a convenient way to organize data. You can, for instance, read a log file in which each line begins with an IP address and store the data as a key using the IP address and the lists of lines in which it appears as the value. You can look up any IP address and immediately see the list of lines after you have read the entire file. The dictionary gathers scattered data and makes it clear.

Del

The operator "del" deletes. In the simplest case, the variable description may be omitted, as though the variable was not specified. Del may also be used to delete or modify entries from the dictionary on list elements or slices.

Data Files
Open) (opens and returns a filehandle which can be used in the normal way to read or write a file. The code f = open('name', 'r') 'will open the file in variable f, ready to read and use f.close) (until it is finished. Using 'w' to compose and 'a' to append instead of 'r.' The special 'rU' mode is the 'Normal' option for text files, which makes it wise to convert different line ends so that they are all a simple '\n.' The regular for-loop works with text files, which run through file lines (this works only with text files, not binary files).

Reading one line at a time has the nice advantage that not every file has to fit into a single memory – perfect for looking at every line in a 10-gigabyte file without consuming 10 gigabytes of memory. The f.readlines() method reads and returns the entire file as a list of its lines. The method f.read() reads the entire file in a single string, which may be a realistic way for dealing with the text at once, as we can see later with regular expressions.

The most simple way to write an f.write(string) is to write data to an open output file. Alternatively, you can use "print," but the syntax is nasty: "print > > f, string." The print syntax in python 3000 is defined as a standard function call with the optional argument file= "print(string, file = f)"

Incremental growth exercise

Don't write the whole thing in one move, create a Python program. Rather, just define the first step, e.g. 'the first step is to remove a word list.' Insert the code to meet that point, then print the data structure and then you can do a sys.exit(0) in a way that will prevent the software from running in its non-done portions. If the milestone code works, you can work on the next milestone code. If you can look at the interpretation of the variables in one state, you can think about how those variables need to be converted to the next state. Python will make some adjustments with this pattern and run the software to see how it operates. Benefit from this fast turnaround to develop your program in small steps.

50 STEP-BY-STEP PYTHON OPEN-SOURCE PROGRAMMING PROJECTS

1. Quiz Challenge: ASCII

Code ASCII

The ASCII code (Pronounced ask-ee) is a code for representing English characters as numbers, with a number assigned from 0 to 127 for each character. The ASCII code for uppercase A for example is 65. The extended ASCII contains 256 characters (using 0 through 255 numbers).

Every character showing up on your keyboard has a unique value. This includes 26 alphabet lowercase letters & 26 uppercase letters, 0 to 9 number digits and a range of punctuation signs and special characters.

Functions chr) (and ord)

Using Python you can easily access a character's ASCII values by using the function comm). For example, ord("A) "returns 65 while chr(65) returns" A.

ASCII Quiz Quiz

The following code to Python is a game based on a quiz. The user attempts to guess the ASCII value of various randomly selected characters. To decrease a life score, the difference between the user's guess and the actual ascii value of the displayed character is used.

The game starts with a lifetime

```python
#The ASCII Quiz Challenge

life = 255
score = -1

while life>0:
    print("_____")
    print("Your life score is " + str(life))
    score+=1
    print("Your score so far: " + str(score))
```

```python
### Generate Random Character and ASCII value
#ascii = random.randint(0,127) #Extended ASCII would go up to 255!
ascii = random.randint(32,126) #Only select printable characters
character = chr(ascii)


### Retrieve User Guess
guess = int(input("What is the ASCII code this charcter: " + character))


### Update life score
if guess == ascii:
    print("Correct Answer. Your life score is reset to 255!")
    life = 255
else:
    print("Incorrect Answer. The correct answer was " + str(ascii))
    difference = abs(guess-ascii)
    print("You lose " + str(difference) + " life points.")
    life = life - difference


print("Game Over!")
print("Your score: " + str(score))
```

2. Thank you, the medical personnel and the key workers!

In this challenge, we will use some python code to draw a rainbow and a "Thank You" message to all medical staff and key workers. Your remit

We wrote the code using Python Turtle but that doesn't produce the expected result.

Could you:

Modify lines 20 to 28 to ensure the code displays the rainbow colors in the correct order

Change lines 30 to 35 to ensure that the stars and text are of the correct colours.

The output of your code should be the same as the above picture.

```
#Rainbow Sequencing Challenge
import turtle
from functions import *
window = turtle.Screen()

red = "#FF0000"
orange = "#FFA600"
yellow = "#FFFF00"
green = "#62FF00"
blue = "#1E56FC"
indigo = "#4800FF"
violet = "#CC00FF"
white = "#FFFFFF"
skyblue = "#69C5FF"

#Fill the canvas with the colour of the sky
window.bgcolor(skyblue)

#Start Drawing the rainbow... You will have to fix this code as it is not displaying the coreect rainbow
drawCircle(0,-360,blue,180)
drawCircle(0,-360,violet,170)
drawCircle(0,-360,yellow,160)
drawCircle(0,-360,indigo,150)

drawCircle(0,-360,red,130)
```

```
drawCircle(0,-360,orange,120)
drawCircle(0,-360,skyblue,110)
drawCircle(0,-360,green,140)


drawStar(-100,130,blue,40)
drawStar(145,130,red,40)


addText(0,150,"Thank you Medical Staff",white,"14pt")
addText(0,120,"and",yellow,"14pt")
addText(0,90,"Key Workers",white,"14pt")
```

3. Create your own music using Python!

We will investigate that we're using Python code to create our own background music and sound effects for use in a retro arcade game for this challenge.

Most music editing software (e.g. Cubase, GarageBand, Logic Pro, FL Studio, etc.) is Digital Audio Workstations (DAW) and allows you to create your own music by adding multi-track audio clips, virtual instruments, and effects. Your music is edited and mixed via a Graphical User Interface.

We use Python code with basic audio clips from the "Eigthbit" library in the example below to recreate some retro arcade game music to be used on an intro / splash screen.

It exhibits some of EarSketch 's key basic features:

Set the tempo

- Import audio clips (on various tracks, at specified times)
- Audio clips are added to timeline
- Add effects (including the effects of fade in, fade-out and delay)
- To repeat a clip using a loop


```
#          python code
#          script_name: Game_Intro.py
```

```
#
#          author: 101Computing
#          description: Background music for intro
#

from earsketch import *

init()
setTempo(120)


clip1 = EIGHT_BIT_ATARI_SFX_004
clip2 = EIGHT_BIT_ATARI_LEAD_011
clip3 = EIGHT_BIT_ATARI_LEAD_010


pointA = 1.75
repeat = 3
pointD = pointA + repeat


#fitMedia(Clip,Track,StartMeasure,EndMeasure)
fitMedia(clip1,1,1,2)
for i in range(0,repeat):
  fitMedia(clip2,2,pointA + i,pointA + i + 1)


fitMedia(clip3,3,pointA,pointD + 1)


#setEffect(Track,effect,parmeter,value)
setEffect(3, VOLUME, GAIN, -10)


#setEffect(Track,effect,parmeter,value,start measure,value,end measure)
#Fade in
```

```
setEffect(1, VOLUME, GAIN, -40, 1, 0, 1.75)
#Delay Effect
setEffect(1, DELAY, DELAY_TIME, 250)
setEffect(2, DELAY, DELAY_TIME, 250)
#Fade Out
setEffect(3, VOLUME, GAIN, -10, pointD, -60, pointD+1)


finish()
```

3. Breakout Tutorial using Pygame: Adding a Brick Wall

This tutorial is the second tutorial in a series of five tutorials about Pygame:

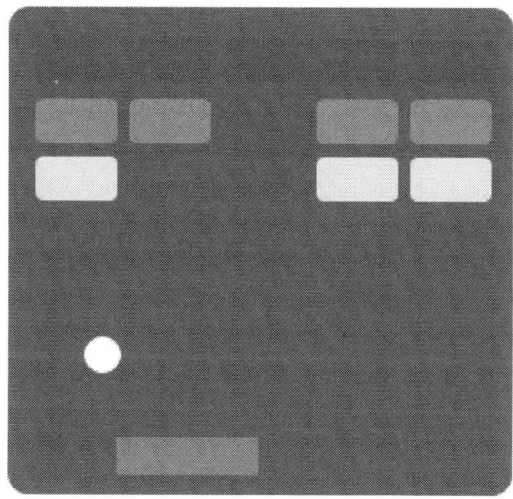

- Tutorial Breakout 1: Launch
- Tutorial Breakout 2: Add the Paddle
- Tutorial Breakout 3: Paddle-control
- Breakout Tutorial 4: Adding a Bouncing Ball
- Breakout Tutorial 5: Adding a Brick Wall
- Extra: How to The Pygame?

The final stage of our tutorial focuses on adding a brick wall to our Breakout game and a scoring system:

- If the ball bounces against a brick the player will score a point.
- If the ball bounces against the bottom edge of the screen the player will lose his life.

- The top of the screen will display both the score and the number of lives.
- If all bricks have been removed a "Level Complete" message will be displayed.
- If the number of lives reaches zero, a "Game Over" message will show up.

The final code for the main.py is set out below. We made several modifications to the code as follows:

- On line 6 we import the Brick class. (Code indicated in the brick.py tab)
- We create three rows of bricks on lines 39 to 57, and add them to the All bricks group.
- On lines 93 to 103 when the ball hit the bottom edge of the screen, we take a lifetime away. If the number of lives is zero, a "Game Over" message is displayed.
- We detect if the ball hits a brick on lines 114 to 129; If that is the case, we remove the brick (using kill) (method) and increase the score by one.

```
#Import the pygame library and initialise the game engine
import pygame
#Let's import the Paddle Class & the Ball Class
from paddle import Paddle
from ball import Ball
from brick import Brick


pygame.init()


# Define some colors
WHITE = (255,255,255)
DARKBLUE = (36,90,190)
LIGHTBLUE = (0,176,240)
RED = (255,0,0)
ORANGE = (255,100,0)
YELLOW = (255,255,0)
```

```python
score = 0
lives = 3

# Open a new window
size = (800, 600)
screen = pygame.display.set_mode(size)
pygame.display.set_caption("Breakout Game")

#This will be a list that will contain all the sprites we intend to use in our game.
all_sprites_list = pygame.sprite.Group()

#Create the Paddle
paddle = Paddle(LIGHTBLUE, 100, 10)
paddle.rect.x = 350
paddle.rect.y = 560

#Create the ball sprite
ball = Ball(WHITE,10,10)
ball.rect.x = 345
ball.rect.y = 195

all_bricks = pygame.sprite.Group()
for i in range(7):
    brick = Brick(RED,80,30)
    brick.rect.x = 60 + i* 100
    brick.rect.y = 60
    all_sprites_list.add(brick)
    all_bricks.add(brick)
for i in range(7):
    brick = Brick(ORANGE,80,30)
```

```python
        brick.rect.x = 60 + i* 100
        brick.rect.y = 100
        all_sprites_list.add(brick)
        all_bricks.add(brick)
for i in range(7):
    brick = Brick(YELLOW,80,30)
    brick.rect.x = 60 + i* 100
    brick.rect.y = 140
    all_sprites_list.add(brick)
    all_bricks.add(brick)


# Add the paddle to the list of sprites
all_sprites_list.add(paddle)
all_sprites_list.add(ball)


# The loop will carry on until the user exit the game (e.g. clicks the close button).
carryOn = True


# The clock will be used to control how fast the screen updates
clock = pygame.time.Clock()


# -------- Main Program Loop -----------
while carryOn:
    # --- Main event loop
    for event in pygame.event.get(): # User did something
        if event.type == pygame.QUIT: # If user clicked close
            carryOn = False # Flag that we are done so we exit this loop


    #Moving the paddle when the use uses the arrow keys
    keys = pygame.key.get_pressed()
```

```python
    if keys[pygame.K_LEFT]:
        paddle.moveLeft(5)
    if keys[pygame.K_RIGHT]:
        paddle.moveRight(5)


    # --- Game logic should go here
    all_sprites_list.update()


    #Check if the ball is bouncing against any of the 4 walls:
    if ball.rect.x>=790:
        ball.velocity[0] = -ball.velocity[0]
    if ball.rect.x<=0:
        ball.velocity[0] = -ball.velocity[0]
    if ball.rect.y>590:
        ball.velocity[1] = -ball.velocity[1]
        lives -= 1
        if lives == 0:
            #Display Game Over Message for 3 seconds
            font = pygame.font.Font(None, 74)
            text = font.render("GAME OVER", 1, WHITE)
            screen.blit(text, (250,300))
            pygame.display.flip()
            pygame.time.wait(3000)


            #Stop the Game
            carryOn=False

    if ball.rect.y<40:
        ball.velocity[1] = -ball.velocity[1]
```

```python
    #Detect collisions between the ball and the paddles
    if pygame.sprite.collide_mask(ball, paddle):
        ball.rect.x -= ball.velocity[0]
        ball.rect.y -= ball.velocity[1]
        ball.bounce()


    #Check if there is a car collision
    brick_collision_list = pygame.sprite.spritecollide(ball,all_bricks,False)
    for brick in brick_collision_list:
        ball.bounce()
        score += 1
        brick.kill()
        if len(all_bricks)==0:
            #Display Level Complete Message for 3 seconds
            font = pygame.font.Font(None, 74)
            text = font.render("LEVEL COMPLETE", 1, WHITE)
            screen.blit(text, (200,300))
            pygame.display.flip()
            pygame.time.wait(3000)


            #Stop the Game
            carryOn=False


    # --- Drawing code should go here
    # First, clear the screen to dark blue.
    screen.fill(DARKBLUE)
    pygame.draw.line(screen, WHITE, [0, 38], [800, 38], 2)


    #Display the score and the number of lives at the top of the screen
    font = pygame.font.Font(None, 34)
```

```
text = font.render("Score: " + str(score), 1, WHITE)
screen.blit(text, (20,10))
text = font.render("Lives: " + str(lives), 1, WHITE)
screen.blit(text, (650,10))


    #Now let's draw all the sprites in one go. (For now we only have 2 sprites!)
    all_sprites_list.draw(screen)


    # --- Go ahead and update the screen with what we've drawn.
    pygame.display.flip()


    # --- Limit to 60 frames per second
    clock.tick(60)


#Once we have exited the main program loop we can stop the game engine:
pygame.quit()
```

4. Shuffling a 2D Array

We would then investigate how and when to create a 2D array to store a value from 1 to 100 in a 10 bra10 array for this challenge. Then we write an algorithm to shuffle this array's content.

1	2	3	4	5	6	7	8	9	10
11	12	13	14	15	16	17	18	19	20
21	22	23	24	25	26	27	28	29	30
31	32	33	34	35	36	37	38	39	40
41	42	43	44	45	46	47	48	49	50
51	52	53	54	55	56	57	58	59	60
61	62	63	64	65	66	67	68	69	70
71	72	73	74	75	76	77	78	79	80
81	82	83	84	85	86	87	88	89	90
91	92	93	94	95	96	97	98	99	100

See the code below to see how to initialize the array to contain all numbers from 1 to 100, and how it will then be displayed on the screen.

```python
#Shuffling a 2D array -
import random


def shuffle(array):
  #Add code here to shuffle the content of the array
  #...
  print("Shuffling the array... (code to be added)")


array = []
#Add numbers from 1 to 100 in a 10x10 array
counter = 1
for i in range(0,10):
  array.append([])
  for j in range(0,10):
    array[i].append(counter)
    counter += 1


#Shuffling the array
shuffle(array)


#Output array on screen:
for i in range(0,10):
  line=""
  for j in range(0,10):
    line = line + str(array[i][j]) + " "
    if array[i][j]<10:
      line = line + " "
  print(line)
```

Your Challenge

The object of this challenge is to add a function to the above code to shuffle all 100 values within the array:

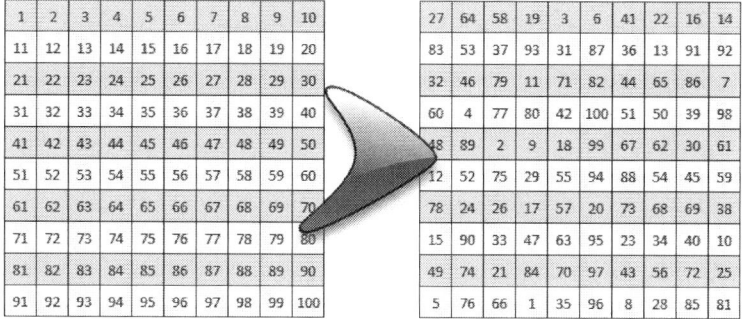

Solution

Check the flowchart below for a solution that would:

- Accesses each value of the array (using two nesting loops),
- Swaps each value: it swaps the value at a random position with another value in the array.

5. Boggle Challenge

Boggle is a game of words based on a 16 letter 44 grid. Each time a new grid is generated as the game is played. This is done in the real game by shaking a cube which contains 16 letter dice. The game's goal is to find words that can be built from sequentially adjacent letters from the 4-4 grid. "Adjacent" letters are those neighboring in horizontal , vertical and diagonal form. Words must be at least three letters long, may include both singular and plural (or other derived forms) separately, but may not use the same letter from the grid more than once per word.

A scoring system can be used by adding the number of letters in each word based on the number of words identified and.

You will re-create a single-player Boggle game using step-by - step approach to this challenge.

Step 1: A random 4×4 grid is generated and displayed

Your first task is to write a script containing 16 letters randomly picked from the alphabet that will randomly generate a 4 al grid.

Note that for letters A (ASCII value 65) to Z (ASCII value 90), you can use the ASCII values to generate a random letter as follows:

`import random`

`letter=chr(random.randint(65,90)) #Generate a random Uppercase letter (based on ASCII code)`

A 4 Sub4 grid can be defined as a 2D array (a Python list of lists). The following code, for example , uses two loops nested to create a 2D array filled with 16 letters "A."

```
grid = []
for row in range(0,4):
    grid.append([])
    for col in range(0,4):
        grid[row].append("A")

print(grid)
```

You have the task of adapting the above code to fill the grid with random letters instead of just using the letter "A."

Then you'll need to fill in the code to display the grid's content using the right format: the output should look like a grid of 4 bus4. (Tip: you need to use the nested loops again!)

letter=chr(random.randint(65,90)) #Generate a random Uppercase letter (based on ASCII code)

print(letter)

Step 2: Inputting and validating words

The next step would be to let user input a word that they spotted on the grid.

To decide whether the word is a valid word that can be generated using adjacent grid letters, you will need your program to. (And make sure that mote cannot be used with the same letter than once).

Step 3: Scoring system

Finally, you can let the user enter several words, and calculate a total score by adding the length of all valid words the user will spot (making sure they don't enter the same word more than once).

6. What 3 Words Localisation

What3words is a geocode system that uses only 3 words to communicate a location on planet Earth, instead of using complex longitude and latitude coordinates. What3words had already assigned a unique 3-word address to every 3 m square in the world which will never change.

The What3words grid contains 57 trillion 3 squares to cover the entire surface of the Earth (510 million km2) and a dictionary of 40,000 words to create enough combinations of 3 words to assign each square a unique address (40,0003 = 64 trillion).

Big Ben, London UK, for example – which is located at Longitude: -0.12461, Latitude:51.500755 – has a 3-word address from: teams.living.bucket

What3words believe this approach can be used in an easy, human-friendly way to communicate very specific locations (with a precision of 3 metres). For example, emergency services in the UK are recommending that every smartphone user download the what3words app, as it can be used to speed up the process of location in the event of an emergency.

What3words API

What3words provides developers with an API to integrate 3-word address conversion into longitude / latitude coordinates, and vice versa into other products / systems.

JSON Data

This API makes use of JSON for data formatting. JSON (JavaScript Object Notation) is a popular lightweight format for data-exchange. Its main benefit is that people can read and write easily and machines can easily parse and generate as you can see in the code.

Code Python

Check our code to see how we call the API, and how we get the requested JSON data and extract it.

To locate and identify the landmarks associated with the following 3-word addresses, you can use this code:

Teams.vive.bucket

Walnuts.octopus.com

Planet.inches.

Dwindling.loses.tree

```python
what3words = ""
while what3words.count(".")!=2:
  what3words = input("Enter 3 words separated by a dot: e.g. teams.living.bucket")


#Our JSON request to retrieve data using a what3words address.
url = "https://www.101computing.net/w3w_proxy.php/convert-to-coordinates?words=" + what3words


response = urllib.request.urlopen(url)
result = json.loads(response.read())


if "words" in result:
  print("What 3 Words: " + result["words"])
  print("Country: " + result["country"])
  print("Longitude: " + str(result["square"]["southwest"]["lng"]))
  print("Latitude: " + str(result["square"]["southwest"]["lat"]))
  print("Nearest Place: " + result["nearestPlace"])
  print("Map URL: " + result["map"])


else:
  if "error" in result:
    if "message" in result["error"]:
      print(result["error"]["message"])
    else:
      print("Unexpected error!")
  else:
    print("Unexpected error!")
```

7. Floating Point Binary Converter

The aim of this challenge is to write a Python program which will receive a binary number expressed using a standardized floating-point representation (using a 5-bit mantissa as well as a 3-bit exponent) as input. Then the program calculates the decimal value which matches the input.

```python
#Floating Point Binary Converter -

binary = input("Input a number in binary using a normalised floating point notation based on a 5-bit mantissa and 3 bit exponent:")

if len(binary)!=8:
    print("Invalid binary number - 8 bits required.")
    exit()

mantissa = binary[:5]
exponent = binary[-3:]

print("Mantissa: " + mantissa)
print("Exponent: " + exponent)

#Complete the code here to work out the decimal value...
```

8. Real-Time Asteroid Watch

Asteroids pass by close to planet Earth every day. NASA closely monitors their trajectory, as some of these could pose a threat to our planet. In this python challenge we will use the NeoWs API to retrieve some real-time data from NASA about these asteroids near Earth.

JSON Data

This API makes use of JSON for data formatting. JSON (JavaScript Object Notation) is a popular lightweight format for data-exchange. Its main advantage is that it is easy for humans to read and write, and machines can easily parse and generate

Python Code

Check our code to see just how we call the API and how we recall and extract the JSON dat requested

```
#Real time Asteroid Watch -
import json, urllib.request, time


today = time.strftime('%Y-%m-%d', time.gmtime())
print("Date: " + today)


#Our JSON request to retrieve data about asteroids approaching planet Earth.
url = "https://api.nasa.gov/neo/rest/v1/feed?start_date=" + today + "&end_date=" + today + "&api_key=DEMO_KEY"


response = urllib.request.urlopen(url)
result = json.loads(response.read())


print("Today " + str(result["element_count"]) + " asteroids will be passing close to planet Earth:")
print("")
asteroids = result["near_earth_objects"]


#Parsing all the JSON data:
for asteroid in asteroids:
    for field in asteroids[asteroid]:
        try:
            print("Asteroid Name: " + field["name"])
            print("Estimated Diameter: " + str(round((field["estimated_diameter"]["meters"]["estimated_diameter_min"]+field["estimated_diameter"]["meters"]["estimated_diameter_max"])/2),0) + " meters")
            print("Close Approach Date & Time: " + field["close_approach_data"][0]["close_approach_date_full"])
```

```python
        print("Velocity: " +
str(field["close_approach_data"][0]["relative_velocity"]["kilometers_per_hour"]) + " km/h")
        print("Distance to Earth: " +
str(field["close_approach_data"][0]["miss_distance"]["kilometers"]) + " km")


        if field["is_potentially_hazardous_asteroid"]:
            print ("This asteroid could be dangerous to planet Earth!")
        else:
            print ("This asteroid poses not threat to planet Earth!")
    except:
        print("Unable to access all data.")
    print("--------------------")
```

9. Padlock Code Challenge

Welcome to our new series of challenges to breaking padlock code.

To work out the padlock code (3-digit number) you'll need to write a computer program for each of these challenges. The solution of the given hint must be output from your program. Then you can insert this combination onto to the padlock to see if it unlocks it!

Python Code

```python
#Padlock Code Challenge -


#A function to find out if a number is prime or not
def isPrime(number):
 prime=True
 for i in range(2,number):
  if number % i ==0:
   prime=False
 return prime



code = 0
```

```
#Update the code below to solve this challenge
for i in range (0,1000):
  code+=1


print("Code:")
print(code)
```

To work out the padlock code (3-digit number) you'll need to write a computer program for each of these challenges. The solution of the given hint must be output from your program. Then you can insert this combination onto the padlock to see if it unlocks it!

```
#Padlock Code Challenge -


#A function to find out if a number is prime or not
def isPrime(number):
  prime=True
  for i in range(2,number):
    if number % i ==0:
      prime=False
  return prime


code = 0
#Update the code below to solve this challenge
for i in range (0,1000):
  code+=1


print("Code:")
print(code)
```

10. Enigma Encoder

The Enigma machine was used to either encrypt or decrypt Enigma messages (Enigma encryption is symmetric, meaning you can use the same settings to encrypt or decrypt a message).

In this challenge, using specific Enigma settings, we will create an enigma encoder program to encrypt and decrypt messages. But we need to get a better understanding of how the Enigma machine actually works before doing so.

INSIDE THE ENIGMA

The enigma machine is a relatively complex encryption machine composed of four main sections:

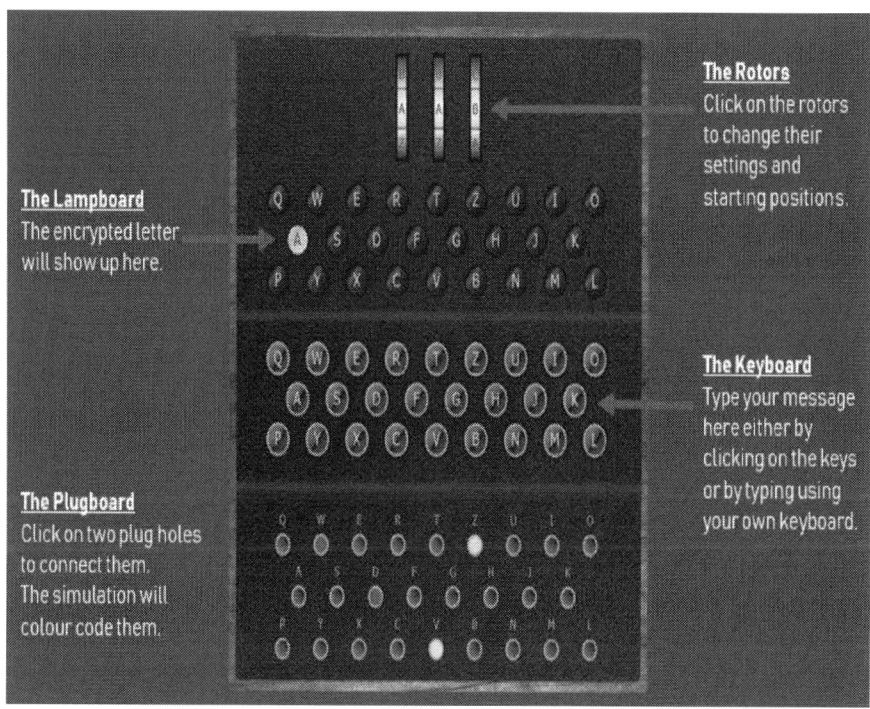

THE KEYBOARD

This same user input is retrieved using the keyboard. The Enigma machine is a machine with symmetric encryption. Which means that the same settings can be used to respectively encrypt or decrypt the message. Hence, the keyboard is used either to enter the plaintext which needs to still be encrypted, or to decrypt the ciphertext.

They have a keyboard consisting of 26 keys for each alphabet letter. This means it will join encrypted messages without any spaces or punctuation signs.

Note how the keyboard starts with QWERTZ rather than QWERTY letters. This is because letter Z is more frequently used in the German language than the letter.

THE MAINTER

Once a key on the keyboard is pressed, it passes through the plugboard which provides the first stage of the encrypted image. It's based on principles of the substitution cipher, a form of encryption of the transposition.

Short wires are used to connect pairs of letters which will be permuted to set up the keyboards. For example, a D will be replaced on the picture below the letter W, and a W letter D will be used as a (red) wire to connect these two letters / plugs. Likewise, letter V would become letter Z, and letter Z would become letter V.

THE ROTORS

After the plugboard, the letter goes in order (from right to left) through the three rotors, each changing it differently using a combination of transposition cipher and Caesar cipher! On engima M3 you can choose from three rotor slots and five rotors. Each rotor is identified using a Roman numeral from I to V. This gives the Enigma machine a few settings: which rotors to use and in which position to position them

Each of the five rotors uses a transposition / permutation cipher to encrypt the letter differently and can be connected with a different Ring setting on the Enigma machine. Another setting is the initial position of the rotors: which letters to start with will you set each rotor (e.g. A / B / C .. /Z is sometimes recorded using numbers in a codebook (01 for A, 02 for B up to 26 for Z). This creates a Shift to Caesar (Caesar Cipher). You can change the position of the rotors on an Enigma machine by turning the 3 wheels.

Various versions of Enigma (e.g. M4) included four rotors which made the encryption process even bigger and the number of possible settings.

What makes it particularly difficult to crack the Enigma code is that the rotor at the right turns by 1 letter each time a key is pressed. Which means the encryption settings for each letter of a message are constantly changing. It also means that it would encrypt a single plaintext letter differently , depending on its position in the message.

The rotors are also connected to each other so that it triggers the rotor in the middle to rotate by one letter when the rotor positioned on the right reaches a particular letter. Similarly, when the middle rotor reaches a specific letter, it triggers the left rotor to turn by one letter.

THE REFLECTOR

Another rotor type within the machine is the reflector. Once the letter has passed through the three rotors from right to left, the reflector will reflect back the electrical current through the rotors, send the encrypted letter from left to right through the rotors for another 3 stages of encryption and then again through the plugboard for a final substitution cipher. Also a permutation cipher is applied to the letter when passing through the reflector.

Various versions of reflectors have been used on various versions of Enigma machines. Each reflector would have a different permutation cipher applied. Enigma M3 machines were either equipped with a Reflector UKW-B or UKW-C. You can apply these two reflectors to our emulator 's rotor settings window (see screenshot above).

THE LAMPBOARD

The lampboard seems to be the final stage of a encryption process which is used to display the output. It consists of 26 light bulbs, one for each letter of the alphabet.

PYTHON ENIGMA INCODER

The following Python program lets you encode and decode messages that use the Enigma encryption.

```
#Enigma Encoder -
```

```
1. # ---------------- Enigma Settings ----------------
2. rotors = ("I","II","III")
3. reflector = "UKW-B"
4. ringSettings ="ABC"
5. ringPositions = "DEF"
6. plugboard = "AT BS DE FM IR KN LZ OW PV XY"
7. # -------------------------------------------------------

8. def caesarShift(str, amount):
    a. output = ""

    b. for i in range(0,len(str)):
        i.  c = str[i]
        ii.  code = ord(c)
        iii.  if ((code >= 65) and (code <= 90)):
            1. c = chr(((code - 65 + amount) % 26) + 65)
        iv.  output = output + c

    c. return output

9. def encode(plaintext):
10.global rotors, reflector,ringSettings,ringPositions,plugboard
11.#Enigma Rotors and reflectors
12.rotor1 = "EKMFLGDQVZNTOWYHXUSPAIBRCJ"
```

```python
13. rotor1Notch = "Q"
14. rotor2 = "AJDKSIRUXBLHWTMCQGZNPYFVOE"
15. rotor2Notch = "E"
16. rotor3 = "BDFHJLCPRTXVZNYEIWGAKMUSQO"
17. rotor3Notch = "V"
18. rotor4 = "ESOVPZJAYQUIRHXLNFTGKDCMWB"
19. rotor4Notch = "J"
20. rotor5 = "VZBRGITYUPSDNHLXAWMJQOFECK"
21. rotor5Notch = "Z"


22. rotorDict = {"I":rotor1,"II":rotor2,"III":rotor3,"IV":rotor4,"V":rotor5}
23. rotorNotchDict =
        {"I":rotor1Notch,"II":rotor2Notch,"III":rotor3Notch,"IV":rotor4Notch,"V":rotor5Notch}


24. reflectorB =
        {"A":"Y","Y":"A","B":"R","R":"B","C":"U","U":"C","D":"H","H":"D","E":"Q","Q":"E","F":"
        S","S":"F","G":"L","L":"G","I":"P","P":"I","J":"X","X":"J","K":"N","N":"K","M":"O","O":"
        M","T":"Z","Z":"T","V":"W","W":"V"}
25. reflectorC =
        {"A":"F","F":"A","B":"V","V":"B","C":"P","P":"C","D":"J","J":"D","E":"I","I":"E","G":"O","
        "O":"G","H":"Y","Y":"H","K":"R","R":"K","L":"Z","Z":"L","M":"X","X":"M","N":"W","W":"
        N","Q":"T","T":"Q","S":"U","U":"S"}


26. alphabet = "ABCDEFGHIJKLMNOPQRSTUVWXYZ"
27. rotorANotch = False
28. rotorBNotch = False
29. rotorCNotch = False


30. if reflector=="UKW-B":
31. reflectorDict = reflectorB
32. else:
33. reflectorDict = reflectorC


34. #A = Left,  B = Mid,  C=Right
35. rotorA = rotorDict[rotors[0]]
36. rotorB = rotorDict[rotors[1]]
37. rotorC = rotorDict[rotors[2]]
38. rotorANotch = rotorNotchDict[rotors[0]]
```

```python
39.rotorBNotch = rotorNotchDict[rotors[1]]
40.rotorCNotch = rotorNotchDict[rotors[2]]


41.rotorALetter = ringPositions[0]
42.rotorBLetter = ringPositions[1]
43.rotorCLetter = ringPositions[2]


44.rotorASetting = ringSettings[0]
45.offsetASetting = alphabet.index(rotorASetting)
46.rotorBSetting = ringSettings[1]
47.offsetBSetting = alphabet.index(rotorBSetting)
48.rotorCSetting = ringSettings[2]
49.offsetCSetting = alphabet.index(rotorCSetting)


50.rotorA = caesarShift(rotorA,offsetASetting)
51.rotorB = caesarShift(rotorB,offsetBSetting)
52.rotorC = caesarShift(rotorC,offsetCSetting)


53.if offsetASetting>0:
54.rotorA = rotorA[26-offsetASetting:] + rotorA[0:26-offsetASetting]
55.if offsetBSetting>0:
56.rotorB = rotorB[26-offsetBSetting:] + rotorB[0:26-offsetBSetting]
57.if offsetCSetting>0:
58.rotorC = rotorC[26-offsetCSetting:] + rotorC[0:26-offsetCSetting]


59.ciphertext = ""


60.#Converplugboard settings into a dictionary
61.plugboardConnections = plugboard.upper().split(" ")
62.plugboardDict = {}
63.for pair in plugboardConnections:
64.if len(pair)==2:
65.plugboardDict[pair[0]] = pair[1]
66.plugboardDict[pair[1]] = pair[0]


67.plaintext = plaintext.upper()
```

```python
68.for letter in plaintext:
69.encryptedLetter = letter


70.if letter in alphabet:
71.#Rotate Rotors - This happens as soon as a key is pressed, before encrypting the
    letter!
72.rotorTrigger = False
73.#Third rotor rotates by 1 for every key being pressed
74.if rotorCLetter == rotorCNotch:
75.rotorTrigger = True
76.rotorCLetter = alphabet[(alphabet.index(rotorCLetter) + 1) % 26]
77.#Check if rotorB needs to rotate
78.if rotorTrigger:
79.rotorTrigger = False
80.if rotorBLetter == rotorBNotch:
81.rotorTrigger = True
82.rotorBLetter = alphabet[(alphabet.index(rotorBLetter) + 1) % 26]


83.#Check if rotorA needs to rotate
84.if (rotorTrigger):
85.rotorTrigger = False
86.rotorALetter = alphabet[(alphabet.index(rotorALetter) + 1) % 26]


87.else:
88.#Check for double step sequence!
89.if rotorBLetter == rotorBNotch:
90.rotorBLetter = alphabet[(alphabet.index(rotorBLetter) + 1) % 26]
91.rotorALetter = alphabet[(alphabet.index(rotorALetter) + 1) % 26]


92.#Implement plugboard encryption!
93.if letter in plugboardDict.keys():
94.if plugboardDict[letter]!="":
95.encryptedLetter = plugboardDict[letter]


96.#Rotors & Reflector Encryption
97.offsetA = alphabet.index(rotorALetter)
98.offsetB = alphabet.index(rotorBLetter)
99.offsetC = alphabet.index(rotorCLetter)
```

```
100.        # Wheel 3 Encryption
101.        pos = alphabet.index(encryptedLetter)
102.        let = rotorC[(pos + offsetC)%26]
103.        pos = alphabet.index(let)
104.        encryptedLetter = alphabet[(pos - offsetC +26)%26]


105.        # Wheel 2 Encryption
106.        pos = alphabet.index(encryptedLetter)
107.        let = rotorB[(pos + offsetB)%26]
108.        pos = alphabet.index(let)
109.        encryptedLetter = alphabet[(pos - offsetB +26)%26]


110.        # Wheel 1 Encryption
111.        pos = alphabet.index(encryptedLetter)
112.        let = rotorA[(pos + offsetA)%26]
113.        pos = alphabet.index(let)
114.        encryptedLetter = alphabet[(pos - offsetA +26)%26]


115.        # Reflector encryption!
116.        if encryptedLetter in reflectorDict.keys():
117.        if reflectorDict[encryptedLetter]!="":
118.        encryptedLetter = reflectorDict[encryptedLetter]


119.        #Back through the rotors
120.        # Wheel 1 Encryption
121.        pos = alphabet.index(encryptedLetter)
122.        let = alphabet[(pos + offsetA)%26]
123.        pos = rotorA.index(let)
124.        encryptedLetter = alphabet[(pos - offsetA +26)%26]


125.        # Wheel 2 Encryption
126.        pos = alphabet.index(encryptedLetter)
127.        let = alphabet[(pos + offsetB)%26]
128.        pos = rotorB.index(let)
129.        encryptedLetter = alphabet[(pos - offsetB +26)%26]
```

```
130.        # Wheel 3 Encryption
131.        pos = alphabet.index(encryptedLetter)
132.        let = alphabet[(pos + offsetC)%26]
133.        pos = rotorC.index(let)
134.        encryptedLetter = alphabet[(pos - offsetC +26)%26]


135.        #Implement plugboard encryption!
136.        if encryptedLetter in plugboardDict.keys():
137.        if plugboardDict[encryptedLetter]!="":
138.        encryptedLetter = plugboardDict[encryptedLetter]


139.        ciphertext = ciphertext + encryptedLetter


140.        return ciphertext


141.        #Main Program Starts Here
142.        print("  ##### Enigma Encoder #####")
143.        print("")
144.        plaintext = input("Enter text to encode or decode:\n")
145.        ciphertext = encode(plaintext)


146.        print("\nEncoded text: \n " + ciphertext)
```

11.Pong Tutorial using Pygame – Adding a Scoring System

Player A score a point if the ball bounces against the screen's right-hand edge while player B score a point if the ball bounces against the screen's left-hand edge. Both scores will show up at the top of the screen.

The final code for the main.py is set out below. We made the following three changes to the code:

- We initialize both player scores to 0 on lines 43 through 45.
- The code detects on lines 72 to 77 when the player scores point.
- How scores are displayed on screen on lines 96 to 101;

 # Import the pygame library and initialise the game engine

```python
1.  import pygame
2.  from paddle import Paddle
3.  from ball import Ball


4.  pygame.init()


5.  # Define some colors
6.  BLACK = (0,0,0)
7.  WHITE = (255,255,255)


8.  # Open a new window
9.  size = (700, 500)
10.screen = pygame.display.set_mode(size)
11.pygame.display.set_caption("Pong")


12.paddleA = Paddle(WHITE, 10, 100)
13.paddleA.rect.x = 20
14.paddleA.rect.y = 200


15.paddleB = Paddle(WHITE, 10, 100)
16.paddleB.rect.x = 670
17.paddleB.rect.y = 200


18.ball = Ball(WHITE,10,10)
19.ball.rect.x = 345
20.ball.rect.y = 195


21.#This will be a list that will contain all the sprites we intend to use in our game.
22.all_sprites_list = pygame.sprite.Group()


23.# Add the car to the list of objects
24.all_sprites_list.add(paddleA)
25.all_sprites_list.add(paddleB)
26.all_sprites_list.add(ball)
```

```
27.# The loop will carry on until the user exit the game (e.g. clicks the close button).
28.carryOn = True


29.# The clock will be used to control how fast the screen updates
30.clock = pygame.time.Clock()


31.#Initialise player scores
32.scoreA = 0
33.scoreB = 0


34.# -------- Main Program Loop ----------
35.while carryOn:
36.# --- Main event loop
37.for event in pygame.event.get(): # User did something
38.if event.type == pygame.QUIT: # If user clicked close
39.carryOn = False # Flag that we are done so we exit this loop
40.elif event.type==pygame.KEYDOWN:
        a.  if event.key==pygame.K_x: #Pressing the x Key will quit the game
        b.  carryOn=False


41.#Moving the paddles when the use uses the arrow keys (player A) or "W/S" keys
    (player B)
42.keys = pygame.key.get_pressed()
43.if keys[pygame.K_w]:
44.paddleA.moveUp(5)
45.if keys[pygame.K_s]:
46.paddleA.moveDown(5)
47.if keys[pygame.K_UP]:
48.paddleB.moveUp(5)
49.if keys[pygame.K_DOWN]:
50.paddleB.moveDown(5)


51.# --- Game logic should go here
52.all_sprites_list.update()
```

```python
53.#Check if the ball is bouncing against any of the 4 walls:
54.if ball.rect.x>=690:
55.scoreA+=1
56.ball.velocity[0] = -ball.velocity[0]
57.if ball.rect.x<=0:
58.scoreB+=1
59.ball.velocity[0] = -ball.velocity[0]
60.if ball.rect.y>490:
61.ball.velocity[1] = -ball.velocity[1]
62.if ball.rect.y<0:
63.ball.velocity[1] = -ball.velocity[1]


64.#Detect collisions between the ball and the paddles
65.if pygame.sprite.collide_mask(ball, paddleA) or pygame.sprite.collide_mask(ball,
      paddleB):
66.ball.bounce()


67.# --- Drawing code should go here
68.# First, clear the screen to black.
69.screen.fill(BLACK)
70.#Draw the net
71.pygame.draw.line(screen, WHITE, [349, 0], [349, 500], 5)


72.#Now let's draw all the sprites in one go. (For now we only have 2 sprites!)
73.all_sprites_list.draw(screen)


74.#Display scores:
75.font = pygame.font.Font(None, 74)
76.text = font.render(str(scoreA), 1, WHITE)
77.screen.blit(text, (250,10))
78.text = font.render(str(scoreB), 1, WHITE)
79.screen.blit(text, (420,10))


80.# --- Go ahead and update the screen with what we've drawn.
81.pygame.display.flip()


82.# --- Limit to 60 frames per second
```

```
83.clock.tick(60)
```

```
84.#Once we have exited the main program loop we can stop the game engine:
   pygame.quit()
```

12. Enigma Daily Settings Generator

The Germans used to change the Enigma settings quite regularly (e.g. once a day), so that if the Allies managed to break their code (find the Enigma settings) they would only have been able to use them for that same day and would have to find the new settings every day. Code books were documents that were highly confidential as if a codebook had been captured or reconstructed, messages could easily be decrypted.

The settings would specify which rotors to use and in which to connect. The Enigma machine originally came with a five rotor box to choose from. Three of the five rotors had been connected on an Enigma M3. The M4 Enigma utilized four rotors selected from a box with up to eight rotors.

The settings would also include the setting of the wheel (how to connect the rotors) and its initial position. Finally the settings would indicate whether the letters to connect to the plugboard by plugging cables in.

#Enigma Daily Settings / Code Book Generator -

from random import randint

```
1.  TITLE = "ENIGMA M3 - UKW-B Reflector - April 1940 - Code Book"
2.  NUMBER_OF_DAYS = 30


3.  def rotor_selection(numberOfRotors):
4.  rotors = ["I","II","III","IV","V"]
5.  alphabet = "ABCDEFGHIJKLMNOPQRSTUVWXYZ"
6.  i = randint(0, numberOfRotors-1)
7.  ii = randint(0, numberOfRotors-1)
8.  while ii==i:
9.  ii = randint(0, numberOfRotors-1)
10. iii = randint(0, numberOfRotors-1)
11. while iii==i or iii==ii:
12. iii = randint(0, numberOfRotors-1)


13. rotor_i = rotors[i]
14. rotor_ii = rotors[ii]
```

```
15. rotor_iii = rotors[iii]


16. settings = rotor_i +  " " + rotor_ii + " " + rotor_iii
17. settings = settings + (" "*(9-len(settings)))
18. return settings


19. def ring_settings(numberOfRotors):  # returns ring settings
20. alphabet = "ABCDEFGHIJKLMNOPQRSTUVWXYZ"
21. settings = ""
22. for i in range(numberOfRotors):
23. rotor = randint(0, 25)
24. settings = settings + alphabet[rotor]
25. return settings


26. def plugboard_settings(numberOfPermutations):  # Plugboard steckering
27. alphabet = "ABCDEFGHIJKLMNOPQRSTUVWXYZ"
28. settings = ""
29. stecksA = []
30. stecksB= []


31. for i in range(numberOfPermutations):
32. a = randint(0, 25)
33. while a in stecksA:
34. a = randint(0, 25)
35. stecksA.append(a)


36. for i in range(numberOfPermutations):
37. b = randint(0, 25)
38. while b in stecksA or b in stecksB:
39. b = randint(0, 25)
40. stecksB.append(b)


41. stecksA.sort()


42. settings=""
43. for i in range(numberOfPermutations):
44. settings = settings + alphabet[stecksA[i]] + alphabet[stecksB[i]] + " "
```

```python
45. settings = settings[:-1]
46. return settings


47. def rotor_positions(numberOfRotors):  # Rotor position
48. alphabet = "ABCDEFGHIJKLMNOPQRSTUVWXYZ"
49. settings = ""
50. for i in range(numberOfRotors):
51. rotor = randint(0, 25)
52. settings = settings + alphabet[rotor]
53. return settings


54. def generateCodeBook(title, numberOfDays):
55. print(title)
56. for day in range(numberOfDays,0,-1):
57. print('+----------------------------------------------+')
58. if day<10:
59. settings = "|  " + str(day) + " | "
60. else:
61. settings = "| " + str(day) + " | "
62. settings = settings  + rotor_selection(5) + " | "
63. settings = settings + ring_settings(3) + " | "
64. settings = settings + plugboard_settings(6) + " | "
65. settings = settings + rotor_positions(3) + " |"
66. print(settings)


67. print('+----------------------------------------------+')


generateCodeBook(TITLE, NUMBER_OF_DAYS)
```

13. Stopping Distance Calculator

In this challenge, we'll write a Python program to estimate a vehicle's total stop distance based on its speed. The distance to the stop consists of two components. The first component is the vehicle's covered reaction distance due to the driver's response time / delay between the moment an obstacle has been spotted on the road as well as the moment the brakes are applied. The second component is the braking distance which would be the distance from which a vehicle will travel when it comes to a complete stop when its brakes are fully applied to. The braking distance is primarily impacted by the vehicle's original speed and the friction coefficient between the tires and the road surface.

We will use a response time (tr) of 1.5 seconds for this challenge, the average response time for a driver. In reality, this response time varies according to the driver's age , experience and condition: e.g. A fatigued driver will have a slower response time than a driver alert.

The common base line value for the μ (pronounced mu) friction coefficient is 0.7. In reality this coefficient varies depending on the road condition (e.g. dry/wet/icy) as well as the tyres' types, condition and pressure.

Our aim is to write an INPUT / PROCESS / OUTPUT based Python program that will:

1. INPUT: Ask the user to enter a car's speed in mph (Miles per hour)
2. PROCESS: Turn that speed to mps (meters per second)
3. PROCESS: apply the formulation for stopping distance (using μ = 0.7 and tr = 1.5s)
4. OUTPUT: Display the vehicle's estimated stop distance in metres.

Complete the Python Code

#Stopping Distance Calculator

```
1.  mu = 0.7 # Friction Coefficient
2.  tr = 1.5 # Response Time
3.  g = 9.81 # Gravity

4.  #INPUT
5.  #Ask the user to enter the speed of the vehicle in mph
6.  #...

7.  #PROCESS
8.  #Convert the speed from miles per hour to meters per second
9.  #...
```

```
10.#Calculate the reaction distance, braking distance and overall total stopping distance
11.#...


12.#OUTPUT
13.#Display the stopping distance in meters
14.#...
```

14. My Weekly Timetable

A school schedule is shown as a 2D table consisting of 5 rows (for each weekday) and 5 columns (number of lessons each day).

Such a table can be stored via a 2-dimensional array (2d Array) in a computer program. This is achieved in python, by constructing a list of lists.

You can then reach any value of a 2D array by proving two indices: row number and column number

Python Challenges

The following 3 tabs include 3 separate tasks, all focused on 2D array access to information called timetable.

What Lecture? Is it Lessons of Today? How many lessons to learn?

Write a program which reads:

1. Asks the user to input a weekday (e.g. Tuesday)
2. Requests the user to enter a time of day (between 1 and 5) (e.g. 2)
3. Retrieve the lesson and question it on that day and time (e.g. Spanish)

Python Code

Use the following code to complete all three challenges mentioned above:

```
#My weekly timetable -
```

```
timetable = []
```

```
#Monday
```

```python
timetable.append(["History","Maths","Computer Science","PE","Music"])
#Tuesday
timetable.append(["English","Spanish","Maths","Geography","Art"])
#Wednesday
timetable.append(["PE","English","Science","Art","PE"])
#Thursday
timetable.append(["Maths","English","Philosohpy","Spanish","Music"])
#Friday
timetable.append(["Science","Drama","History","Geography","Science"])


#Complete the code from here
```

The following lines of code will help you solve each of the three challenges.

```python
#INPUT
day = input("Day of the week?").title()
period = int(input("Lesson number (1 to 5):"))
while period<1 or period>5:
    period = int(input("Lesson number (1 to 5):"))


#PROCESS
lesson=""
if day=="Monday":
    lesson = timetable[0][period-1]
elif day=="Tuesday":
    lesson = timetable[1][period-1]
elif day=="Wednesday":
    lesson = timetable[2][period-1]
elif day=="Thursday":
    lesson = timetable[3][period-1]
elif day=="Friday":
    lesson = timetable[4][period-1]
```

```
else:
    print("Not a valid week day!")


#OUTPUT
if lesson!="":
    print("On " + day + ", lesson " + str(period) + " you have " + lesson + ".")
```

15. Cell Phone Trilateration Algorithm

Mobile phone tracking is a mechanism for detecting a cell phone's location, whether stationary or on the move. Localization may occur either through the multilateralisation of radio signals between multiple cell towers and the telephone, or simply through GPS.

Mobile positioning is used by telecommunications providers to estimate a cell phone's location and allows the mobile user to be provided location-based services and/or information.

Multilateration / Cell Phone Trilateration

Trilateration of cell towers (sometimes called triangulation) is used to identify the phone's location. A cell phone constantly emits roaming radio signals that three or more cell towers can pick up allowing the triangulation to function. Trilateration estimates measure the co-ordinates of a mobile device using the co-ordinates (longitude, latitude) of the nearest cell towers as well as the approximate distance between the device and the cell towers (e.g. either based on the signal intensity or by calculating the time delay that a signal takes to return from the phone to the towers).

In this challenge we will analyze the mathematical equations used in calculations for trilateration. Using a 2D problem model based on (x, y) coordinates (as an alternative to longitude / latitude coordinates) we can simplify the operation.

Python Implementing

Now that we understand the math required in a trilateration calculation, let's implement those equations in a Python algorithm and use a function that takes 9 parameters (X_1, Y_1 R_1, X_2, Y_2 $R_2, X_3, Y_3 R_3$) and returns the (x , y) intersection point coordinates of the three circles.

Your job is to complete the trackPhone) (code which we started for you:

```
#Cell Phone Trilateration Algorithm -
import draw
```

```
#A function to apply trilateration formulas to return the (x,y) intersection point of three circles
def trackPhone(x1,y1,r1,x2,y2,r2,x3,y3,r3):
    A = 2*x2 - 2*x1
    B = 2*y2 - 2*y1
    C = r1**2 - r2**2 - x1**2 + x2**2 - y1**2 + y2**2
    D = 2*x3 - 2*x2
    E = 2*y3 - 2*y2
    F = r2**2 - r3**2 - x2**2 + x3**2 - y2**2 + y3**2
    x = (C*E - F*B) / (E*A - B*D)
    y = (C*D - A*F) / (B*D - A*E)
    return x,y


#Generate and represent data to be used by the trilateration algorithm
x1,y1,r1,x2,y2,r2,x3,y3,r3 = draw.drawCellTowers()


#Apply trilateration algorithm to locate phone
x,y = trackPhone(x1,y1,r1,x2,y2,r2,x3,y3,r3)


#Output phone location / coordinates
print("Cell Phone Location:")
print(x,y)
```

16. Weight on the Moon Calculator

Your weight is an indicator of how much gravity planet Earth exerts on your body. On planet Earth the magnitude of gravity is 9.81 N / Kg (Newtons per kilogram). Since the Moon has only one-sixth of Earth's gravity, you 'd be weighing less up on it. Gravity on the Moon has a magnitude of 1.622 N/Kg.

Therefore, we can measure the weight on the Moon using the following formula:

We will write a short Python program for this task, based on the model Input / Process / Output. Our programme:

189

1.INPUT:

Ask the user to enter their weight in kg and store the value in a weightOnEarth variable.

2. PROCESS:

Apply the formula to measure the corresponding lunar weight, and store it in a weightOnMoon variable.

3. OUTPUT:

Show weight on screen on the Moon.

Python Code

```
#Weight on the Moon Calculator
#Input
weightOnEarth = float(input("Enter your weight/mass in kg:"))
#Process - Calculate weight on the Moon, rounded to 2 decimal places.
weightOnMoon = round( weightOnEarth * 1.622 / 9.81 , 2)
#Output
print("Your weight on the Moon is: " + str(weightOnMoon) + "kg.")
```

17. Lissajous Curve Tracing Algorithm

Lissajous curves are a family of curves described by the parametric equations that follow:

$$x(t) = A \sin(at + \delta)$$

$$y(t) = B \sin(bt)$$

Lissajous curves have applications in the fields of physics, astronomy and others. Below are a few examples of Lissajous curves that you will be able to replicate by modifying the values of constant A and B in the Python code in the Python.

Lissajous Curve using Python Turtle

```
#Python Turtle - Lissajous Curve -
import turtle
```

```python
from math import cos,sin
from time import sleep


window = turtle.Screen()
window.bgcolor("#FFFFFF")


myPen = turtle.Turtle()
myPen.hideturtle()
myPen.tracer(0)
myPen.speed(0)
myPen.pensize(3)
myPen.color("#AA00AA")


myPen.penup()


A = 100
B = 100
a = 3
b = 4
delta = 3.14/2
t=0


for i in range(0,1000):
    t+=0.01
    #Apply Lissajous Parametric Equations
    x = A * sin(a*t + delta)
    y = B * sin(b*t)

    myPen.goto(x,y)
    myPen.pendown()
```

```
myPen.getscreen().update()
```

```
sleep(0.5)
```

18. The Honeycomb Challenge

Honeycomb is a collection of hexagonal cavities (wax cells), formed by bees for storing honey and eggs.

In this challenge we are going to use a series of iterative algorithms to draw a pattern of the honeycomb.

First, we'll be creating a single hexagonal cavity draw **function**. Our drawCavity () function takes in three parameters:

- x-x coordinates the hexagon position.
- Y-x coordinates the hexagon position.
- EdgeLength-the length of the hexagon edge in pixels.

```
#The honeycomb challenge -
import turtle
myPen = turtle.Turtle()
myPen.shape("arrow")


myPen.color("#a86f14")
myPen.fillcolor("#efb456")
myPen.pensize(2)
myPen.delay(10) #Set the speed of the turtle


#A Procedue to draw a pentagonal cavity at a given (x,y) position.
def drawCavity(x,y,edgeLength):
```

```
myPen.penup()
myPen.goto(x,y)
myPen.pendown()
myPen.begin_fill()
for i in range(0,6):
    myPen.forward(edgeLength)
    myPen.left(60)
myPen.end_fill()



#Main Program Starts Here
#Comlpete this code to draw a full honeycomb pattern
for x in range(-150,150,60):
    drawCavity(x,150,20)



myPen.hideturtle()
```

19. Sudoku Generator Algorithm

You have the job of creating an algorithm used to construct a Sudoku Grid. The Sudoku grid created should have enough clues (numbers in cells) to be solvable, which would result in a unique solution.

Sudoku?

Number-placement puzzle is a Sudoku game. The goal is to fill a 9-shaped grid with digits so that each column, each row, and each of the nine 3-shaped subgrids that make up the grid (also known as "boxes," "lines," or "regions") contain all the 1-9 digits. The puzzle setter provides a partially finished grid which has a single solution for a well-positioned puzzle.

Our target for this challenge is not to produce a Sudoku solver algorithm but rather to construct an algorithm that a puzzle setter can use to construct a well-positioned Sudoku grid: a grid with a unique solution. The output of our algorithm may for example be a grid

Have you known?

Sudoku fanatics have long believed that a Sudoku puzzle will contain the smallest number of starting clues is 17. There are also numerous examples of grids with 17 clues that have a specific solution but we never found a well-positioned grid with only 16 clues. This means the minimum number of clues a grid can have is 17.

This main fact can be useful in helping you to more effectively answer this challenge.

Sudoku Solver algorithm

The Sudoku Generator algorithm might well need to use a Sudoku Solver Algorithm to test for solvency of a generated grid and to verify that it only provides one solution.

Sudoku Solver Algorithm's most common form is based on a backtracking algorithm used to investigate all possible solutions for a given grid.

Extension Task:

Sudoku puzzles are also given such a degree of difficulty as "Beginner – Intermediate – Advanced – Professional."

How to adapt your algorithm to estimate the degree of difficulty of a Sudoku grid?

Do different algorithms should be used to create Sudoku grids for a particular level of difficulty?

Solution

We base our solution on 5 steps:

1. Generate a complete numbers grid (full filled in). This move is more complicated as it seems we can't just produce numbers at random to fill in the grid. We must ensure that all numbers are put on the grid in compliance with the Sudoku rules. To do so, a sudoku solver algorithm (backtracking algorithm) is used which we will apply to an empty grid. We'll add a random element to this solver algorithm to ensure that each time we run it; a new grid is created.
2. Then we shall delete 1 value at a time from our complete list.
3. We will apply a sudoku solver algorithm each time a value is removed to see if the grid can still be solved and to count the number of solutions it leads to.
4. If there is only one solution in the resulting grid, we can carry on the process from phase 2. If we aren't going to have to put the money that we took back in the system.
5. We can repeat the same method many times (from step 2) using a different value each time to try and extract additional numbers, which leads to a more complicated grid to solve. The number of attempts that we will use to go through this process will affect the level of complexity of the resulting grid.

```python
1.  #Sudoku Generator Algorithm
2.  import turtle
3.  from random import randint, shuffle
4.  from time import sleep


5.  #initialise empty 9 by 9 grid
6.  grid = []
7.  grid.append([0, 0, 0, 0, 0, 0, 0, 0, 0])
8.  grid.append([0, 0, 0, 0, 0, 0, 0, 0, 0])
9.  grid.append([0, 0, 0, 0, 0, 0, 0, 0, 0])
10.     grid.append([0, 0, 0, 0, 0, 0, 0, 0, 0])
11.     grid.append([0, 0, 0, 0, 0, 0, 0, 0, 0])
12.     grid.append([0, 0, 0, 0, 0, 0, 0, 0, 0])
13.     grid.append([0, 0, 0, 0, 0, 0, 0, 0, 0])
14.     grid.append([0, 0, 0, 0, 0, 0, 0, 0, 0])
15.     grid.append([0, 0, 0, 0, 0, 0, 0, 0, 0])


16.     myPen = turtle.Turtle()
17.     myPen.tracer(0)
18.     myPen.speed(0)
19.     myPen.color("#000000")
20.     myPen.hideturtle()
21.     topLeft_x=-150
22.     topLeft_y=150


23.     def text(message,x,y,size):
24.     FONT = ('Arial', size, 'normal')
25.     myPen.penup()
26.     myPen.goto(x,y)
27.     myPen.write(message,align="left",font=FONT)


28.     #A procedure to draw the grid on screen using Python Turtle
29.     def drawGrid(grid):
30.     intDim=35
31.     for row in range(0,10):
32.     if (row%3)==0:
33.     myPen.pensize(3)
34.     else:
35.     myPen.pensize(1)
```

```
36.        myPen.penup()
37.        myPen.goto(topLeft_x,topLeft_y-row*intDim)
38.        myPen.pendown()
39.        myPen.goto(topLeft_x+9*intDim,topLeft_y-row*intDim)
40.        for col in range(0,10):
41.            if (col%3)==0:
42.                myPen.pensize(3)
43.            else:
44.                myPen.pensize(1)
45.            myPen.penup()
46.            myPen.goto(topLeft_x+col*intDim,topLeft_y)
47.            myPen.pendown()
48.            myPen.goto(topLeft_x+col*intDim,topLeft_y-9*intDim)


49.        for row in range (0,9):
50.            for col in range (0,9):
51.                if grid[row][col]!=0:
52.                    text(grid[row][col],topLeft_x+col*intDim+9,topLeft_y-row*intDim-
       intDim+8,18)



53.    #A function to check if the grid is full
54.    def checkGrid(grid):
55.        for row in range(0,9):
56.            for col in range(0,9):
57.                if grid[row][col]==0:
58.                    return False


59.        #We have a complete grid!
60.        return True



61.    #A backtracking/recursive function to check all possible combinations of
       numbers until a solution is found
62.    def solveGrid(grid):
63.        global counter
64.        #Find next empty cell
65.        for i in range(0,81):
66.            row=i//9
```

```
67.        col=i%9
68.          if grid[row][col]==0:
69.          for value in range (1,10):
70.            #Check that this value has not already be used on this row
71.            if not(value in grid[row]):
72.              #Check that this value has not already be used on this column
73.              if not value in
(grid[0][col],grid[1][col],grid[2][col],grid[3][col],grid[4][col],grid[5][col],grid[6
][col],grid[7][col],grid[8][col]):
74.              #Identify which of the 9 squares we are working on
75.              square=[]
76.              if row<3:
77.                if col<3:
     a. square=[grid[i][0:3] for i in range(0,3)]
78.              elif col<6:
     a. square=[grid[i][3:6] for i in range(0,3)]
79.              else:
     a. square=[grid[i][6:9] for i in range(0,3)]
80.              elif row<6:
81.                if col<3:
     a. square=[grid[i][0:3] for i in range(3,6)]
82.              elif col<6:
     a. square=[grid[i][3:6] for i in range(3,6)]
83.              else:
     a. square=[grid[i][6:9] for i in range(3,6)]
84.              else:
85.                if col<3:
     a. square=[grid[i][0:3] for i in range(6,9)]
86.              elif col<6:
     a. square=[grid[i][3:6] for i in range(6,9)]
87.              else:
     a. square=[grid[i][6:9] for i in range(6,9)]
88.              #Check that this value has not already be used on this 3x3 square
89.              if not value in (square[0] + square[1] + square[2]):
90.                grid[row][col]=value
91.                if checkGrid(grid):
     a. counter+=1
     b. break
92.                else:
     a. if solveGrid(grid):
     b. return True
93.              break
94.          grid[row][col]=0
```

197

```python
95.      numberList=[1,2,3,4,5,6,7,8,9]
96.      #shuffle(numberList)


97.      #A backtracking/recursive function to check all possible combinations of
         numbers until a solution is found
98.      def fillGrid(grid):
99.      global counter
100.     #Find next empty cell
101.     for i in range(0,81):
102.     row=i//9
103.     col=i%9
104.     if grid[row][col]==0:
105.     shuffle(numberList)
106.     for value in numberList:
107.     #Check that this value has not already be used on this row
108.     if not(value in grid[row]):
109.     #Check that this value has not already be used on this column
110.     if not value in
(grid[0][col],grid[1][col],grid[2][col],grid[3][col],grid[4][col],grid[5][col],grid[6
][col],grid[7][col],grid[8][col]):
111.     #Identify which of the 9 squares we are working on
112.     square=[]
113.     if row<3:
114.     if col<3:
     a. square=[grid[i][0:3] for i in range(0,3)]
115.     elif col<6:
     a. square=[grid[i][3:6] for i in range(0,3)]
116.     else:
     a. square=[grid[i][6:9] for i in range(0,3)]
117.     elif row<6:
118.     if col<3:
     a. square=[grid[i][0:3] for i in range(3,6)]
119.     elif col<6:
     a. square=[grid[i][3:6] for i in range(3,6)]
120.     else:
     a. square=[grid[i][6:9] for i in range(3,6)]
121.     else:
122.     if col<3:
     a. square=[grid[i][0:3] for i in range(6,9)]
123.     elif col<6:
```

```
        a. square=[grid[i][3:6] for i in range(6,9)]
124.    else:
        a. square=[grid[i][6:9] for i in range(6,9)]
125.    #Check that this value has not already be used on this 3x3 square
126.    if not value in (square[0] + square[1] + square[2]):
127.        grid[row][col]=value
128.        if checkGrid(grid):
        a. return True
129.        else:
        a. if fillGrid(grid):
        b. return True
130.        break
131.        grid[row][col]=0


132.    #Generate a Fully Solved Grid
133.    fillGrid(grid)
134.    drawGrid(grid)
135.    myPen.getscreen().update()
136.    sleep(1)


137.    #Start Removing Numbers one by one


138.    #A higher number of attempts will end up removing more numbers from
    the grid
139.    #Potentially resulting in more difficiult grids to solve!
140.    attempts = 5
141.    counter=1
142.    while attempts>0:
143.        #Select a random cell that is not already empty
144.        row = randint(0,8)
145.        col = randint(0,8)
146.        while grid[row][col]==0:
147.            row = randint(0,8)
148.            col = randint(0,8)
149.        #Remember its cell value in case we need to put it back
150.        backup = grid[row][col]
151.        grid[row][col]=0
```

```
152.        #Take a full copy of the grid
153.        copyGrid = []
154.        for r in range(0,9):
155.          copyGrid.append([])
156.          for c in range(0,9):
157.            copyGrid[r].append(grid[r][c])


158.        #Count the number of solutions that this grid has (using a backtracking
            approach implemented in the solveGrid() function)
159.        counter=0
160.        solveGrid(copyGrid)
161.        #If the number of solution is different from 1 then we need to cancel the
            change by putting the value we took away back in the grid
162.        if counter!=1:
163.          grid[row][col]=backup
164.        #We could stop here, but we can also have another attempt with a
            different cell just to try to remove more numbers
165.        attempts -= 1


166.        myPen.clear()
167.        drawGrid(grid)
168.        myPen.getscreen().update()


print("Sudoku Grid Ready")
```

20. Chemical Elements Quiz

The goal of this challenge is to construct a quiz based on the periodic table 's list of chemical elements, based on the following requirements:

- Contains 10 questions to the quiz.
- Each question shows the element name (e.g., Aluminum) and asks the user to enter the element symbol (e.g. Al).
- The user score 2 points for every correct answer, and the user loses 1 point for every incorrect answer.
- In the negative values the score cannot go.
- After each question a feedback with the correct answer is given.

- Shows the final score (out of 20) at the conclusion of the quiz.

Python Dictionary

A Python dictionary is a mapping of values by unique keys. A colon (:) distinguishes each key from its value, the objects are separated by commas), (and the entire set of key / value pairs is enclosed in curly braces}.

For this task, we'll use a dictionary data structure of store all of the periodic table's chemical elements using the symbol of element as the key and the element name as the meaning. Z.B.

Python Quiz:

We began the code for the Chemical Elements Quiz as well as created the Python dictionary which contains all 118 periodic table chemical elements.

Your job is to complete the code for implementing the full quiz, based on the requirements listed above.

```
#Chemical Elements Quiz -
import random


elements = {"Ac":"Actinium","Ag":"Silver","Al":"Aluminum","Am":"Americium",
"Ar":"Argon","As":"Arsenic","At":"Astatine","Au":"Gold","B":"Boron","Ba":"Barium",
"Be":"Beryllium","Bh":"Bohrium","Bi":"Bismuth","Bk":"Berkelium","Br":"Bromine",
"C":"Carbon","Ca":"Calcium","Cd":"Cadmium","Ce":"Cerium","Cf":"Californium",
"Cl":"Chlorine","Cm":"Curium","Cn":"Copernicium","Co":"Cobalt","Cr":"Chromium",
"Cs":"Cesium","Cu":"Copper","Db":"Dubnium","Ds":"Darmstadtium","Dy":"Dysprosium",
"Er":"Erbium","Es":"Einsteinium","Eu":"Europium","F":"Fluorine","Fe":"Iron",
"Fl":"Flerovium","Fm":"Fermium","Fr":"Francium","Ga":"Gallium","Gd":"Gadolinium",
"Ge":"Germanium","H":"Hydrogen","He":"Helium","Hf":"Hafnium","Hg":"Mercury",
"Ho":"Holmium","Hs":"Hassium","I":"Iodine","In":"Indium","Ir":"Iridium",
"K":"Potassium","Kr":"Krypton","La":"Lanthanum","Li":"Lithium","Lr":"Lawrencium",
"Lu":"Lutetium","Lv":"Livermorium","Mc":"Moscovium","Md":"Mendelevium",
"Mg":"Magnesium","Mn":"Manganese","Mo":"Molybdenum","Mt":"Meitnerium",
```

```
"N":"Nitrogen","Na":"Sodium","Nb":"Niobium","Nd":"Neodymium","Ne":"Neon",
"Nh":"Nihonium","Ni":"Nickel","No":"Nobelium","Np":"Neptunium","O":"Oxygen",
"Og":"Oganesson","Os":"Osmium","P":"Phosphorus","Pa":"Protactinium","Pb":"Lead",
"Pd":"Palladium","Pm":"Promethium","Po":"Polonium","Pr":"Praseodymium",
"Pt":"Platinum","Pu":"Plutonium","Ra":"Radium","Rb":"Rubidium","Re":"Rhenium",
"Rf":"Rutherfordium","Rg":"Roentgenium","Rh":"Rhodium","Rn":"Radon",
"Ru":"Ruthenium","S":"Sulfur","Sb":"Antimony","Sc":"Scandium","Se":"Selenium",
"Sg":"Seaborgium","Si":"Silicon","Sm":"Samarium","Sn":"Tin","Sr":"Strontium",
"Ta":"Tantalum","Tb":"Terbium","Tc":"Technetium","Te":"Tellurium","Th":"Thorium",
"Ti":"Titanium","Tl":"Thallium","Tm":"Thulium","Ts":"Tennessine","U":"Uranium",
"V":"Vanadium","W":"Tungsten","Xe":"Xenon","Y":"Yttrium","Yb":"Ytterbium",
"Zn":"Zinc","Zr":"Zirconium"}


print("H-Mg-Ti-O-Au-Ni-Pt-Er-W-Xe-Zn-Li")
print("Pd                    Na")
print("Cu   Chemical Elements Quiz   Fe")
print("Sc                    Te")
print("H-Mg-Ti-O-Au-Ni-Pt-Er-W-Xe-Zn-Li")
print("")


#Select a random element from the dictionary
symbol = random.choice(elements.keys())
element = elements[symbol]


print(symbol + " - " + element)
```

21. Airport Code Lookup Check

We will introduce a small Python program on this challenge to:

- Ask the user to enter a 3-letter airport code (e.g. LHR) on one of the world's top 20 busiest airports.

- Enter the Airport name that matches the code.

We will use official International Air Transport Association (IATA) codes for this programme.

To make our software more stable, we will add a few **validation checks** that are used to verify if an airport code is legitimate. Our procedure for validation is to:

- Transform user input (airport code) automatically to uppercase
- Ensure that the given airport code is exactly 3 characters long (**Length Check**)
- Ensure that the given airport code is one of the top 20 airport codes (**Lookup Check**)

We will use a dictionary data structure which contains all 20 airport codes and their full names to carry out our lookup search.

A dictionary is a data structure that includes an unordered array of pairs of key / value. In our examples the keys are the airport codes, and the values are the names of the entire airport.

Python Code

Test the code below to validate a 3 letter airport code by testing both the duration and the lookup.

```
#Airport Code Lookup Check -

#Define a dictionary of the top 20 busiest airports in the world (in 2018)
airports = {"ATL":"Hartsfield–Jackson Atlanta International Airport",
    "PEK":"Beijing Capital International Airport",
        "DXB":"Dubai International Airport",
        "LAX":"Los Angeles International Airport",
        "HND":"Tokyo Haneda Airport",
        "ORD":"O'Hare International Airport (Chicago)",
        "LHR":"London Heathrow Airport",
        "SAR":"Hong Kong International Airport",
        "PVG":"Shanghai Pudong International Airport",
        "CDG":"Paris-Charles de Gaulle Airport",
        "AMS":"Amsterdam Airport Schiphol",
        "DEL":"Indira Gandhi International Airport (Delhi)",
```

```python
        "CAN":"Guangzhou Baiyun International Airport",
        "FRA":"Frankfurt Airport",
        "DFW":"Dallas/Fort Worth International Airport",
        "ICN":"Seoul Incheon International Airport",
        "IST":"Istanbul Atatürk Airport",
        "CGK":"Soekarno-Hatta International Airport",
        "SIN":"Singapore Changi Airport",
        "DEN":"Denver International Airport",
    }


code = input("Enter a 3-letter airport code:").upper()


#Apply a legnth check on the airport code to only accept 3 letter codes.
while len(code)!=3:
  print("Invalid airport code.")
  code = input("Enter a 3-letter airport code:").upper()


#Apply a lookup check to ensure the code is recognised (part of the dictionary)
while not code in airports:
  print("Airpot code not recognised. Please try again with a different airport code.")
  code = input("Enter a 3-letter airport code:").upper()


#Output
print(airports[code])
```

22. Pentagram Challenge

A polygon is a straight-line plane structure (2D). It is made up of vertices and rims.

A polygon is regular when the angles are all equal and the sides are all equal. For example, a regular pentagon is composed of 5 vertices and 5 equal size edges. A regular pentagon's vertices are distributed likewise on a circle. This outer circle is called a circumcircle, and it connects all polygon vertices (corner points). The circumcircle radius is the polygon radius, as well. The trigonometric formulae can be used to figure out the (x, y) coordinates of each vertex of a regular pentagon. (See screenshot to the right).

Using this method, we can use a Python script to measure the 5 vertices of a regular pentagon (x, y) coordinates and store them in a list of [x, y] sub-lists.

Star Shape

A pentagram is a polygon that represents a 5-pointed star. The outer vertices (the star points) form a regular pentagon. The star 's inner vertices also form a smaller regular pentagon, "inner."

So, we can use a similar method to measure the (x, y) coordinates of both our pentagram's "outer" and "inner" vertices.

Python Turtle

We completed the code for calculating a standard pentagon's co-ordinates (using the code given above) and generated a function called drawPolygon) (that uses Python Turtle to draw a polygon on screen.

```
#Pentagram Challenge -
import turtle, math
myPen = turtle.Turtle()
myPen.shape("arrow")
myPen.pencolor("purple")
myPen.pensize(2)
myPen.speed(1000)


#A Procedure to draw a polygon from a list of vertices.
def drawPolygon(polygon):
  myPen.penup()
  myPen.goto(polygon[0][0],polygon[0][1])
  myPen.pendown()
```

```
for i in range(1,len(polygon)):
    myPen.goto(polygon[i][0],polygon[i][1])


myPen.goto(polygon[0][0],polygon[0][1])



#A polygon can be stored as a list of vertices
pentagon=[]
R = 150
for n in range(0,5):
    x = R*math.cos(math.radians(90+n*72))
    y = R*math.sin(math.radians(90+n*72))
    pentagon.append([x,y])


drawPolygon(pentagon)
myPen.hideturtle()
```

22. The Shoelace Algorithm

The shoelace formula or algorithm for shoelace is a mathematical algorithm to determine the **area of a simple polygon** whose vertices are represented in the plane by their Cartesian coordinates.

The method is to cross-multiply the corresponding coordinates of the various vertices of a polygon in order to find its location. Because of the constant cross-multiplication for the coordinates that make up the polygon, it is called the shoelace rule, as binding shoelaces. (See table underneath). This algorithm has applications, among other fields, in 2D and 3D computer graphics, in surveying or forestry.

You'll need to apply the shoelace algorithm to:

- List all of the anticlockwise vertices. (E.g. A, B , C, D, E) in a row, and record the x and y coordinates in two separate table columns;
- Measure the sum of each x coordinate multiplying by the y coordinate in the row below (wrapping back to the first line when you reach the bottom of the table);

- Measure the sum of each y coordinate multiplying by the x coordinate in the row below (wrapping back to the first line when you reach the bottom of the table);
- Subtract from the first the second sum, obtain the absolute value (Absolute Dfference|sum1-sum2|,
- Divide the resulting value by 2 to obtain the actual polygon area.

Using Python, The Shoelace Algorithm:

We will define a polygon as a set of vertices, listed in anticlockwise order, to implement the shoelace algorithm. Each vertex will be a list of 2 values: its co-ordinates x and y.

```python
#The Shoelace Algorithm -


def polygonArea(vertices):
    #A function to apply the Shoelace algorithm
    numberOfVertices = len(vertices)
    sum1 = 0
    sum2 = 0


    for i in range(0,numberOfVertices-1):
        sum1 = sum1 + vertices[i][0] * vertices[i+1][1]
        sum2 = sum2 + vertices[i][1] * vertices[i+1][0]


    #Add xn.y1
    sum1 = sum1 + vertices[numberOfVertices-1][0]*vertices[0][1]
    #Add x1.yn
    sum2 = sum2 + vertices[0][0]*vertices[numberOfVertices-1][1]


    area = abs(sum1 - sum2) / 2
    return area


#Vertices (x,y) Coordinates
A = [2,7]
B = [10,1]
```

207

```
C = [8,6]
D = [11,7]
E = [7,10]
#Define a polygon as being a list of vertices, (on anticlockwise order)
polygon = [A,B,C,D,E]


area = polygonArea(polygon)
print("Polygon Vertices:")
print(polygon)
print("")
print("Area = " + str(area) + "cm2")
```

23. Sorting Algorithms using Python

In several cases computers are used to sort vast volumes of data. Although this may seem like a simple task to complete, much research has centered on finding the most efficient algorithms for sorting large quantities of data.

Four of the most important algorithms for sorting a data set are:

- **Bubble Sort Algorithm,**
- **Insertion Sort Algorithm,**
- **Merge Sort Algorithm.**
- **Selection Sort Algorithm,**

Below we implemented many of these algorithms, using Python to sort out a set list of values.

Insertion Sort
The insertion sort is an **iterative** algorithm (using nested loops).

```
#Insertion Sort Algorithm


def insertion_sort(list):
    for i in range(len(list)):
```

```
        currentValue = list[i]
        position = i


    while position > 0 and list[position - 1] > currentValue:
            # Swap the number down the list
        list[position] = list[position - 1]
        position = position - 1


    list[position] = currentValue
    print(list)



myList = [14, 7, 86, 39, 4, 23, 56, 44]
insertion_sort(myList)
```

24. Random Password Generator

We'll use a Python script to create a random password of 8 characters to answer this request. A new password is created at random each time the program is running. The created passwords will be 8 characters long, and must include the following characters in any order:

- A to Z 2 upper case letters,
- 2 letters with lower case from a to z,
- 2 digits 0 through 9,
- 2 Signs of punctuation like!? "This, #, etc.

To overcome this challenge, we will need to create random characters and use the ASCII code to do so.

ASCII code

The ASCII code (Pronounced ask-ee) is a code for representing English characters as numbers, with a number assigned from 0 to 127 for each character. The ASCII code for upper case M, for example, is 77. The extended ASCII code has 256 characters (using numbers ranging from 0 to 255).

Using Python, you can easily access a character's ASCII values by using the function comm).
For eg, ord("M) "returns 77 while chr(77) returns" M

Looking at the list of most commonly used ASCII codes you can find that there is an ASCII code between 65 (= A) and 90 (= Z) for all upper-case letters from A to Z. Thus, we can use the following Python code to create a random uppercase letter between A and Z:

Python Code

You can use the above flowchart and our ASCII helpsheet to fill in the code given below.

```python
import random


#A function do shuffle all the characters of a string
def shuffle(string):
    tempList = list(string)
    random.shuffle(tempList)
    return ''.join(tempList)


#Main program starts here
uppercaseLetter1=chr(random.randint(65,90)) #Generate a random Uppercase letter (based on ASCII code)
uppercaseLetter2=chr(random.randint(65,90)) #Generate a random Uppercase letter (based on ASCII code)
#Generate more characters here
#....


#Generate password using all the characters, in random order
password = uppercaseLetter1 + uppercaseLetter2 # + ....
password = shuffle(password)


#Ouput
print(password)
```

25. Weather Forecast API

The goal of this challenge is to write a computer program which will show a 5-day weather forecast for a specific location selected by the end user.

You are scheduled to:

- Retrieve the city from the end user (input),
- Use the Open Weather Map API to get a current weather forecast for this area,
- Decode the information retrieved;
- Show a 5 day weather forecast for the area selected. (Output)

To get an API key, you will need to log in.

You will then be able to make the appropriate API calls, like the one mentioned in the tabs below.

OR XML or JSON?

JSON and XML are two commonly used Open Data Interchange options.

Initially the only option for open data interchange was XML (eXtensible Markup Language). Yet the field of open data sharing has grown quite a lot over the years. For various reasons, the more lightweight JSON (JavaScript Object Notation) has become a common alternative to XML, one of the main reasons being that JSON is more portable, quicker, and lighter to process / parse (in terms of memory requirements).

The Open Weather Map API allows you to choose the data format to be collected using either the format JSON or XML. (See below for examples). But you have to determine which format you want to use.

The following two challenges can be read and completed which show how to use a **JSON API using Python code**. These challenges will help you decide how to make an API call and how to parse a simple collection of JSON data.

- ISS Real-Time Tracker
- Currency Converter

Open Weather Map API

Here are only a few examples of how to access JSON or XML data sets using the Open Weather Map API.

API Call

https://api.openweathermap.org/data/2.5/weather?q=London&appid=...

Output

{

"coord":{"lon":-0.13,"lat":51.51},

"weather":[{"id":300,"main":"Drizzle","description":"light intensity drizzle","icon":"09d"}],

"base":"stations",

"main":{"temp":280.32,"pressure":1012,"humidity":81,"temp_min":279.15,"temp_max":281.15},

"visibility":10000,

"wind":{"speed":4.1,"deg":80},

"clouds":{"all":90},

"dt":1485789600,

"sys":{"type":1,"id":5091,"message":0.0103,"country":"GB","sunrise":1485762037,"sunset":1485794875},

"id":2643743,

"name":"London",

"cod":200

}

26. Currency Converter

Our goal is to create a currency converter that will help us convert a amount of money from currency to currency.

Currency exchange rates are constantly changing, which is why we have opted not to keep all the exchange rates in our code up-to - date. We would also obtain up-to - date currency exchange rates by making calls to an API providing the latest rates.

Python Code

Check our code to see how we call the API, and how we get the requested JSON data and extract it.

```
#Currency Converter
import json, urllib.request
```

```python
#See full lists of valid currencies on https://free.currencyconverterapi.com/api/v6/currencies
validCurrencies = ["EUR","GBP","USD","JPY"]


#Display banner
print("$£¥€$£¥€$£¥€$£¥€$£¥€$£¥€$£¥€$£¥€$£¥€")
print("$£¥€                    $£¥€")
print("$£¥€    Currency Converter    $£¥€")
print("$£¥€                    $£¥€")
print("$£¥€$£¥€$£¥€$£¥€$£¥€$£¥€$£¥€$£¥€$£¥€")
print("")
print("List of currencies: ")
print("  GBP - British Pound £")
print("  JPY - Japanese Yen ¥")
print("  EUR - Euro €")
print("  USD - US Dollar $")
print("")


#Initialise key variables
currencyFrom = ""
currencyTo = ""
amount = 0


#Retrieve user inputs
while not currencyFrom in validCurrencies:
  currencyFrom = input("Enter Currency to convert From: (e.g. GBP)").upper()


while not currencyTo in validCurrencies:
  currencyTo = input("Enter Currency to convert To: (e.g. EUR)").upper()


amount = float(input("Enter amount to convert: (e.g. 10.00)"))
```

```
#A JSON request to retrieve the required exchange rate
url = "https://free.currencyconverterapi.com/api/v6/convert?q="+currencyFrom + "_" +
currencyTo +"&compact=y"
response = urllib.request.urlopen(url)
result = json.loads(response.read())


#Let's extract the required information
exchangeRate=result[currencyFrom + "_" + currencyTo]
rate = exchangeRate["val"]


#Output exchange rate and converted amount
print("")
print("Exchange rate: 1 " + currencyFrom + " = " + str(rate) + " " + currencyTo)
print(str(amount) + " " + currencyFrom + " = " + ("{0:.2f}".format(amount*rate)) + " " +
currencyTo)
```

27. Real-Time ISS Tracker

The International Space Station (ISS) travels at approximately 28,000 km / h and circles the Earth 16 times a day, about a 90 minute! In this python challenge we'll use an open source API (Open Notify) to get some real-time data from Nasa about the ISS spot.

Our objective is to obtain the International Space Station 's current longitude and latitude, and use this knowledge to plot it on the globe.

Note that we will also use the Free Notify API to retrieve current astronaut numbers in space and retrieve all of their names and the spacecraft on which they are.

Both of these APIs format the **data using JSON**. JSON (JavaScript Object Notation) is a common lightweight format for data-exchange. Its main advantage is that it is easy for humans to read and write, and machines can easily interpret and produce as you can see in the code below.

Python Code

Check our code to see how we call the API, and how we get the requested JSON data and extract it. You may need to display this trinket in full-screen display to see the ISS 'location on the world map. An infinite "while Real" loop is used to continuously update the ISS 's location on the globe, with a delay of 5 seconds between each iteration.

```python
#Real time ISS tracker -

import json, turtle, urllib.request, time

#A first JSON request to retrieve the name of all the astronauts currently in space.
url = "http://api.open-notify.org/astros.json"
response = urllib.request.urlopen(url)
result = json.loads(response.read())
print("There are currently " + str(result["number"]) + " astronauts in space:")
print("")

people = result["people"]

for p in people:
   print(p["name"] + " on board of " + p["craft"])

#Display information on world map using Python Turtle
screen = turtle.Screen()
screen.setup(720, 360)
screen.setworldcoordinates(-180, -90, 180, 90)
#Load the world map picture
screen.bgpic("world-map.gif")
```

```python
screen.register_shape("iss.gif")
iss = turtle.Turtle()
iss.shape("iss.gif")
iss.setheading(45)
iss.penup()


while True:
    #A JSON request to retrieve the current longitude and latitude of the IIS space station (real time)
    url = "http://api.open-notify.org/iss-now.json"
    response = urllib.request.urlopen(url)
    result = json.loads(response.read())


    #Let's extract the required information
    location =result["iss_position"]
    lat = location["latitude"]
    lon = location["longitude"]


    #Output informationon screen
    print("\nLatitude: " + str(lat))
    print("Longitude: " +str(lon))


    #Plot the ISS on the map
    iss.goto(lon, lat)
    #refresh position every 5 seconds
    time.sleep(5)
```

28. 3D Snowman

3D Snowman

Mentioned in Computer Science, Python-Intermediate, Python Challenges on December 14, 2018

We'll use Glowscript in this blog post to create a snowman 3D animation.

Audio Recording

Our goal is to build our snowman by adding various 3D shapes including circles, tubes, cones, etc .. We will then construct a composite object to combine these shapes into a single object together. Finally, when looping, we can use an infinite to move / rotate the snowman around the Y axis.

Glow / vPython? ...

To complete this challenge and learn all the 3D shapes that you can use in Glowscript,

(x , y, z) Coordinates

Complete the code

We started out the code for you. To further customize this snowman your task is to complete this code. (The animation can be previewed using Google Chrome)

```
# 3D Snowman: 3D animation using Glowscript


belly=sphere(color=vector(1,1,1),pos=vec(0,0,0),radius=10, shininess=10)

head=sphere(color=vector(1,1,1),pos=vec(0,14,0),radius=7, shininess=10)

treeTrunk=cylinder(color=vector(0.5,0.2,0),pos=vector(22,-10,0),axis=vector(0,3,0),
radius=2)

tree=cone(color=vector(0,0.5,0.1),pos=vector(22,-7,0),axis=vector(0,30,0),radius=8)


#Group all objects into one compound
snowman = compound([belly,head,treeTrunk,tree])


#Animate/rotate the snowman
theta=0.1
```

```
framerate=20

while True:
    rate(framerate)
    snowman.rotate(angle=theta, axis=vector(0,1,0), origin=vector(0,0,0))
```

29. Target Detection Algorithm

Most spacecraft are equipped with laser cannons to destroy enemy spaceships in Star Wars movies. These spaceships have built-in targeting computers to assist the pilot, which allow them to aim the cannon and warn them when their aim is within reach. If that is the case, the pilot is told by the algorithm with the following message:

We retrieved the code that was used in the Star Wars Tie Fighter spacecraft. Using the code to guide the laser cannon. This spaceship is not however equipped with a target selection algorithm to tell the pilot when to fire.

Python Code

Your goal is to upgrade this code from line 60 to detect when the enemy's spacecraft is within laser cannon reach:

```
# Target Detecion Algorithm -
# Complete the code from line 60

from processing import *
from math import cos, sin, radians
from random import randint

delay = 10

def setup():
    strokeWeight(1)
    frameRate(20)
```

```
size(400,400)


def drawLine(x1,y1,x2,y2):
    global X,Y
    #Draw a line on screen
    line(x1+X,y1+Y,x2+X,y2+Y)


def drawSpaceship(xA,yA,xB,yB,xC,yC,color):
    stroke(color[0],color[1],color[2])
    strokeWeight(4)
    line(xA,yA,xB,yB)
    line(xB,yB,xC,yC)
    line(xC,yC,xA,yA)


def drawGrid():
    background(10,10,10)


    #Draw grid lines
    stroke(255,185,0)
    strokeWeight(1)
    for i in range(-2000,2000,1000):
        drawLine(-2000,i,-40,i/50)
        drawLine(2000,i,40,i/50)
        drawLine(i,-2000,i/50,-40)
        drawLine(i,2000,i/50,40)
    for i in range(-2000,2000,40):
        drawLine(i,i,i,-i)
        drawLine(i,-i,-i,-i)
```

```
    strokeWeight(2)
    drawLine(-2000,0,-20,0)
    drawLine(20,0,2000,0)
    drawLine(0,-2000,0,-20)
    drawLine(0,20,0,2000)


def startGame():
  global X,Y,xA,yA,xB,yB,xC,yC


  X = (mouse.x);
  Y = (mouse.y);
  print(X,Y)


  drawGrid()
  targetAcquired=False


  """
  Complete code here to check if the mouse pointer (X,Y)
  is within the ABC triangle (xA,yA,xB,yB,xC,yC)
  If so reset targetAcquired to True
  """


  if targetAcquired:
    #Turn spaceship to red
    drawSpaceship(xA,yA,xB,yB,xC,yC,(255,0,0))
    f = createFont("Arial",36,True)
    textFont(f,36)
    fill(255)
```

```
        text("Target Acquired!",70,360)
    else:
        drawSpaceship(xA,yA,xB,yB,xC,yC,(255,255,255))

    fc = environment.frameCount

#Randomly position spaceship on grid by generatring coodinates of vertices A, B and C.
xA=randint(60,340)
yA=randint(60,340)
xB=xA-randint(30,50)
yB=yA+randint(30,50)
xC=xA+randint(30,50)
yC=yA+randint(30,50)
draw = startGame
run()
```

30. The Pizzaiolo's Puzzle

A pizzaiolo (a pizza maker) was asked to make a very big pizza, sprinkle some Parmesan cheese uniformly on the pizza and spread a full jar of black olives (about 80 olives) on the pizza.

He has chosen to find a formula for distributing the olives on the pizza uniformly to make sure:

- The pie is filled with olives,
- Olives are relatively equidistant between themselves,

The model from Fermat's Spiral & Vogel

After doing some analysis, he was captivated to find out how to use the Vogel model to measure each olive 's polar coordinates to be applied to his pizza:

- Where the angle is θ,

221

- r is the distance or radius from the centre;
- The olive index number is n,
- C is a constant element to scal,
- The 137.508 ° angle is the golden angle that is approximated by the Fibonacci number ratios.

Python Code

The following Python Turtle illustrates how to use Vogel's model to solve the puzzle in our pizzaiolo:

```python
#The Pizzaiolo's Puzzle -
import turtle
import math
from random import randint


myPen = turtle.Turtle()
myPen.tracer(0)
myPen.speed(0)
screen = turtle.Screen()
screen.bgcolor("#FFFFFF")
myPen.penup()
myPen.goto(0,0)


def drawPizza(x,y,radius):
    myPen.penup()
    myPen.goto(x,y-radius)
    myPen.pendown()
    myPen.color("#f4c542")
    myPen.pensize(6)
    myPen.fillcolor("#c42513")
    myPen.begin_fill()
    myPen.circle(radius)
    myPen.end_fill()
```

```python
def drawOlive(x,y,radius):
    myPen.pensize(1)
    myPen.penup()
    myPen.goto(x,y-radius)
    myPen.pendown()
    myPen.color("#000000")
    myPen.fillcolor("#000000")
    myPen.begin_fill()
    myPen.circle(radius)
    myPen.end_fill()


#Draw the Pizza
drawPizza(0,0,180)


c=18 #scaling factor
for n in range(80):
    #Generate Polar Coordinates using Vogel's Model
    r = c*(n**0.5)
    teta = n*137.508
    #Convert polar coordinates to Cartesian coordinates using trigonometric formulas (SOHCAHTOA)
    x = r*math.cos(math.radians(teta))
    y = r*math.sin(math.radians(teta))


    drawOlive(x,y,4)


myPen.hideturtle()
myPen.getscreen().update()
```

31. Word Unscramble Challenge

We will create a Word Unscramble quiz in this challenge where the machine will randomly pick up words from a given list, scramble the word's letters, produce the scrambled word (anagram) and ask the user to guess the original word. The user will be given 1 point for every correct answer.

Taking a look at the flowchart above, answer the following questions:

- Where are the Score and Total variables initialized?
- Where is the score incremented by 1 variable?
- Where is a declared / initialised list?
- Where and what iteration is used for?
- Where and for what form of variety is used?
- Where is the scramble) (subroutine / feature called?
- Where is a sentence used for input?
- Where is concatenation of string used?

Python Code

We began the code for you, and implemented the feature scramble).

Your job is to complete this code from line 29, following the steps set out in the flowchart.

```
#Word Unscramble Challenge
from random import shuffle


#A function to scramble a word!
def scramble(word):
    #Convert word from a string to a list of letters
    letters=list(word)
    #Shuffle list
    shuffle(letters)
    #convert list back to a string
    scrambledWord = "".join(letters)
    return scrambledWord
```

```
#Main Program Starts Here
words = ["mouse","keyboard","monitor","printer","harddrive","speakers"]


#Display welcome banner
print("ABCDEFGHIJKLMNOPQRSTUVWXYZ")
print("A                        Z")
print("A    Word Unscramble    Z")
print("A      Input, Output      Z")
print("A   & Storage Devices    Z")
print("A                        Z")
print("ABCDEFGHIJKLMNOPQRSTUVWXYZ")
print("")


score = 0
#Complete the code here...
```

32. Lunar Craters Challenge

The floor of the Moon is replete with thousands of craters. This are caused by collision with the lunar surface by asteroids and meteorites. In this challenge we will use Python Turtle with a random set of craters to create a Moon drawing.

This challenge includes the random location of craters of different sizes (radius) on the Moon's surface. The generation of random (x , y) coordinates is fairly straightforward, but the challenge is to make sure that the craters fit within the moon's disk:

We started out the code for you. You will fill in the code in the first tab below. You may also compare two different methods used to address this challenge:

• Solution 1: Use of polar and trigonometric formulae (SOHCAHTOA)

• Solution 2: Use of Cartesian Coordinates and the Theorem of Pythagoras

We started the code for you, but not all of the craters fit within the disk representing the Moon with this code. Your job is to modify this code to ensure all of the craters fit within the disk representing the Moon's surface.

```python
#Lunar Craters Challenge -
import turtle
import math
from random import randint


myPen = turtle.Turtle()
myPen.tracer(0)
myPen.speed(0)
screen = turtle.Screen()
screen.bgcolor("#111155")
myPen.color("#888888")
myPen.pensize(3)
myPen.penup()
myPen.goto(0,0)


def drawMoon(x,y,radius):
  myPen.penup()
  myPen.goto(x,y-radius)
  myPen.pendown()
  myPen.fillcolor("#AAAAAA")
  myPen.begin_fill()
  myPen.circle(radius)
  myPen.end_fill()


def drawCrater(x,y,radius):
  myPen.pensize(1)
  myPen.penup()
```

```
myPen.goto(x,y-radius)
myPen.pendown()
myPen.fillcolor("#AAAAAA")
myPen.begin_fill()
myPen.circle(radius)
myPen.end_fill()


#Draw the Moon
MOON_RADIUS = 160
drawMoon(0,0,MOON_RADIUS)
#Add 20 craters on the Moon's surface
for i in range(20):
    x = randint(-MOON_RADIUS,MOON_RADIUS)
    y = randint(-MOON_RADIUS,MOON_RADIUS)
    radius = randint(3,50)
    drawCrater(x,y,radius)


myPen.hideturtle()
myPen.getscreen().update()
```

33. Recursive vs. Iterative Palindrome Check

For this task we will explore two algorithms used to figure out whether or not a term is a palindrome. The first algorithm employs an iterative approach, while the second algorithm uses a recursive approach.

Iterative Approach

An iterative approach relates to the use of a loop that can be:

- A count-controlled loop (for example the FOR loop)
- A loop regulated by condition (e.g. WHILE loop or REPEAT Before loop)

We will use a loop to search all the letters in the first half of the word for our iterative palindrome search algorithm, and compare them with the letters in the second half of the word (in reverse order). If all matches then the term is a palindrome.

227

```python
#Iterative Palindrome Check
def isPalindrome(word):
    midPoint = len(word)//2
    palindrome = True
    for i in range(0,midPoint):
        left = word[i]
        right = word[len(word)-i-1]
        if left!=right:
            palindrome=False
            break
    return palindrome
```

```python
word = input("Enter a word or sentence:")
#Length check - we need a word of at least 2 characters
while len(word)<2:
    word = input("Try again - Enter a word or sentence with at least 2 characters.")
```

```python
if isPalindrome(word):
    print("This is a palindrome.")
else:
    print("This is not a palindrome.")
```

Recursive Apporach

A function that is recursive is one that:

- The call to itself contains,
- Has the state of stoppage to stop the recursion.
- We will use a function to check our recursive palindrome algorithm which:
- Make sure the word is at least two characters long:

228

- If the word is less than two characters then the feature stops the recursion (stop condition) and returns True since the word is a palindrome.
- If the word is two or more characters long, the feature checks that the word's first and last letter are the same as:
- If they are the same, the feature will extract the word in the middle (remove the first letter and the last letter) and name the new shortest word to itself.
- If the term is different, then it is not a palindrome. Here the function prevents the recursion (stop condition), and returns False.

```
#Recursive Palindrome Check -
def isPalindrome(word):
  if len(word)<2:
    return True   # Stop the recursion
  else:
    firstLetter = word[0]
    lastLetter = word[len(word)-1]
    if firstLetter == lastLetter:
      middleWord = word[1:len(word)-1]
      print(firstLetter + "==" + lastLetter)
      print("Now checking if '" + middleWord + "' is a palindrome.")
      return isPalindrome(middleWord)  #recursive call
    else:
      print(firstLetter + "!=" + lastLetter)
      return False   # Stop the recursion


word = input("Enter a word or sentence:")
#Length check - we need a word of at least 2 characters
while len(word)<2:
  word = input("Try again - Enter a word or sentence with at least 2 characters.")


if isPalindrome(word):
  print("This is a palindrome.")
else:
  print("This is not a palindrome.")
```

229

34. The Rail Fence Cipher

The rail fence cipher (quite often called zigzag cipher) is indeed a transposition cipher that uses a simple algorithm to jumble up the order of the letters of a message.

The rail fence cipher works by writing the message across the page on alternating lines, and then reading each line in turn.

Your Challenge

You'll need to write two python programs for this task, one to encrypt a message (plaintext to ciphertext), and one to decode an encoded message (plaintext to plaintext). We have generated flowcharts of both the encoder and the decoder algorithms to help you with this challenge.

```
#The Rail Fence Cipher -


plaintext = input("Type a message to encode:")

#Convert plaintext to UPPERCASE

plaintext = plaintext.upper()

#Remove white spaces from plaintext

plaintext = plaintext.replace(" ", "")


#Complete the code from here
```

35. Semaphore Code Using Python Turtle

Flag semaphore is a telegraphy device that uses visual signals with handheld flags to relay information at distances. Information is encoded by flag location. The existing flag semanphore system uses two short poles for square flags, which a signalman keeps to signal alphabet letters and numbers in various locations. The signalman holds one pole in each hand, and in one of eight possible directions extends each arm. At sea, the flags are red and yellow, while white and blue on land.

Python Turtle Code

We have created an animation that scans all of a message 's characters and animates the signalman to show the correct semaphor flags for each character in the message.

```python
# Semaphore Code Using Python Turtle -
from turtle import *
from shapes import *
from time import sleep


#We use a {dictionary} to store the angle position of both arms for each letter of the alphabet
semaphore = {
 "A":(225,-90),
 "B":(180,-90),
 "C":(135,-90),
 "D":(90,-90),
 "E":(-90,45),
 "F":(-90,0),
 "G":(-90,-45),
 "H":(180,225),
 "I":(135,225),
 "J":(90,0),
 "K":(225,90),
 "L":(225,45),
 "M":(225,0),
 "N":(225,-45),
 "O":(180,-135),
 "P":(180,90),
 "Q":(180,45),
 "R":(180,0),
 "S":(180,-45),
```

```python
    "T":(135,90),
    "U":(135,45),
    "V":(90,-45),
    "W":(45,0),
    "X":(45,-45),
    "Y":(135,0),
    "Z":(0,-45),
    " ":(-90,-90)}


myPen = Turtle()
myPen.shape("arrow")
myPen.tracer(0)
myPen.speed(0)
window = turtle.Screen()
window.bgcolor("white")
myPen.hideturtle()
#let's draw the signalman


message="ABCDEFGHIJKLMNOPQRSTUVWXYZ"


for letter in message:
  turtle.clear()
  draw_signalman(turtle)
  #Draw First Flag
  angle = semaphore[letter][0]
  if angle>=90:
    draw_left_arm(turtle,angle)
  else:
    draw_right_arm(turtle,angle)
  #Draw Second Flag
```

```
angle = semaphore[letter][1]
if angle>90:
    draw_left_arm(turtle,angle)
else:
    draw_right_arm(turtle,angle)


myPen.getscreen().update()
sleep(1)
```

36. Is my credit card valid?

We will use the Luhn Algorithm to verify in this challenge if a debit card or credit card number is a legitimate card number.

This approach is used for verifying whether your card number is a legitimate credit card number any time you scan or enter your credit card number (e.g. when you pay online). This system can be used to quickly identify mistyped credit card numbers or to identify when someone tries to enter a fake / credit card number. Remember that it is not 100 percent effective, so to prevent any invalid card numbers is only used as a pre-check. If this first test passes, then more rigorous tests will be carried out for approval of the online transaction.

The Algorithm by Luhn

The Luhn Algorithm is composed of four main steps:

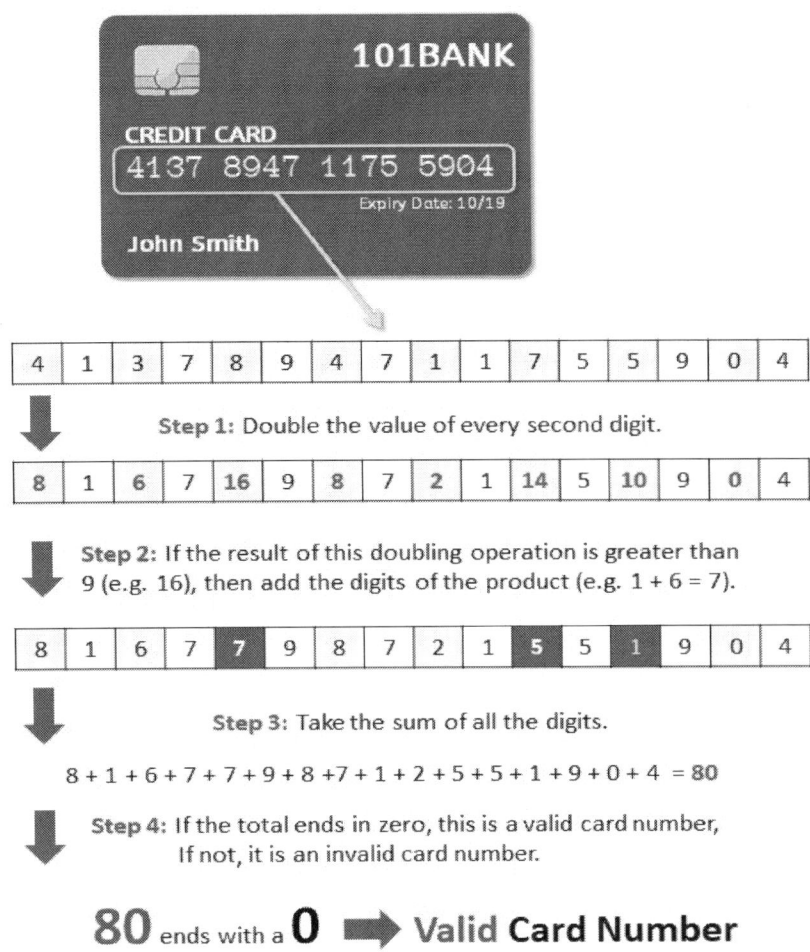

Step 1: Double the value of every second digit.

Step 2: If the result of this doubling operation is greater than 9 (e.g. 16), then add the digits of the product (e.g. 1 + 6 = 7).

Step 3: Take the sum of all the digits.

8 + 1 + 6 + 7 + 7 + 9 + 8 + 7 + 1 + 2 + 5 + 5 + 1 + 9 + 0 + 4 = 80

Step 4: If the total ends in zero, this is a valid card number, If not, it is an invalid card number.

80 ends with a **0** ➡ **Valid Card Number**

Write program that asks the end-user to enter a 16-digit number of cards.

Your software will then apply the Luhn algorithm to evaluate and output whether this number of cards is valid or not.

```
#Is My Credit Card Number Valid?
cardNumber = input("Enter a 16-digit card number:")
#Complete the code here to implement the Luhn Algorithm
```

37. Intersection Point

The goal of this challenge is to write a script which allows the uer to input the two straight lines equation (Line 1: y = ax+b, Line 2: y = cx+d). Then the program calculates the intersection point co-ordinates if such a point exists!

Your Code

Complete your code, using the steps mentioned in the flowchart above.

```
#Intersection point of two lines -
print("Line 1: y = ax + b")
a = float(input("a?"))
b = float(input("b?"))
print("y = " + str(a) + "x" + " + " + str(b))
print("Line 2: y = cx + d")
#Complete the code here...
```

38. My Python Turtle Roller Coaster

In this challenge we are going to use Python Turtle to draw a roller coaster track.

We created three procedures that you should use when drawing the track. Each procedure takes the following two parameters:

- StraightLine(distance, speed): Straight line drawing. The distance is given as just a number of pixels (e.g. 100) as well as the speed as a number between 1 and 6 to represent when the hill (low speed) or hill (high speed) of the roller coaster is going up.
- TurnLeft(angle, radius): draw a specified angle turn / arc in degrees (e.g. 180 for a twist), and a radius to show how sharp a turn is (Sharp turn = low radius, e.g. 10).
- TurnRight(angle, radius): Just like above but turn right.

Our Coaster Roller (Overhead view)

#Python Turtle Roller Coaster -

```
import turtle
import math


myTrack = turtle.Turtle()
myTrack.speed(100)


screen = turtle.Screen()
screen.bgcolor("#7ace67")
```

```
myTrack.color("#5e1d1d")
myTrack.pensize(6)
myTrack.penup()
myTrack.goto(0,0)
myTrack.pendown()


def straightLine(distance,speed):
  for i in range(0,distance,speed):
    myTrack.forward(speed)


def turnLeft(angle,radius):
  step = 10*3.14*radius/360
  for i in range(0,angle,5):
    myTrack.left(5)
    myTrack.forward(step)


def turnRight(angle,radius):
  step = 10*3.14*radius/360
  for i in range(0,angle,5):
    myTrack.right(5)
    myTrack.forward(step)



#Drawing the roller coaster track:
straightLine(85,3) #Uphill - slow speed
turnLeft(90,60)
straightLine(50,3) #Uphill - slow speed
turnRight(180,20) #Sharp U turn
straightLine(240,6)  #Downhill - fast speed
turnRight(135,30)
```

```
straightLine(120,6)  #Downhill - fast speed
turnLeft(90,40)
turnRight(90,40)
turnLeft(90,40)
turnRight(135,40)
straightLine(160,3) #Uphill - slow speed
turnRight(145,40)
straightLine(160,6) #Downhill - fast speed
turnLeft(65,40)
```

39. Happy New Year Animation

In this challenge we'll use Python code to create the text-based (ASCII) animation to be used before the new year as a final countdown!

Our countdown timer to count down from 5 to 0 is based on a loop. It will also use the time library's sleep) (function to allow 1 second between each loop iteration.

```
#Happy New Year Animation -
import os
import time
#Initialise settings
start=5
message=">     Happy New Year!     <"

#Start the countdown
for counter in range(start,0,-1):
    print(counter)
    time.sleep(1)
    os.system('clear')
```

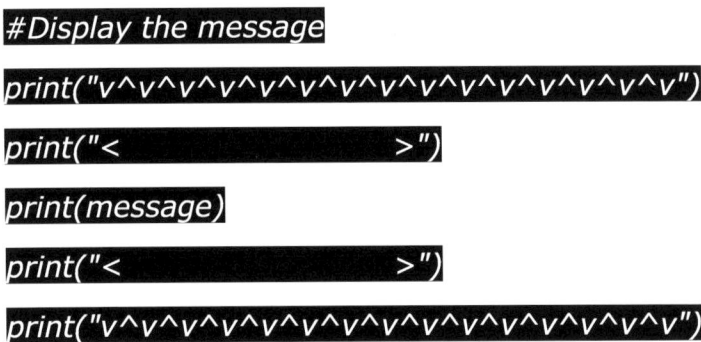

```
#Display the message
print("v^v^v^v^v^v^v^v^v^v^v^v^v^v")
print("<                    >")
print(message)
print("<                    >")
print("v^v^v^v^v^v^v^v^v^v^v^v^v^v")
```

40. Guitar Chords Reader

The concept behind this python challenge is to write a python program to help guitar players learn new songs and practice them.

Our software can read all the chords used in a song and display a visual representation / chart of the chord being played and animate them.

Let's first reconsider what are the main chords when playing the guitar

The code that appears under each chord indicates the finger location as defined on each table. Using this code to:

- "x" means an unplayed series,
- "0" means an open string played,
- A number tells you who cares about putting your finger on.

Python Code

The following python code utilizes various data structures:

- Chords are a dictionary in which each chord (e.g. C) is given a "free notation" like "x32010"
- SongChords is a list of all the chords used in the song in question

Your # 1 Challenge

By adding more chords to the dictionary you can boost the challenge.

Then you can add your own songs to this code and let the user determine which songs they want to visualise.

Your # 2 Challenge

How do you further strengthen this code by showing the lyrics alongside the chords being played?

#Guitar Chords Reader

```
import time
import os


#A Python Dictionary matching chord names with "fret notation"
chords = {"C": "x32010", "A":"x02220", "G": "320033", "E": "022100", "D": "xx0232", "F": "x3321x", "Am": "x02210", "Dm": "xx0231", "Em": "022000"}


#A procedure to display where to position your fingers to play a given chord
def displayChord(chord):
  fretNotation = chords[chord]

  print("  " + chord)
  nut=""
  for string in fretNotation:
   if string=="x":
     nut=nut+"x"  # x means don't play this string
   else:
     nut = nut + "_"
  print(nut) #Guitar Nut
  for fretNumber in range(1,5):
   fret=""
   for string in fretNotation:
    if string==str(fretNumber):
       fret=fret+"O"
    else:
       fret = fret + "|"
   print(fret)
```

239

```
#Main Program Starts Here
song = "C,D,G,Em,C,D,G,Em"


#Let's read this song, one chord at a time
songChords = song.split(",")
for chord in songChords:
    displayChord(chord)
    time.sleep(2)
    #Clear the screen
    os.system("cls")
```

41. Text Based Animations

In this challenge we are going to use Python code to create text-based animations (ASCII). Each of these animations uses a main loop repeating the given code every 0.2 seconds, and clearing the screen between two iterations (frames)

#Rocket Animation -

```
import os
import time


def animate_rocket():
    distancefromtop = 20
    while true:
        print("\n" * distancefromtop)
        print("        /\        ")
        print("        ||        ")
        print("        ||        ")
        print("       /|\        ")
        time.sleep(0.2)
```

240

```
    os.system('clear')
    distancefromtop -= 1
    if distancefromtop <0:
        distancefromtop = 20


#main program starts here....
animate_rocket()
```

Your Task

Using similar approach to create your own text-based animation. You can start by tuning up any of the above animations.

42. Adding a Splash Screen to your Python Projects

Add a Splash to your Python Projects

Typically a splash screen appears for a few seconds when a game or program is being launched. It which contain basic details such as the game name and the version number thereof.

The following Python trinket demonstrates how a simple text-based splash screen can be easily created to reuse in your current projects:


```
#My Splash Screen
import os
import time
def splash_screen(seconds):
    print("\n")
    print(" *********************")
    print(" *                   *")
    print(" *   SPLASH SCREEN   *")
    print(" *        v1.0       *")
    print(" *                   *")
    print(" *********************")
```

```
  time.sleep(seconds)
  os.system('clear')
#Main Program Starts Here....
splash_screen(3)
username=input("Type your username:")
```

Progress bar added to the Python projects

A progress bar is indeed a graphical control feature that visualizes the progress of an extended computer process, such as download, upload or installation of data. Often a textual representation of improvement in a percent format is followed by the graphics.

```
#My Progress Bar -
import os
import time


def progress_bar(seconds):
  for progress in range(0,seconds+1):
   percent = (progress * 100) // seconds
   print("\n")
    print("Loading...")
   print("<" + ("=" * progress) + (" " * (seconds-progress)) + "> " + str(percent) + "%")
   print("\n")
    time.sleep(1)
    os.system('clear')
#Main Program Starts Here....
progress_bar(10)
username=input("Type your username:")
```

43. Football Results Tracker

You were asked to develop a software that would keep track of Major League football scores.

Your program will store results of matches in a text file using the format below:

home team;away team;home score;away score;

For example, your Text file may contain the following information after a few games:

Chelsea;Everton;2;0;
Liverpool;Arsenal;4;0;
Crystal Palace;Swansea City;0;2;
Newcastle United;West Ham United;3;0;
Manchester United;Leicester City;2;0;
Manchester City;Everton;1;1;
Swansea City;Manchester United;0;4;
Liverpool;Crystal Palace;1;0;

Task 1:

Your programme, which should include:

- Insert option and add a new line / match score to the text file. The software would do so:
- Ask the user to fill in the Home team name,
- Ask the user to fill in the Away team name,
- Ask the user to input the Home Score (number of home team goals scored),
- Ask the user to enter the Away Score (number of goals scored by the team outside),
- At the end of the text file add all of this detail.

Task 2:

Develop another choice for the software where it wants:

- Ask the user to display all scores on the screen using the format below:

Home Score: Away Score-Away Team

Task 3:

Build a third alternative where you want the software to:

- Allow the user to enter a team name to show all of this team 's data.
- Determine and show a team's number of points; understanding the team scores 3 points for a victory, 1 point for a draw and 0 point for a loss.

Top-Down Modular Design

This diagram describes our system 's principal components:

Python Code

We began the code with implementing a simple menu structure for you. You are charged with implementing code for each of the three options:

```python
#Football Results Tracker
def displayBanner():
    print("  _____ ")
    print(" |                                       |")
    print(" |          Premier League               |")
    print(" |          Results Tracker              |")
    print(" |                                       |")
    print("___|_____|___ ")
    print("")


def displayMenu():
    print("")
    print(" > Option 1: Add a new match score")
    print(" > Option 2: Display all scores")
    print(" > Option 3: Search all scores of a team")
    print(" > Option 4: Exit")
    print("")


#Main Program Starts Here
displayBanner()
displayMenu()


choice = input("Choose an option between 1 and 4.")
```

```
if choice == "4":
    print "Good bye!"
```

44. Four-in-a-row challenge!

You will use Python Code in this topic post to complete this simulation of the connect 4 game.

First, you'll have to reverse-engineer the code issued. The code used so far is to:

- Use Python Turtle to view the 6 Um7 grid.
- Put tokens on the gird at random, turning over (yellow and red).
- Use drawGrid) (to reset the grid on the panel.

The code given uses a variable called connect4, which is used to store integer values in a two-dimensional array (620). A 2D-array in Python is a list of the sets. Within this array a 0 is an empty location, a 1 is a yellow token and a 2 is a red token.

Your Task:

Complete the checkIfWinner) (function (from line 39) to check whether the game continues after putting the token, or if the player has placed 4 tokens in a row, column or diagonal. If so, the winner's color value is returned by the function (1 for Yellow, 2 for Red, 0 if no winner)

```
#Four-in-a-row Challenge -
import turtle
from random import randint
from time import sleep
YELLOW=1
RED=2


#Draw the grid on screen with all the tokens
def drawGrid(grid):
    global RED, YELLOW
    #Clear the screen
    #myPen.clear()
    myPen.setheading(0)
```

```python
    myPen.goto(-150,130)
    for row in range (0,6):
        for col in range (0,7):
                if grid[row][col]==0:
                    myPen.fillcolor("#FFFFFF")
                elif grid[row][col]==RED:
                    myPen.fillcolor("#FF0000")
                elif grid[row][col]==YELLOW:
                    myPen.fillcolor("#FFFF00")

                myPen.begin_fill()
                myPen.circle(25)
                myPen.end_fill()

                myPen.penup()
                myPen.forward(50)
                myPen.pendown()
        myPen.setheading(270)
        myPen.penup()
        myPen.forward(50)
        myPen.setheading(180)
        myPen.forward(50*7)
        myPen.setheading(0)
        myPen.getscreen().update()


def checkIfWinner(grid, color):
    #--------------------COMPLETE THE CODE HERE --------------------------
    # Check if 4 in a row / column or diagonal
    # Returns color if so!
    #--------------------------------------------------------------------
```

```python
    #Returns 0 if not
    return 0


#Main Program Starts Here
myPen = turtle.Turtle()
myPen.hideturtle()
myPen.speed(500)
window = turtle.Screen()
window.bgcolor("#2288FF")
myPen.color("#2288FF")
myPen.tracer(0)
myPen.speed(0)


#Initialise empty 6 by 7 connect4 grid
connect4=[]
for row in range(0,6):
    connect4.append([])
    for col in range(0,7):
        connect4[row].append(0)


#Play the game, take it in turn. Up to 42 turns
for turn in range(1,43):
    #Randomly pick an column that is not full
    column = randint(0,6)
    while connect4[0][column]!=0:
        #This column is already full, pick another one
        column = randint(0,6)


    #Make the token slide to the bottom of the grid (Stacked on top of any other existing tokens)
    row=5
```

```python
while connect4[row][column]!=0:
 row=row - 1


#Find out the colour of the current player (1 or 2)
playerColor = (turn % 2) + 1
#Place the token on the grid
connect4[row][column]=playerColor
#Draw the grid
drawGrid(connect4)


#Check if this token wins the game
winner = checkIfWinner(connect4, playerColor)
if winner==RED:
  myPen.penup()
  myPen.color("#FF0000")
  myPen.goto(-70, -170)
  myPen.write("RED Wins!", None, None, "24pt bold")
  myPen.getscreen().update()
  break  #Stop the game
elif winner==YELLOW:
  myPen.penup()
  myPen.color("#FFFF00")
  myPen.goto(-80, -170)
  myPen.write("Yellow Wins!", None, None, "24pt bold")
  myPen.getscreen().update()
  break  #Stop the game


sleep(0.2)
```

45. Langton's Ant

Langton's Ant is a cellular automaton that uses some very simple rules to model an ant traveling on a grid of cells.

The ant is randomly placed on a 2D-grid of white cells at the start of the simulation. Even the ant has a path (either facing upwards, downwards, left or right).

The ant then moves with the following rules, according to the color of the cell in which it is currently seated:

1. If the cell is white, the ant turns to black and turns 90 ° to the right.
2. When the cell is black it turns white and the ant turns 90 ° left.
3. The ant then continues to the next cell, and repeats step 1.

These basic rules contribute to complicated behaviours. There are three distinct types of behaviour, when starting on a white grid:

1. Simplicity: It produces very simple patterns throughout the first few hundred moves which are mostly symmetric.
2. Chaos: A wide, irregular pattern of black and white squares appears after some hundred moves. The ant follows a pseudo-random path up to about ten thousand levels.
3. Emerging order: The ant eventually begins to create a repetitive 104-step "highway" sequence that persists forever.

Eventually, all finite initial configurations tested converge to the same recurrent pattern, indicating that the "highway" is an attractor of Langton's ant but no one has been able to prove that this is valid for all such initial configurations.

Python Code (Using Python Turtle)

Below is our Langton's Ant model implemented using Python Turtle. Notice that we have had to apply one rule to the model on a fixed-size 2D grid:

• Simulation ends on a fixed-size 2D-scale when the ant hits the scale edge.

#Langton's Ant -

```
import turtle
import time
```

```python
from random import randint

#Change this value to speed up or slow down this animation
animationSpeed=2


gridSize = 15
myPen = turtle.Turtle()
myPen.shape("turtle")
myPen.tracer(0)
myPen.speed(0)
myPen.color("#000000")
topLeft_x=-180
topLeft_y=180


#Draw the grid on screen (intDim is the width of a cell on the grid)
def drawGrid(grid,intDim):
  global gridSize
  global ant_row, ant_col, ant_direction
  #Clear the screen
  myPen.clear()
  for i in range(0,gridSize+1):
    myPen.penup()
    myPen.goto(topLeft_x,topLeft_y-i*intDim)
    myPen.pendown()
    myPen.goto(topLeft_x+gridSize*intDim,topLeft_y-i*intDim)
  for i in range(0,gridSize+1):
    myPen.penup()
    myPen.goto(topLeft_x+i*intDim,topLeft_y)
    myPen.pendown()
    myPen.goto(topLeft_x+i*intDim,topLeft_y-gridSize*intDim)
```

```python
for i in range(0,gridSize):
    myPen.penup()
    myPen.goto(topLeft_x+i*intDim+10,topLeft_y+10)
    myPen.write(chr(65+i))
for i in range(1,gridSize+1):
    myPen.penup()
    myPen.goto(topLeft_x-15,topLeft_y-i*intDim+10)
    myPen.write(str(i))


myPen.setheading(0)
myPen.goto(topLeft_x,topLeft_y-intDim)
for row in range (0,gridSize):
    for col in range (0,gridSize):
        if grid[row][col]>0:
            box(intDim)
        myPen.penup()
        if row==ant_row and col==ant_col:
            myPen.color("#FF0000")
            x = myPen.xcor()
            y = myPen.ycor()
            myPen.goto(x+12,y+12)
            myPen.setheading(ant_direction)
            myPen.stamp()
            myPen.goto(x,y)
            myPen.color("#000000")
            myPen.setheading(0)

        myPen.forward(intDim)
        myPen.pendown()
    myPen.setheading(270)
```

```python
    myPen.penup()
    myPen.forward(intDim)
    myPen.setheading(180)
    myPen.forward(intDim*gridSize)
    myPen.setheading(0)
    myPen.pendown()


# This function draws a box by drawing each side of the square and using the fill function
def box(intDim):
    myPen.begin_fill()
    # 0 deg.
    myPen.forward(intDim)
    myPen.left(90)
    # 90 deg.
    myPen.forward(intDim)
    myPen.left(90)
    # 180 deg.
    myPen.forward(intDim)
    myPen.left(90)
    # 270 deg.
    myPen.forward(intDim)
    myPen.end_fill()
    myPen.setheading(0)


#Randomely populate the grid
def randomGrid():
    global gridSize
    grid = []
```

```python
    for row in range(0,gridSize):
        grid.append([])
        for col in range(0,gridSize):
            grid[row].append(randint(0,1))
    return grid


#Create an empty grid
def emptyGrid():
    global gridSize
    grid = []
    for row in range(0,gridSize):
        grid.append([])
        for col in range(0,gridSize):
            grid[row].append(0)
    return grid


##################### MAIN PROGRAM STARTS HERE #####################
gridSize = 15
grid=emptyGrid()


#Position the Ant
ant_row = randint(5,10)
ant_col = randint(5,10)
ant_direction = randint(0,3)*90


#Start animating the grid
while ant_row>=0 and ant_row<gridSize and ant_col>=0 and ant_col<gridSize :
    #Change the direction of the ant based on the colour of the cell it's on
    if grid[ant_row][ant_col]==0:
```

```
    ant_direction-=90
  if ant_direction<0:
    ant_direction+=360
else:
  ant_direction+=90
  if ant_direction>=360:
    ant_direction-=360


  drawGrid(grid,25) #25 is the width of each square on the grid
  myPen.getscreen().update()
  time.sleep(1/animationSpeed)
  #Apply Langton's Ant rules
  #Change the colour of the cell the ant was on
  if grid[ant_row][ant_col]==0:
    grid[ant_row][ant_col]=1
  else:
    grid[ant_row][ant_col]=0


  #Move ant by 1 cell in the new direction
  if ant_direction==0:
    ant_col+=1
  elif ant_direction==90:
    ant_row-=1
  elif ant_direction==180:
    ant_col-=1
  elif ant_direction==270:
    ant_row+=1
```

Your Task

This code can be completed by adding several ants to this model or starting with a random grid of black and white cells rather than just an empty grid of white cells.

46. Python Turtle – Protractor Challenge

Python turtle? Let's get

You can understand the purpose of each Python Turtle Instruction by looking at the following code:

- turtle.color("red")
- turtle.forward(100)
- turtle.right(90)
- turtle.left(45)
- turtle.penup()
- turtle.pendown()
- turtle.goto(0,0)
- turtle.circle(50)
- turtle.setHeading(45)

(X, Y) Coalitions?

The canvas on which we draw (using Python Turtle) is 400 pixels wide by 400 pixels tall.

Look at the canvas below to see how (x , y) coordinates function:

Protractor Challenge:

A protractor is a tool used to calculate or draw angles in Maths.

Our challenge is to use Python to draw a protractor on screen, using all the graduations for a 0 ° to 180 ° scale.

#Python Turtle Protractor -

```
import turtle
myPen = turtle.Turtle()
myPen.shape("turtle")
myPen.speed(500)
myPen.color("#333333")
```

```
myPen.penup()
myPen.goto(-10,0)
myPen.pendown()
myPen.setheading(0)
myPen.forward(20)
myPen.penup()
myPen.goto(0,-10)
myPen.pendown()
myPen.setheading(90)
myPen.forward(20)


#Add the code to draw all the graduations




myPen.penup()
myPen.goto(-80,-50)
myPen.write("My Protractor", None, None, "22pt bold")


myPen.hideturtle()
```

47. The Social Network

Six Degrees of Separation

The Six degrees of separation is a concept originally established in 1929 that can be applied to social networks like Facebook.

It is based on the premise that all human beings in the world are six or less steps apart from each other so that a chain of statements "a friend of a friend" can be made in a maximum of six steps to link any two persons.

Using a Diagram:

To check this definition, we will use a graph data structure in which all graph nodes will represent the members of a small social network that contains 100 members.

The interactions between the nodes will represent relationships of friendship between two members.

Then we'll ask the end-user to enter 2 names and use an algorithm to find out the shortest chain of friendships between these two members (if any).

Using Python Graphs

Most programming languages do provide direct graph support as a form of data. For example, Python does not have a data structure for graphs. Graphs can however be constructed from lists and dictionaries. For example, here is the Python code which represents the connections from the graph above:

Shortest Path Algorithm

The shortest path algorithm would be based on a recursive function used to find all the chain / paths of friendship that can be found between two members, and determine which one is the shortest path (the path with the smallest number of nodes).

We also have a stopping condition to avoid exploring a path that would be longer than the shortest path found so far to make this algorithm more efficient.

```python
def find_shortest_path(graph, start, end, shortestLength=-1, path=[]):
    path = path + [start]
    if start == end:
        return path
    if not graph.has_key(start):
        return None
    shortest = None
    for node in graph[start]:
        if node not in path:
            if shortestLength==-1 or len(path)<(shortestLength-1):
                newpath = find_shortest_path(graph, node, end, shortestLength, path)
                if newpath:
                    if not shortest or len(newpath) < len(shortest):
                        shortest = newpath
                        shortestLength = len(newpath)
    return shortest
```

Python Code

Check the code below to find the shortest path between two members, using the find shortest path) (algorithm. Then it is used for measuring the degree of separation (based on the chain length).

```python
#The Social Network
from members import members


def find_shortest_path(graph, start, end, shortestLength=-1, path=[]):
    path = path + [start]
    if start == end:
        return path
    if not graph.has_key(start):
        return None
    shortest = None
    for node in graph[start]:
        if node not in path:
            if shortestLength==-1 or len(path)<(shortestLength-1):
                newpath = find_shortest_path(graph, node, end, shortestLength, path)
                if newpath:
                    if not shortest or len(newpath) < len(shortest):
                        shortest = newpath
                        shortestLength = len(newpath)
    return shortest


#Main Program Starts Here
member1="Naomi"
member2="Sahil"
print("Member 1: " + member1)
print("Member 2: " + member2)
print("\nSearching the shortest friendship chain... \n")
path=find_shortest_path(members,member1,member2)
print("Friendship Chain: ")
```

258

```
print(path)
print("Degrees of Separation: ")
print(len(path)-1)
```

48. Python Turtle Spirograph

In this topic theme we will build a spirograph using Python Turtle to draw various types of curves.

Do You know?

A Spirograph is a geometric drawing tool that produces the varieties theoretically recognized mathematical roulette curves as hypotrochoids and epitrochoids. It was built and first marketed by British engineer Denys Fisher in 1965.

Python Turtle Spirograph: (Hypotrochoid)

#Python Turtle -

```
import turtle
from math import cos,sin
from time import sleep


window = turtle.Screen()
window.bgcolor("#FFFFFF")


mySpirograph = turtle.Turtle()
mySpirograph.hideturtle()
mySpirograph.tracer(0)
mySpirograph.speed(0)
mySpirograph.pensize(2)


myPen = turtle.Turtle()
myPen.hideturtle()
myPen.tracer(0)
```

```python
myPen.speed(0)
myPen.pensize(3)
myPen.color("#AA00AA")


R = 125
r = 75
d = 125


angle = 0


myPen.penup()
myPen.goto(R-r+d,0)
myPen.pendown()


theta = 0.2
steps = int(6*3.14/theta)


for t in range(0,steps):
    mySpirograph.clear()
    mySpirograph.penup()
    mySpirograph.setheading(0)
    mySpirograph.goto(0,-R)
    mySpirograph.color("#999999")
    mySpirograph.pendown()
    mySpirograph.circle(R)
    angle+=theta


    x = (R - r) * cos(angle)
    y = (R - r) * sin(angle)
    mySpirograph.penup()
    mySpirograph.goto(x,y-r)
    mySpirograph.color("#222222")
```

```
mySpirograph.pendown()
mySpirograph.circle(r)
mySpirograph.penup()
mySpirograph.goto(x,y)
mySpirograph.dot(5)


x = (R - r) * cos(angle) + d * cos(((R-r)/r)*angle)
y = (R - r) * sin(angle) - d * sin(((R-r)/r)*angle)
mySpirograph.pendown()
mySpirograph.goto(x,y)
#mySpirograph.setheading((R-r)*degrees(angle)/r)
#mySpirograph.forward(d)
mySpirograph.dot(5)
myPen.goto(mySpirograph.pos())


mySpirograph.getscreen().update()
sleep(0.05)


sleep(0.5)
#Hide Spirograph
mySpirograph.clear()
mySpirograph.getscreen().update()
```

49. Insertion Sort Algorithm

The Insertion sort algorithm is one of Computer Science 's key sorting algorithms.

First, the algorithm considers a list's first value to be a sorted sub-list (of one value to start with). This iterative algorithm then tests each value, one by one, in the remaining value list. It inserts the value in the correct position in the sorted sub-list of the data set, moving higher ranked elements up as needed.

This algorithm is a relatively efficient O(n2) algorithm for small lists and mostly sorted lists, and is often used as part of even more sophisticated algorithms.

Python Implementation of the Insertion Sort algorithm

The Python code below helps you to see how a small set of values (from 1 to 9) sort an Insertion algorithm. Every time you run this code the list of values is shuffled.

```
#Insertion Sort Algorithm -
import turtle
from random import shuffle
from time import sleep

myPen = turtle.Turtle()
myPen.tracer(0)
myPen.speed(0)
myPen.color("#000000")
myPen.hideturtle()

topLeft_x=-180
topLeft_y=160
intDim=30
gap = 40

def text(message,x,y,size):
    FONT = ('Arial', size, 'normal')
    X=myPen.xcor()
    Y=myPen.ycor()
    myPen.penup()
    myPen.goto(x,y)
    myPen.color("#000000")
    myPen.write(message,align="left",font=FONT)
    myPen.goto(X,Y)
    myPen.pendown()
```

```python
#A procedure to draw the grid on screen using Python Turtle
def drawList(list,numberOfIterations):
  global topLeft_x,topLeft_y,intDim
  myPen.penup()
  myPen.goto(topLeft_x,topLeft_y)
  myPen.pendown()

  for i in range(0,len(list)):
    #myPen.goto(topLeft_x+i*intDim,topLeft_y-intDim)
    if i<numberOfIterations:
      myPen.fillcolor("#FF00FF")
    else:
      myPen.fillcolor("#FFFFFF")

    myPen.begin_fill()
    for side in range(0,4):
      myPen.forward(intDim)
      myPen.left(90)
    myPen.end_fill()

    myPen.forward(intDim)
    text(list[i],topLeft_x+i*intDim+8,topLeft_y+5,20)

def highlightValue(list,position,color):
  global topLeft_x,topLeft_y,intDim,gap
  myPen.penup()
  myPen.goto(topLeft_x+position*intDim,topLeft_y+gap)
  myPen.pendown()
  myPen.fillcolor(color)
  myPen.begin_fill()
  for side in range(0,4):
```

```
    myPen.forward(intDim)
    myPen.left(90)
myPen.forward(intDim)
myPen.end_fill()
myPen.end_fill()


text(list[position],topLeft_x+position*intDim+8,topLeft_y+5+gap,20)
myPen.getscreen().update()
sleep(0.2)


#A function to sort a list using an insertion Sort Algorithm
def insertionSort(list):
    global topLeft_y,intDim,gap
    drawList(list,1)
    topLeft_y = topLeft_y - gap
    myPen.getscreen().update()
    sleep(1)
    numberOfIterations = 1

    for i in range(1, len(list)):
        highlightValue(list,i,"#FFAAFF")
        highlightValue(list,i,"#FFFFFF")
        j = i-1
        key = list[i]
        while (list[j] > key) and (j >= 0):
            highlightValue(list,j,"#CCCCCC")
            list[j+1] = list[j]
            highlightValue(list,j,"#FF00FF")
            j -= 1
        list[j+1] = key
        numberOfIterations += 1
        drawList(list,numberOfIterations)
```

```
    topLeft_y = topLeft_y - gap
    myPen.getscreen().update()
    sleep(0.5)
    text("Insertion Sort Complete", topLeft_x,topLeft_y+10,20)
    myPen.getscreen().update()
list = [1,2,3,4,5,6,7,8,9]
shuffle(list)
insertionSort(list)
```

50. Bubble Sort Algorithm

One of the main sorting algorithms used in Computer Science is the Bubble sort algorithm. It is a fairly easy algorithm to implement, and is especially useful when finding a list 's top x values.

The algorithm begins at data set start. It compares the first two values and it replaces them if the first is greater than the second. For any pair of adjacent values, it continues to do this until the end of the data collection. It then begins again with the first two elements, repeated until there have been no swaps at the last move.

The average and worst-case output of this algorithm is O(n2), thus, it is rarely used to sort massive, unordered data sets. Bubble sort could be used to sort out a small number of items which is much more efficient on data sets where the values are almost sorted already.

Python Implementation of a Bubble Sort algorithm

The Python code below helps you to see how to sort a Bubble algorithm with a limited collection of values (from 1 to 9). Any time you run this code the list of values is shuffled.


```
#Bubble Sort Algorithm -
import turtle
from random import shuffle
from time import sleep

myPen = turtle.Turtle()
myPen.tracer(0)
myPen.speed(0)
```

```python
myPen.color("#000000")
myPen.hideturtle()


topLeft_x=-180
topLeft_y=160
intDim=30
gap = 40


def text(message,x,y,size):
    FONT = ('Arial', size, 'normal')
    X=myPen.xcor()
    Y=myPen.ycor()
    myPen.penup()
    myPen.goto(x,y)
    myPen.color("#000000")
    myPen.write(message,align="left",font=FONT)
    myPen.goto(X,Y)
    myPen.pendown()


#A procedure to draw the grid on screen using Python Turtle
def drawList(list,numberOfIterations):
    global topLeft_x,topLeft_y,intDim
    myPen.penup()
    myPen.goto(topLeft_x,topLeft_y)
    myPen.pendown()


    for i in range(0,len(list)):
        #myPen.goto(topLeft_x+i*intDim,topLeft_y-intDim)
        if i<len(list)-numberOfIterations:
            myPen.fillcolor("#FFFFFF")
        else:
            myPen.fillcolor("#FF00FF")
```

```python
    myPen.begin_fill()
    for side in range(0,4):
        myPen.forward(intDim)
        myPen.left(90)
    myPen.end_fill()

    myPen.forward(intDim)
    text(list[i],topLeft_x+i*intDim+8,topLeft_y+5,20)


def highlightValues(list,position,color1,color2):
    global topLeft_x,topLeft_y,intDim,gap
    myPen.penup()
    myPen.goto(topLeft_x+position*intDim,topLeft_y+gap)
    myPen.pendown()
    myPen.fillcolor(color1)
    myPen.begin_fill()
    for step in range(0,2):
        for side in range(0,4):
            myPen.forward(intDim)
            myPen.left(90)
        myPen.forward(intDim)
        myPen.end_fill()
        myPen.fillcolor(color2)
        myPen.begin_fill()
    myPen.end_fill()

    text(list[position],topLeft_x+position*intDim+8,topLeft_y+5+gap,20)
    text(list[position+1],topLeft_x+(position+1)*intDim+8,topLeft_y+5+gap,20)
    myPen.getscreen().update()
    if color1!="#FFFFFF":
        sleep(0.2)
```

```python
#A function to sort a list using a Bubble Sort Algorithm
def bubbleSort(list):
    global topLeft_y,intDim,gap
    drawList(list,-1)
    topLeft_y = topLeft_y - gap
    drawList(list,-1)
    topLeft_y = topLeft_y - gap
    myPen.getscreen().update()
    sleep(1)
    numberOfIterations = 0
    changed = True
    while changed:
        changed = False
        for i in range(0, len(list) - numberOfIterations-1):
            highlightValues(list,i,"#CCCCCC","#CCCCCC")
            if list[i] > list[i+1]:
                highlightValues(list,i,"#FF66FF","#FF66FF")
                #swap values
                list[i], list[i+1] = list[i+1], list[i]
                highlightValues(list,i,"#FF66FF","#FF66FF")
                changed = True
            if i>=len(list) - numberOfIterations:
                highlightValues(list,i,"#FFFFFF","#FFFFFF")
            else:
                highlightValues(list,i,"#FFFFFF","#FF00FF")
        numberOfIterations += 1
        drawList(list,numberOfIterations)
        topLeft_y = topLeft_y - gap
        myPen.getscreen().update()
        sleep(0.5)
    text("Bubble Sort Complete", topLeft_x,topLeft_y,20)
```

```
  myPen.getscreen().update()
list = [1,2,3,4,5,6,7,8,9]
shuffle(list)
bubbleSort(list)
```

CONCLUSION

Python programming is an ever more critical aspect of a programmer's education in today's workplace. As a dynamic language that focuses on readability and succinct design philosophy, Python is a common option for use in scripting. It is more versatile than compiled languages, like other interpretive languages, and it could be used to bind different structures together. Python is indeed a versatile language with numerous applications in growing fields.

Python is a popular software programming language. Raspberry Pi, Python's primary programming language, is the single board computer project for teaching student computer programming. Moreover, much of the One Laptop program per Child XO has been written in Python. A python is also a popular tool for theoretical mathematics and computational computing at the other end of the learning spectrum. As the production of educational software continues to expand, Python will become an increasingly important language.

Python is also a favorite language for AI use in addition to educational applications. Since Python is a written language with comprehensive text processing tools, module design, and simplicity in syntax, it is a natural option for natural language processing applications.

Python is also used as a web application scripting language. For example, Google's App Engine, the cloud computing platform through developing and hosting web apps, has adopted Python as being one of the available languages. Python is also used as a software communication system between computers for web applications such as Dropbox. Since the development of the web application is an increasingly growing area, programmers would like to learn Python to keep their skills up to date.

Python is also very useful as a modern Perl-like scripting language that can be used to bind various systems together. Due to the fact that Python is a basic part of many operating systems based in Linux and Unix and since Python is commonly used in the information security industry, Python is a valuable tool for system administrators and programmers to learn.

Python training is becoming an increasingly important language for programming. Python has a wide range of applications in many growing areas due to its flexibility. Both programmers and system managers will do well to take up some knowledge of Python to up-to-date their abilities.

PYTHON FOR DATA ANALYSIS

The Ultimate step by step Beginners' Guide to Learning Python 3.0 Data analysis

Mark Slatkin

INTRODUCTION

Since the late 1980s, Python has been active and is regarded as a mature programming language. The Python language developers perform extensive feature and regression tests so that each new release ensures that the language is bug-free and stable.

Good developers often use the various programming paradigms to reduce the amount of time and effort needed to develop large and complex applications. Python supports several commonly used programming styles like other modern programming languages including, procedural, functional object-oriented, and imperative. It also enables automated memory management and a dynamic system type. Programmers can therefore use the language to develop large and complex software applications.

Currently, Python is available on major operating systems such as Windows, Mac OS X, Linux, and Unix. The desktop GUI applications can therefore be deployed on multiple platforms in the programming language. The programmers can further speed up the development of cross-platform GUI applications by using frames such as Kivy, wxPython, and PyGtk. Several reports have shown that Python is widely used for numerical and scientific applications. While in Python, developers can use tools like Scipy, Pandas, IPython, and the Python Imaging Library to write scientific and numerical applications.

CHAPTER ONE

PYTHON-DATA ANALYSIS

Data analysis requires a significant number of cleaning, processing, and transforming data collection in order to benefit from it. Python is typically used as a programming language for analyzing data since several tools, such as Pandas and Bokeh, Jupyter Notebook, are written in python and can be implemented easily instead of digging your own data analysis libraries.

• The following data exploration sequence uses Python as the programming language during various stages of the study of a data collection.

I. Part 1 offers an insight into how you can act and explain what you want to understand.

II. Part 2 outlines the transformation and categorization of an easier-to-analyze data set.

III. Part 3 illustrates how the outcomes of your data analysis can be visualized.

• PyData 101 provides slides to one of the leading Python ecosystem developers about how you can concentrate on data science while new.

• The Python Data Science Handbook is available online for free, but we also recommend that you purchase the book because it is a great resource to learn the subject.

• PyData TV provides all PyData conference series videos. Professionals and developers who compose the analytical libraries also deliver the conference presentations, so there is a wealth of knowledge that is not generally collected elsewhere.

• Python Plotting is a fantastic guide on how to use basic data displays to bootstrap your data set understanding. The development involves histograms, the study of time series, distributed plots, and different types of bar charts.

• This "Agile Analytics" series has three elements explaining how to function in a data science team and how to run one if you are a manager:

I. Part 1: Positive stuff

II. Part 2: Bad stuff

III. Part 3: Adaptations

• Learning the Seattle Bicycle counts work habits offer an excellent example of how to use open data, from Seattle in this case, to play with Python and pandas, and then to map it by using ski-learns. This form of research can be performed on virtually every data set in order to find its patterns.

• Exploring the story shapes with Python and feel APIs is a fantastic reading with a resolution background, plenty of insight into how to replicate the findings with your own code and several charts that demonstrate how feeling analysis can extract information from text blocks.

• How to automate the construction of AWS high-tech virtual machines for data science projects through the establishment of an Amazon Web Services development environment so that you can analyze your data without needing a high-end computer. Refer to AWS Introduction for Data Scientists for another tutorial showing how to set up additional widely used AWS data science resources.

• Overview of bugs.python.org uses the collected data from the development of CPython to display the most common version issues and problems in the history of the project.

• Diverse and convergent data analysis phases analyze the flow of most data scientists and research projects in the discovery, synthesis, modeling, and narration processes.

• Forget about privacy: anyway, a particular form of article is terrible to target. It's a broad observation rather than a guide on a specific subject of data analysis. The author argues that the collection of data is typically easy, but that the dirty analysis often results in little insight that can be identified. Overall, this is a well-written piece of thinking that will make you pause and wonder, "Do we really have to collect this user data?"

• Gender distribution with the Convolutionary Neural Networks in North Korean posters is an important post using convolutionary neural networks to classify gender on North Korean posters. A good example of how data analysis can solve problems that would take a long time for someone to find out without a computer is the study of that messy dataset and the results it generated using some Python glue code with various open-source libraries.

• Time Series Python Analysis: An introduction demonstrates how the Prophet library is used to conduct time-series analysis on a collection of data.

• Cryptocurrency version uses the panda's library to clean a cryptocurrency data set and to transfer data to a system that the author needs to do for research.

• Cryptocurrency version uses the panda's library to clean a cryptocurrency data set and to transfer data to a system that the author needs to do for research.

• Mobile Python Data Formalization and Cleaning Libraries offers a brief overview of libraries such as Arrow and Dora to ease the processing of the knowledge before the research is completed.

• Reviewing a million files in robots.txt discusses what the robots.txt file is, why it matters, how to download a lot, and analyze it with NumPy.

• The Google BigQuery Python Aid module for the secure analysis of common licenses on GitHub Projects uses a huge three terabyte data set given by GitHub.

• Cleaning and preparation of Python data is an example of how pandas are used to perform the "boring" part of a data analysis task and turn dirty data into a more reliable, organized format.

• 9 obscure data science Python libraries have many lesser-known but still very useful libraries for the analysis of knowledge like gymnastics and fuzzy-wuzzy.

• Nvidia's data analysis series, machine learning, and deep learning are worth to read and how the problem areas are broken down

WHY PYTHON IS ESSENTIAL FOR DATA ANALYSIS

Python is the world-renowned programming language to better handle your data for a range of causes.
We live in the digital age of high-tech, intelligent devices, and mobile solutions. Data is a fundamental aspect of any company and company. It is essential that the data flow is collected, processed, analyzed, done as quickly as possible. Today, the volume of data can be

large, making the handling of information time expensive and consuming. Because of this, the data science industry is growing quickly, creating new opportunities and vacancies.

Practical applications in Embedded Systems for AI and ML

Many new methods of recording, storing, and analyzing data have now emerged to effectively extract cognitive information and gain insights and knowledge. You cannot just select from a list of options, functionality, and tools, but you can also use them for processing operations and leveraging methods to convert information to knowledge and insights through reports or visualization.

There are a number of prominent programming languages for data reduction. Some of them are C, C++, R, Java, JavaScript, and Python. Each of them offers distinctive features, options, and tools that meet your different requirements. Some are better for particular industry needs than others. For instance, one industry survey states that Python is a leader in improving fintech software and other areas of application.

Two main factors make Python particularly a widely-used programming language in science computing:
- The amazing ecosystem;
- A huge proportion of data-oriented function packages which can accelerate up and simplify data processing and save time.

In addition, Python is first used to update data analysis. It is among those languages that are constantly being developed. Thereby Python is called the leading language with more potential than other programming languages in the field of data science.

What makes Python a great data analysis option?

Python is a cross-functional, consummately interpreted language with many advantages. The object-based programming language is often used for streamlining huge complex sets of data. Moreover, Python has more unrhythmic RAD capabilities with dynamic semantics (Rapid development of application) and is also heavily used for the script. Python can be applied in another way – as a coupling language.
Another advantage of Python is its high readability that helps engineers save time by typing fewer code lines for the performance of tasks. Python is fast and jibs well with data analysis. And that is due to the strong support of a variety of open-source libraries, including but not restricted to computer programming, for different purposes. Therefore, it is not at all surprising that it is stated to be the preferred data science programming language. There is a range of unique features, which makes Python a number one data analysis option. Seeing is faithful. Let's just overlook every single option one by one.

Easy to Learn

You have the idea that Python is widely recognized by its clear syntax and readability because you are involved in development for web services, mobile applications, or coding. Yes, these are the most well-known language features. Moreover, a low and therefore fast learning curve is Python's next preeminence when compared with older languages.
Ruby, C #, Java, and others, particularly entry-level programmers, are much more difficult to master. Python focuses on simplicity and readability, which offer data analysts/scientists a

range of helpful options simultaneously. Newbies can therefore easily use their very simple syntax to develop viable solutions even for difficult cases. This is all with fewer lines of code used, most notably. It's a perfect tool for beginners because of this.

Well-sponsored

You probably know that having the knowledge of using some tools free of charge is a difficult task to get decent support. However, this is not the case with Python. Despite the great simplicity, situations can arise if you still need help with Python. Python is widely utilized in the industry alongside academic fields and has a wide range of useful libraries with lots of supporting and helpful materials. The great advantage is that all libraries are free of charge. The greater the language's popularity, the more cognitive information about real user experience is provided. Therefore, you have access to a user-contributed code; stack overflow, documents, mailing lists, etc. Users worldwide can ask advice and help from more experienced programmers when necessary.

Flexibilities

There are no cool options. Let us, therefore, observe another reason why Python is a fantastic data processing option. The hyper flexibility that makes Python highly sought after by data scientists and analysts is another strong feature of the language. This enables data models to be built, data sets to be systematized, ML-powered algorithms, web services, and data mining to be implemented in a short period of time to complete different tasks. Yes, Python is such an advantage that the data science industry needs an ideal solution.

Scalability

The feature of this Python is described immediately after flexibility, not by accident but because it is closely related to the previous option. Python is much faster and more scalable in comparison with other languages such as R, Go, and Rust. Python is therefore good for various uses in various fields that can solve a wide range of problems. This is why many firms migrated to Python. Furthermore, this language is perfect for all types of RAD (as stated above). In addition, the data analysis is on the list of industries in which language can be successfully applied.

Great collection of libraries

As we mentioned earlier, Python is now one of the most widely supported languages. It has a long list of completely free libraries for all users. This is a key factor that gives Python a strong push, and in data science as well. If you are more than likely involved in this field, you are aware of names such as SciPy, Pandas, statsmodels, and other libraries, which are widely used in the data science community. Note that the libraries are constantly expanding and offer robust solutions. Herewith, you can easily find a solution without any additional costs.

Exceeding the Community of Python

It's some sort of open-source language. This means that you have at least two major advantages. Python is free and uses a community-based development model. Yes, this and the preceding paragraph are also inextricably linked. In addition to open-source libraries like data visualization, ML, statistics, and manipulation, Python also has a huge community base with training pieces and forums available.

This is how people around the world can share experiences, thoughts, and knowledge and provide solutions, codes, and questions. We recommend that you go to the Python Package Index if you are interested in learning about the various aspects of Python.

Tools for graphics and visualization

It is known that visual information can be understood, operated, and remembered much more easily. Here is another portion of a piece of good news for you. A range of visualization options is available. That makes Python a must for all data science and not only for data analysis. By creating different charts, graphs, and interactive web-ready plots, you can make the data more accessible and easier to use. Yes, Python enables you to get a good sense of data.

Extended Analytical package Tools available

Just after you collect data, you're going to handle it. Python is highly appropriate for this purpose. Therefore, we cannot but mention the integrated data analytics tools of Python in order to find the perfect tool for complex data processing or self-service analysis. Dozens of data mining companies around the world use Python to reduce data. Python is also able to easily penetrate patterns and to correlate information in large sets and to give better insights into the performance assessment along with other critical matrices.

Your business success depends directly on the ability to draw knowledge and insights from data to make effective strategic decisions, remain competitive, and progress. Python is the world-renowned programming language to better manage your data for a variety of reasons.

Python is one of the easiest languages to learn, simple to use, the best price ever (it's really free!). It offers an excellent set of features. Although Python is an open-source language, a large community still supports it. All this makes Python perfect for programming newbies. Furthermore, Python is scalable and flexible enough to be used in various fields and for diverse purposes.

USING PYTHON AS GLUE

There is no more boring conversation than everyone agrees.

Many people like to say that Python is a wonderful language of glue. This segment will hopefully convince you that this is true. Python's first adopters for science were normal people who used it to glue large application codes on supercomputers together. It was not only much more convenient to code in Python than in a shell script and Perl, but it also made it relatively easy to extend Python to create new classes and types that are specifically adapted to the problems that have been solved. Numeric emerged as an array-like object from the interactions of these early contributors to pass data between these applications.

As Numeric matured and developed into NumPy, more code was written directly to NumPy. This code is often fast enough for production, but sometimes you still have to access compiled code. Either to achieve that last bit of efficiency from the algorithm or to make access to widely available codes written in C / C++ or Fortran easier.

This part will review many of the tools available in other compiled languages for accessing code. There are numerous resources available to learn other compiled libraries from Python and this segment is not intended to make you an expert. The main objective is to make you aware of some options so that you know what to do.

Call other Python compiled libraries

While Python is a good language, its dynamic character leads to overhead so that some code (i.e. raw calculations inside loops) are up to 10 to 100 times slower than the equivalent code written into a statically compiled language. It can also make the memory use larger than needed as temporary arrays are created and destroyed while computing. For many different computer needs, extra slow-down and memory use (at least for time- or memory-critical parts of your code) often cannot be spared. One of the most common necessities is to call a rapid machine code (e.g. compiled with C / C++ or Fortran) from Python code. The reason Python is such an excellent high-level language for scientific and engineering programming is the fact that this is quite easy to do.

They are two fundamental approaches to calling compiled code: the writing of an extension module and the import command to Python or the call of a share-Bibliothek subroutine from Python directly with the ctype module. The most common method is to write an extension module.

Hand-generated wrappers

In writing an extension module, extension modules were discussed. The basic way in which compiled code is interfaced is to write an extension module and build a module method calling the compiled code. Your method should use the PyArg ParseTuple call to convert between Python objects and C data types for improved readability. A built-in converter is probably already available for standard C data types. You may need to write your own converter for others and use the 'O &' string, which allows you to specify a function that is used to convert from Python to any C-structure.

The next step in the wrapper is to call the underlying function once the conversion to a suitable C-structure and C data type has been performed. This is easy if the underlying function is C or C++. However, you need to know how Fortran's subroutines are called from C / C++ with your compiler and platform to call Fortran code. This can vary slightly between platforms and compilers (which is another reason why f2py simplifies life for Fortran code interactions), but usually underlines a lack of a name, and the fact that all variables are referenced (i.e. that all arguments are points).

The advantage of the hand-made wrapper is that the C-library is fully controlled and named, which can lead to a narrow and tight interface with minimal overhead. The drawback is that you have to enter, debug, and maintain C-code although most can be adapted with the time-honored "cut-past-and-modify" technique from other expansion modules. Since the procedure is fairly regimented for calling for additional C-code, code generation procedures have been developed to facilitate this process. One of the techniques of code generation is distributed to NumPy and enables easy integration with Fortran and (simple) C code. This package, f2py, is briefly covered in the following section.

F2py

F2py allows you to automatically build an extension module that uses Fortran code 77/90/95 to interface routines. It can parse the Fortran 77/90/95 code and automatedly generate Python signatures to the subroutines that it encounters, or you can guide how to build a definition-file (or modify the f2py-produced) of the subroutine interfaces to Python.

Cython

Cython is a Python compiler, which adds (optional) static speed typing and allows C or C++ code to be mixed in your modules. It produces extensions C or C++ that can be compiled and imported into the Python code.

If you're writing an extension module that also includes your own algorithmic code, Cython is a good match. Among its features is the ability to work with multidimensional arrays easily and quickly.

Note that Cython is a generator extension module only. Unlike f2py, the extension module (must be done as usual) is not automatically compiled and linked. It provides a modified distutil class called build ext, that allows you to build a.pyx-source extension module.

Ctypes

Ctypes is an extension module for Python, included in stdlib, that allows you to call an arbitrary feature directly from Python in a shared library. This approach enables you to interface directly from Python with C-code. This opens up a huge number of Python libraries. The drawback, however, was that coding errors can lead to hideous program crashes very easily (as in C) because the parameters are checked by small types or boundaries. This is especially true when the array data is passed to a raw memory location as a pointer. It is then your responsibility not to access the memory outside the actual array area. If, however, you don't mind the dangerous way of living a little ctypes, you can use a large common library quickly (or write extended functionality in your own shared library).

Because the ctypes approach exposes the compiled code to a raw interface, user mistakes are not always tolerant. The robust use of the module for ctypes typically involves an added layer of Python code to verify the data types and the boundaries of objects passed to the subroutine. This additional test layer (to mention not convert ctypes to C-data types performed by ctypes) makes the layout lighter than a hand-written enhanced version module interface. However, this overhead should be negligible if the C routine does a lot of work. Ctypes is an easy way to write a valuable interface in (shared) code library if you are a wonderful Python programmer with weak C capabilities.

You must use ctypes

1. Have a library shared.

2. Load the library shared.

3. Convert python objects into arguments that are understood by the type.

4. Call the library function with ctypes arguments.

Having a common library

There are several requirements for a shared library that can be used with platform-specific types. This guide assumes that you know how to make a shared library on your system (or have a common library at your disposal). Objects to be remembered are:

A shared library must be specially compiled (e.g. using the -shared flag with gcc).

On certain platforms (e.g. Windows), a common library requires a .def file to specify the export functions. For instance, a mylib.def file could contain:

Mylib.dll LIBRARY

EXPORTS Expo

Cool component 1

Cool component 2

Alternatively, you can use the declspec(dllexport) storage class specifier in the C-definition of the function, to avoid this def file requirement.

Python distutils are unable to create a standard shared library in a cross-platform way (a shared extension module is a "special" library, which Python understands). Thus, a major drawback of ctyps at the time this book is that it is hard to distribute a Python extension that utilizes ctypes and contains your own code that should be compiled on the user's system as a shared library.

Loading the common library

One simple but reliable way to load the shared library is by using the cdll ctype object to get the exact pathname and load it:

lib = ctypes.cdll(<path name >)

However, when Windows accesses a cdll method attribute, the first DLL is loaded by a name presented in the current directory or on the PATH directory. To load the absolute name of the path requires some fineness for cross-platform work because the shared libraries are expanded differently. There is a ctypes.util.find library tool, which can simplify the process of loading the library, but is not foolproof. Multiple platforms have various default extensions for shared libraries (eg ... dll – Windows,.so – Linux,.dylib – Mac OS X). Complicating matters. This should also be considered if you use ctypes to wrap code that needs to focus on several platforms.

NumPy provides the ctypeslib.load library convenience function (name, path). This component takes the title of the shared library and a path where the shared library is located (including any prefixes like "lib" but excluding extension). It comes back a library object, or increases an OSError if the library cannot be found or the module ctypes can not be found, it raises the ImportError. (Windows users: the ctype library object loaded with load library is always loaded if a calling agreement cdecels it. For ways to load libraries with other calling conventions, check the ctype library information under ctypes.windll and/or ctypes.oledll).

The functions in the shared library are available as ctypes library object attributes (returned from the ctypeslib.load library) or as objects with lib['func name'] syntax. The latter method is especially useful if the name of the function contains characters not allowed in variable Python names.

Arguments conversion

The none object is converted instantly to a NULL pointer as required to similar ctypes arguments Python ints / longs, strings, and unicode objects. All other objects in Python must be converted to specific types of cypes. There are two ways to integrate ctypes with other objects around this restriction.

1. Do not enter the function object's argtypes attribute and define the as parameter method for the object in which you want to pass. The as parameter method must return a Python int that is directly passed to the function.

2. Set the attribute of argtypes to list which entries contain objects from a class method called param that knows how to convert your object into an object that ctypes can comprehend (int / long, string, unicode, and object with the as parameter attribute).

NumPy uses both methods with a second method preference because it can be safer. The ctypes ndarray attribute returns an object with an as parameter attribute that returns an integer that represents the address of the ndarray associated with it. This means that you can transmit this ctype object attribute to a function that expects a pointer to your ndarray data. If the data pointer is passed to inappropriate arrays, the caller should make sure that the ntarray object is of the correct type, form, and has the correct flags or risky crashes.

NumPy gives the class factory basis ndpointer in the numpy.ctypeslib module to implement the second method. This class factory basis produces a relevant class, which can be placed in the ctypes attribute entry. The class will contain a ctypes method from a param to convert any ndarray passed to the function to an object recognized by ctypes. During this conversion, all features of the ndarray that were indicated by the user in the call to ndpointer are monitored. Aspects of the ndarray that can be checked include data type, the number of dimensions, the form, and/or the flag status on any passed array. The return value of the from param method is a ctypes attribute of the array, which can be directly used by ctypes because it contains the as parameter attribute pointing to the array area.

The ndarray ctypes attribute has further attributes that can be convenient to pass additional array information into the ctypes function. The attributes shape, data, and steps can provide types of ctypes that match the data area, shape, and array steps. The data attribute returns a c void p which indicates the area of the data. The shape and steps allow each ctype integer range to be returned (or None representing a NULL point, if a 0-d array). The base array type is a type integer that is the same size as the platform pointer. Also available are data as({type}), shape as(<base ctype >), and strides as(<base ctype >). These return the data as a category object of your choice and the shape/strides arrays of the base type of your choice. For convenience, the module ctypeslib also contains c intp as ctypes integer data type whose size is the same as the size c void p on the platform.

Strengths of Python

Python code looks syntactically like executable pseudocode. The creation of Python programs is five to ten times faster than with C / C++, while Java is three to five times faster. In certain instances, an application prototype can be written without writing C / C++/Java code in Python. The prototype is often sufficiently usable and works well enough to be the final product, thus saving considerable time for production. In other examples, the prototype can be partly or in full translated into C++ or Java — the object-oriented nature of Python makes the translation easy.

The correct strategy is often to write just the performance-crucial elements for the C++ or Java application and to use Python to monitor and configure all higher-level applications. There are numerous examples of applications that began as pure C++ code to which Python has been introduced as an extension language. The Python framework has increased with each new version, while the overall performance, usability, and usability of the framework have also increased. (e.g. Case Study: Commercial Python, Greg Stein, Microsoft, 6th International Python Conference, and UvA and CMU Project Alice VR.)

Python has a strong web-based presence. It is suitable for CGI programming, with interfaces in all major commercial databases (Unix, Windows, and Mac). Python has a library that interfaces with the main web protocols and the Internet, and has HTML parsing and toolkits for a generation. When they were smaller, Python was a major development language for Infoseek. At least one organization (Digital Creations) offers a suite of Python server-side software. Finally, Python was used to run a web browser (Grail).

In the field of distributed systems, Python is also well known. It is one of the major languages provided by the ILU of the Xerox PARC (ILU), and many distributed applications have been developed into Python using ILU. Python is also used by the University of Queensland, Australia's Hector group.

Python is finally well integrated with the Windows frameworks. Python programs can communicate and even offer new COM and DCOM services (which can not be used with Visual Basic!). Python can also be used in the Microsoft Active Scripting architecture as a scripting engine.

Using Python as a language for integration

Related to the subject of this Workshop, Python is also used as an integration language to tie existing components together ("steer"). The strategy here is to build Python extension modules (written in C / C++) that provide the Python programmer with the functionality of the large components written in C / C++. The "glue" module is important because Python can not call the functions of the C / C++ directly; the Python data types and the C / C++ data types are translated by the glue extensions; and error testing, with the exception of the Python error return values.

The presence of SWIG simplifies the development of glue extensions, reading header files containing function and method prototypes, and automatically generating the appropriate conversion type and error checking code. If the underlying code (usually the C code) does not use an object-oriented model, the glue extension may be wrapped in a Python module that specifies the correct class hierarchy and assigns essential performance operations to the C code.

Python can be used to build better software, and different types of programmers can function together on a project. For example, C / C++ programmers can implement successful numerical algorithms during the development of a scientific application, while scientists from the same project can write programs from Python that test and use these algorithms. The scientist requires no low-level programming language, and the programmer C / C++ requires no knowledge of the science involved.

Without Python, a large volume of C / C++ code sometimes needs to be written just to provide a sufficiently versatile input mechanism for scientists to provide the software with its data in all the variations required for experimental installation (for example). A more flexible input mechanism can be used for Python in a much shorter period or the ultimate flexible input mechanism can be Python itself. The Lawrence Livermore National Laboratories uses Python to finally substitute a scripting language (BASIS) built in-house to the same effect; BASIS began as a simple input mechanism for Fortran programs and has gradually gained many scripting language features (variables, conditions, loops, procedures, and so forth) with the awkwardness.

Python is suitable for oddball integration work because it has interfaces for so many different modules in very different application domains. It can connect a commercial database to a number-crossing code, add a graphical user interface to a network management tool, send emails from an application with virtual reality.

PYTHON NUMPY

Numpy Python

Numpy is an array-processing application for general purposes. It offers a multidimensional high-performance array object and software for working with such arrays. It is the basic kit for Python's scientific computing.

Numpy can also be used as an effective multi-dimensional generic data container in addition to its obvious scientific utilization.

Numpy can also be used as an effective multi-dimensional generic data container in addition to its obvious scientific utilization.

Numpy Arrays

Array in Numpy is a table of elements, all of which are the same form and indexed with a number of positive integer numbers. In Numpy, the number of array dimensions is called the array rank. A number of integer numbers giving the array size over-dimensional are known as the array form. An array class is called ndarray in Numpy. Numpy elements are accessed with square brackets and can be initialized via nested python lists.

Build a Numpy Array

Arrays in Numpy can be generated in many ways, with a variety of ranks that determine the array size. Arrays can also be generated using different data types including lists, tuples, etc. The resulting array type is derived from the sequence element sort.

Note: The array form can be specified specifically during array development.

Program for Python

Arrays development

Numpy import as np

Build an array of rank 1

Arr = NP ([1, 2, 3])

Print("Ranked Array 1:\n,"arr)

Build an array of rank 2

arr = np.array([[1, 2, 3], Array = np.

[4, 5 and 6])

Print("Rank 2 array:\n, "arr)

 # Build an array from tuple

arr = np.array((1,3,2))

print("\nArray created using "

"Tuple passed:\n," ar)

Output:

Rank 1 array:

[1 2 3]

Rank 2 array:

[[1 2 3]

[4 5 6]]

Array created with passed tuple:

[1 3 2]

Enable the index array

In a numpy array, the index array can be indexed or accessed in multiple ways. Slicing is performed to print a number of arrays. Slicing an array defines a range in a new array that is used to print out a range of elements in the original array. As a sliced array contains a variety of elements of the original array, the material adjustment using a sliced array affects the content of the original array.

Demonstration software Python

Numpy array indexing

Numpy import as np

Initial Array

Arr = array([[-1, 2, 0 , 5], Arr = array np.

[4, -0.5, 6, 0],

[2.6, 0, 7, 8],

[3, -7, 4, 2.0]])

Print("Subsequent Array:)

Print(arr)

Printing a range of Array

use the slicing form

sliced arr = arr[:2,: :2]

print ("Array with first 2 rows and"

    " alternate columns(0 and 2):\n", sliced_arr)

```
# Printing elements at
# specific Indices
Index_arr = arr[[1, 1, 0, 3],
[3, 2, 1, 0]]
print ("\nElements at indices (1, 3), "
"(1, 2), (0, 1), (3, 0):\n", Index_arr)
```

Output:

```
Initial Array:
[[-1.   2.   0.   4. ]
 [ 4.  -0.5  6.   0. ]
 [ 2.6  0.   7.   8. ]
 [ 3.  -7.   4.   2. ]]
First 2 rows array and alternative columns(0 and 2):
[[-1.   0.]
 [ 4.   6.]]


Elements at indices (1, 3), (1, 2), (0, 1), (3, 0):
 [ 0. 54.  2.  3.]
```

Operations of Simple Array

In NumPy arrays, a large variety of operations may be carried out on a single array or array combination. This includes some simple math operations, as well as single and binary operations.

```
# Python demonstration program
# primary processing on single array
import numpy as np

# Defining Array 1
a = np.array([[1, 2],
```

```
                [3, 4]])

# Defining Array 2
b = np.array([[4, 3],
            [2, 1]])

# Add 1 to each element
print ("Add 1 to each element:", a + 1)

# Subtract 2 of each element
print ("\Subtract 2 of each element:", b - 2)

# sum of array elements
# Performing Unary operations
print ("\nSum of all array "
        "elements: ", a.sum())

# Adding two arrays
# Performing Binary operations
print ("\nArray sum:\n", a + b)
```

Output:

Add 1 to each element:

 [[2 3]

 [4 5]]

Subtract 2 from every element:

 [[2 1]

 [0 -1]]

Sum of all array elements: 10

Array sum:

 [[5 5]

 [5 5]]

Numpy Data Forms

Every array of Numpy is a table of elements (usually numbers) of the same form, indexed by a multitude of positive integer numbers. Every ndarray has a data type (dtype) object associated with it. The object (dtype) of this data type provides details on the array structure. The ndarray values are stored in a buffer that can be considered as an adjoining block of memory bytes that the object type can interpret. Numpy offers a wide collection of numerical data types to construct arrays. When Array is generated, Numpy tries to devise a datatype, but functions that generate arrays typically often provide an optional argument to define the data type explicitly.

Building a Datatype object

In Numpy, Arrays data types should not be specified unless a particular datatype is needed. Numpy attempts to formulate the data form for arrays that are not predefined in the builder feature.

WHAT IS MATPLOTLIB PYTHON

Data handling is a skillful art. There is a huge amount of data consumed and wasted in the trendy technological world. Thus the efficient handling of this data becomes the main objective of data science. We can use different programming languages to handle data sets that include operations such as marketing, statistics measurement, sales, graphic platform plotting, etc.

Matplotlib Python Description

Data can be plotted extensively through Matplotlib, a plotting library that can be displayed in Python scripts. Graphs are a part of data visualization, and Matplotlib is used to accomplish this property.

To provide object-oriented APIs for inserting plots into applications Matplotlib uses a variety of general-purpose GUI tools, such as Tkinter, wxPython, QT, etc. John D. Hunter was the person who wrote Matplotlib, and Michael Droettboom was the lead developer. Python SciPy is one of the free and open-source Python libraries that is used primarily for technical and scientific computing. Matplotlib is popularly used in SciPy as most scientific calculations need graphs and diagrams to be plotted.

Python (Matplotlib) vs. MATLAB

Python Programming	MATLAB
It is a free open source programming language.	MATLAB is a business platform. Therefore, it's not secure.
Matplotlib is more versatile and plottable.	Plotting is not as flexible and capable as the plotting of Python.
Python has a wide variety of libraries in which to operate.	Adding libraries and working with them in MATLAB is difficult.
Python is a programming language that is easy to read and efficient.	MATLAB isn't as good as Python.
Matplotlib plotting in Python is easier.	MATLAB data visualization takes time and effort.
Additionally, an integrated development environment (IDE) needs to be implemented.	In the MATLAB environment, IDE will be given.
In different systems, code can be used. It's the web.	The portability of code is limited.
Namespace in Python is supported.	MATLAB core supports no namespace.

Types of Matplotlib python

The visualization of the data is the graphical representation of the data generating images to map the connections between the data values. There are several visualization tools on the market that allow automated charts or graphs to be created by collecting data from various sources. Python is a very simple programming language, widely employed on the market to meet business needs in the field of data science work. Python has its own software packages for charts or graphs.

Matplotlib is a module used to view 2D graphics in Python. In python shell, scripts, web application servers, and other GUI toolkits, the Matplotlib can be used. Python offers various types of plot for displaying the data, such as Bargraph, Scatterplot, Histogram, Pie plot, Area Plot. Now let us speak in-depth about these forms of Matplotlib.

1. Matplotlib bar graph

The bar charts are used to compare data, where changes can be calculated over a period of time. It can be horizontally or vertically represented. The longer the counter, the larger the value.

Example code:

Python

```
  I.   from matplotlib import pyplot as plt
 II.   plt.bar([0.25,1.25,2.25,3.25,4.25],[30,40,10,80,20],
III.   label="Male",color='c',width=.5)
 IV.   plt.bar([0.75,1.75,2.75,3.75,4.75],[50,30,20,50,60],
  V.   label="Female", color='g',width=.5)
 VI.   plt.legend()
VII.   plt.xlabel('Days')
VIII.  plt.ylabel('Bed rest(hrs)')
 IX.   plt.title('Information')
  X.   plt.show()
```

2. Matplotlib Using Histogram

The histogram is used to distribute the data, while the bar graph compares the two entities. During arrays or long list data, histograms are preferred. Take as an example a population age can be plotted with regard to the bin. The bin describes the range of values in a number of intervals. In the following example bins, an interval of 10 containing elements 0 to 9, then 10 to 19, and so on is created.

Example code:

Python

```
  I.   import matplotlib.pyplot as plt
 II.   population_age =
       [22,55,62,45,21,22,34,42,42,4,2,102,95,85,55,110,120,70,65,55,111,115,80,
       75,65,54,44,43,42,48]
III.   bins = [0,10,20,30,40,50,60,70,80,90,100]
 IV.   plt.hist(population_age, bins, histtype='bar', rwidth=0.8)
  V.   plt.xlabel('age groups')
 VI.   plt.ylabel('Number of people')
```

VII.   plt.title('Histogram')

VIII.   plt.show()

3. Matplotlib Scatter Plot

When comparing the data variables, disperse parts are preferred to identify the relationship between two and independent variables. The data is shown as a collection of points, each having a variable value which shows the direction on the horizontal axis and the position on the vertical axis of the other variable.

Example code:

Python

```
  I.    import matplotlib.pyplot as plt
 II.    x1 = [1,1.5,2,2.5,3,3.5,3.6]
III.    y1 = [7.5,8,8.5,9,9.5,10,10.5]
 IV.    x2=[8,8.5,9,9.5,10,10.5,11]
  V.    y2=[3,3.5,3.7,4,4.5,5,5.2]
 VI.    plt.scatter(x1,y1, label='high bp low heartrate',color='r')
VII.    plt.scatter(x2,y2,label='low bp high heartrate',color='b')
VIII.    plt.title('Scatter Plot')
 IX.    plt.xlabel('x')
  X.    plt.ylabel('y')
 XI.    plt.legend()
XII.    plt.show()
```

4. Area Plot Using Matplotlib

The plots of the region were often called stack plots. It's quite close to the plots on the graph. For two or more similar classes that make up a whole category, area plots will be used for monitoring changes over time.

Example:

Python

```
  I.    import matplotlib.pyplot as plt
 II.    days = [1,2,3,4,5]
```

III.   age =[72,82,61,11,27]

IV.   weight =[17,28,72,52,32]

V.   plt.plot([],[],color='c', label='age', linewidth=5)

VI.   plt.plot([],[],color='g', label='weight', linewidth=5)

VII.   plt.stackplot(days,age,weight,colors=['c','g'])

VIII.   plt.xlabel('x')

IX.   plt.ylabel('y')

X.   plt.title('Area Plot')

XI.   plt.legend()

XII.   plt.show()

5. Matplotlib Pie Chart

A pie chart is a circular diagram divided into segments or pieces. The proportional data or percentage where every piece of the pie represents a group is represented.

Example:

Python

I.   import matplotlib.pyplot as plt

II.   slices = [12,25,50,36]

III.   activities = ['Prescription drugs','clinical services','hospital services','other services']

IV.   cols = ['c','m','r','g']

V.   plt.pie(slices,

VI.   labels=activities,

VII.   colors=cols,

VIII.   startangle=90,

IX.   shadow= True,

X.   explode=(0,0.1,0,0),

XI.   autopct='%1.1f%%')

XII.   plt.title('Pie Plot')

XIII.   plt.show()

CHAPTER TWO

GET STARTED USING PYTHON ON WINDOWS FOR BEGINNERS

Set up your environment for development

We recommend that you install Python from the Microsoft Store for beginners new to Python. The Microsoft Store uses the basic Python3 interpreter, but also provides automatic updates and manages the PATH settings for the current user (avoid the need for admin access). This is particularly helpful if you are in an educational setting or an organization that limits permissions or administrative access to your computer.

We suggest a different setup for your development environment for you to use Python on Windows for web development. Instead of directly installing on Windows, we suggest that Python be installed and used via the Linux Windows Subsystem. See for help: Start using Python for Windows web development. If you want to automate common tasks on your framework, check out our guide: Start using Python for scripting and automation on Windows. You may want to allow the installation of the special Python update from python.org or suggest downloading an alternative such as Anaconda, PyPy, Jython, IrónPython, WinPython, etc. for certain advanced scenarios (like having to directly access / modify Python's installed files, create copies of binaries, or use Python DLLs). We would only recommend this if you are a more experienced Python programmer for a certain purpose.

Python Update

I. Installing Python via the Microsoft Store:
II. Go to the Start menu, type "Microsoft Shop," select the path to open a shop.
III. If the shop is open, choose Search from the top-right menu and type "Python." Open "Python 3.7" from the App performance. Choose Get.
IV. When the download and installation process is finished, Python will open Windows PowerShell using the Start menu (lower left icon of Windows). If PowerShell has been opened, enter the version of Python to verify that Python3 has enabled.
V. The Python installation of the Microsoft Store consists of pip, the standard package manager. Pip helps you to install and manage additional packages, not in the main Python library. In the pip —version, you can also check that pip is available to install and manage packages.

Install Artist Visual Code

You can use IntelliSense (code completion help), Linting (helping you to prevent errors in your code), debug support (helps you find errors in your code after running it), code snippets (templates for re-usable block code), and unit testing (try the user interface with different types of input).

The VS Code contains also the built-in terminal which allows you to create a seamless workflow between both the editor and command line by opening a Python command line with a Windows PowerShell, Command prompt, or whatever you prefer.

I. Download VS App for Windows to run VS App.

II. You must also install the Python extension once VS Code is installed. You can select the open or VS code VS Marketplace link to install the Python extension and search for Python from the extensions menu (Ctrl+Shift+X).

III. Python is an interpreted language, and you have to say VS Code which interpreter to use in order to execute Python code. We recommend that you stick to Python 3.7 unless you have a particular reason to choose anything else. If the Python extension has been installed, pick a Python 3 interpreter by opening Ctrl+Shift+P. Start by typing the Python command. Pick the Interpreter to scan then choose the command. You can also use the Python Environment option in the bottom Status Bar if available (a selected interpreter may already be displayed). A list of available interpreters, including virtual worlds, can be found automatically by VS Code. See Setting up Python environments if you don't see the right interpreter.

IV. To open a window, choose View > Terminal, or use the Ctrl+' shortcut (with the character backtick). PowerShell is the main terminal.

V. Open Python inside your VS code terminal simply by entering the command: python

VI. Check out the Python interpreter by entering: print. Python will return your statement "Hello World".

Git installation (optional)

If you plan to share or host your projects on an open-source platform with others on your Python code, VS Technology supports Git for version control. The VS Code's Source Control tab monitors any changes and has typical Git commands incorporated right into the user interface (add, attach, push, pull). To power the Source Control Panel, you must first install Git.

I. Download and update Git on the git-scm website for Windows.

II. There is an Update Wizard that will ask you a range of questions about your Git installation settings. All default settings are recommended unless you have a particular reason to change anything.
III. GitHub guides will help you get started if you have never worked with Git before.

Tutorial for some basics of Python

Python is a 'high-level programming language,' and its central philosophy of design concerns the readability of code and a syntax that enables programmers to express ideas within a few lines of code.'

Python is a script that is interpreted. Unlike languages that you have compiled in which the code you write must be translated to the machine code to be run through the processor on your computer, the Python code is directly passed on and run directly to an interpreter. You just type in and run your file. Let's do it!

I. Enter the Python to run the Python 3 interpreter with your PowerShell command line open. (Some instructions may also operate with the command py or python3). You will know that you are good because you will see a > > > prompt with three larger symbols.
II. There are some built-in methods to make changes in Python strings. Build a variable with: = 'Hello World! '. To enter a new line, click Enter.
III. Print with: print(value) the number. The text "Hello World!" is shown.
IV. Find your string variable's length, how many characters you use, with len(variable). This will indicate that 12 characters are used. (Note that in the total length the blank space is counted as a character.)
V. Convert your vector string to top-case letters: number.upper). Convert now to lowercase letters your string variable: variable.lower).
VI. Count how many times the string variable uses the letter "l": number.count("l).
VII. In your string list, search for a particular character, let's find a point of exclamation with variable.find!"). This indicates that the exclamation point is in the 11th position of the string character.
VIII. Replace the point of the exclamation by a question mark: variable.replace!"? (""").
IX. You can either enter exit), (quit), (or pick Ctrl-Z to exit Python.

Python tutorial with VS code

The VS Code team has built a great Python tutorial to start how to build a Hello World program with Python, to run the software file, to set up and run the debugger, and to install packages like matplotlib and NumPy in a virtual setting.

I. Go to this directory and open it in VS Code: Open PowerShell and create the empty folder called "hello"

Console:
mkdir hello
cd hello
code.

II. As VS Code opens, display your new hello folder in the left-hand explorer window, open a command-line window on the lower panel of VS Code by pressing Ctrl+' or choosing View > Terminal. Starting VS Code in a folder makes this folder your "workspace." VS Code saves settings in.vscode/settings.json unique to that environment, which are different from globally stored user settings.
III. Continue the VS code tutorial: Build a source code file of Python Hello World.

Build a simple Pygame game

Ygame is a common Python simulation kit – it enables students to learn programming while making something fun. In a new window, Pygame shows graphics such that the WSL command line solution will not work. However, if you have installed Python in this tutorial via the Microsoft Store, it will work fine.

I. If Python is installed, install Pygame from the command line (or terminal inside VS Code) by typing -U pygame —user to python-m pip update.
II. Try installing the sample game: python -m pygame.examples.aliens
III. All right, the game is going to open a window. When you finish playing, close the window.

Here's how you can start to write your own game.

I. Open PowerShell (or Windows Command Prompt) and create a blank "bounce" folder. Navigate to this folder and create the "bounce.py" file. Open the VS Code folder:

PowerShell:

```
mkdir bounce

cd bounce

new-item bounce.py

code.
```

II. Invoke the below Python code (or copy and paste it) using the VS code:

```python
Python
import sys, pygame

pygame.init()

size = width, height = 640, 480
dx = 1
dy = 1
x= 163
y = 120
black = (0,0,0)
white = (255,255,255)

screen = pygame.display.set_mode(size)

while 1:

    for event in pygame.event.get():
        if event.type == pygame.QUIT: sys.exit()

    x += dx
    y += dy
```

```python
if x < 0 or x > width:
    dx = -dx

if y < 0 or y > height:
    dy = -dy

screen.fill(black)

pygame.draw.circle(screen, white, (x,y), 8)

pygame.display.flip()
```

III. Save it as: bounce.py.

IV. Run it by accessing the: python bounce.py from PowerShell Terminal.

TOP 10 PYTHON PACKAGES WITH EXAMPLES

Python's simplicity is a big reason why it is one of the most popular programming languages. It is used in a broad range of disciplines, from basic physics science, machine learning, artificial intelligence (AI) to application development.

This widespread use is made possible partly by a broad standard library providing a variety of facilities designed to improve Python's flexibility and portability. This is augmented by the increasing number of Python Package Index (PyPI) packages and projects, which not only provide expanding Python capabilities to more field-specific applications but also improve Python's general usability. Here you can find a list of the most common packages downloaded from the Python Package Index.

Top 10 packages for Pythons (Popular and Useful)

Among the many different use cases in Python, some packages are particularly useful. If you use Python for ML or web applications, the following 10 packages deserve to be recognized and can only boost your experience with Python. We will begin with the absolutely necessary and end with the only essential:

1. Pip: Pip is the basic way to install and manage packages in Python as we have mentioned in a previous segment. Every Python distribution comes as standard to allow you to install, uninstall, upgrade, etc. on the command line. For instance, to install a specific PyPI piped package, run:

pip install "SomePackage"

Or for a specific package version:

pip install "SomePackage == 1.0"

The pip allows multiple sources to be installed and is not limited to the installation of PyPI-packages.

2. Six: Six is a Python 2 and 3 compatible library, which is particularly important in view of the number of applications that are currently being converted from Python 2 to 3 organizations, due to the death of Python 2. Six reconciles Python 2 and 3 variations and adapts on the basis of which version works locally. This enables Python programmers to write without much difficulty code compatible with both versions of Python.

For instance, iterating dictionary keys in Python 3 is done by:

for item in dictionary.items():

    #do something

In Python 2, iteration is done by:

for item in dictionary.iteritems():

    #do something

With Six, the syntax is:

import six

for item in six.iteritems(dictionary):

    #do something

3. The dateutil module provides a variety of date and time handling capabilities, such as calculating gap distance between various arbitrary dates, handling time zone data, and parsing datetime objects. It builds on Python's datetime module, which is simple and easy to use.

For Instance: to get the current local time,

from datetime import *

300

from dateutil.relativedelta import *

now = datetime.now()

To add an arbitrary number of months, days, and hours:

now + relativedelta(months=1, weeks=1, hour=10)

Or to query when the next Wednesday will occur:

now + relativedelta(weekday=WE(+1))

These are just a few instances, but the interface in general follows this pattern. The package is easy but can boost your Python experience dramatically when handling time series data.

4. Requests: Python requests are an HTTP library. It's based on urllib3 (another Python HTTP client), but it has a much easier and much more elegant syntax. It also incorporates a variety of other Python libraries to optimize flexibility while reducing complexity. The use of Urllib3 alone (or the combined urllib and urllib2) means that more flexibility and greater control are possible and more work is needed on the user's side. Therefore, requests are the chosen HTTP client in almost all Python instances. You can find the complete list of features here.

For example, here is how to make a Spotify request (no authentication necessary):

import requests

r = requests.get

r.status_code

A status code in the 200s shows success. The headers, encoding, and a host of other information can be extracted from here:

print(r.headers)

print(r.encoding)

5. Docutils: The Documentation Utility project offers a collection of tools for editing plaintext documents quickly in more usable file formats, including XMS, HTML, or LaTeX. For the most common processes, the project has built several front-end tools. This includes reading the input file, proper decoding (Parser tool), and composing the new file (Writer tool). The command prompt syntax follows a common structure for each of these tools:

toolname [options] [<source> [<destination>]]

6. Setuptools: The packages throughout this list are not included in Python's regular distribution, as stated earlier. So how does one deliver a shipment from a third party? The

integrated tool for this is known as distutils, which initially created a standard method to bundle Python code.

When third-party packages evolved, a divergence from the standard was achieved, this allowed the packages themselves to be more flexible and usable. Setuptools are the officially recommended method for doing this. It maintains all the functionality provided by distutils, extends to PyPI managed third party packages, and even those not. Pip and other Python installer packages work well.

The manual is very comprehensive for guidance on how to build your own package.

The syntax is as follows:

```
from setuptools import setup

setup(name='package_name',

version='0.1',

description='an example of a package',

url=' user/example_package',

author='Dante',

author_email='dante@example.com',

license='MIT',

packages=['example'],

zip_safe=False)
```

7. Pytest: Checking the reliability of code as a programmer is not only good practice, it is even simpler with pytest. The pytest package offers a simple bug-finding platform. Parallel checking, self-detection of test functions or modules, subset checking, and other customized functions can be carried out.

An instance of a small test:

```
# content of test_sample.py

def inc(x):

    return x + 1

def >test_answer():

    assert inc(3) == 5
```

8. NumPy: NumPy is the most popular package in Python for scientific and mathematical computing. It inaugurates n-dimensional arrays and matrices that are required for

sophisticated math. It requires basic operations on arrays such as sorting, shaping, and other mathematical matrix operations.

For instance, two 2×2 complex matrices are generated and the sum is printed:

```
import numpy as np
a = np.array([[1+2j, 2+1j], [3, 4]])
b = np.array([[5, 6+6j], [7, 8+4j]])
print(a+b)
```

And to take the complex conjugate of one of them:

```
np.conj(a)
```

9. Pandas: The DataFrame package introduces the new data structure, multidimensional, heterogeneous data and optimized for tabular. The package suply intuitive and practical ways to clean and manipulate your data after it has been converted to this format.

Manipulations such as merge, groupby, join, concatenated, or fill data may be executed in a single line, to replace and impute null values. The package developers have the primary objective of producing the most powerful data analysis and manipulation tool available in every language in the world — a daunting task they can actually achieve.

Creating a DataFrame:

```
import pandas as pd
df_1 = pd.DataFrame({'col1': [1,2], 'col2': [3,4]})
```

And to concatenate two dataframes together:

```
df_2 = pd.DataFrame({'col3': [5,6], 'col4': [7,8]})
df = pd.concat([df_1,df_2], axis = 1)
```

To perform a simple filtering operation, extracting the row that meets the logical condition:

```
df[df.col3 == 5]
```

10. SciPy: The SciPy kit builds on NumPy by offering scientific computation-critical functions and algorithms in technical areas. These are slightly more advanced than NumPy's operations, including optimization, interpolation, transformation, clustering, and data integration algorithms. These operations are necessary if any sort of data analysis is carried out or ML-based models are created.

In order to display interpolation, we use NumPy to construct some arbitrary data points and then compare various interpolation methods:

```
from scipy.interpolate import interp1d

import pylab

x = np.linspace(0, 5, 10)

y = np.exp(x) / np.cos(np.pi * x)

f_nearest = interp1d(x, y, kind='nearest')

f_linear  = interp1d(x, y)

f_cubic   = interp1d(x, y, kind='cubic')

x2 = np.linspace(0, 5, 100)

pylab.plot(x, y, 'o', label='data points')

pylab.plot(x2, f_nearest(x2), label='nearest')

pylab.plot(x2, f_linear(x2), label='linear')

pylab.plot(x2, f_cubic(x2), label='cubic')

pylab.legend()

pylab.show()
```

PYTHON CONFERENCES

Python Conferences

The culture of Python aims to coordinate regional low-cost events worldwide. Since then, other regional conferences have entered existing events such as EuroPython and PyCon, but instead, Python is often popular in different open source conferences.

Africa

- PyConNG (Nigeria)
- PyConZim (Zimbabwe)

Americas

- PyCon (North America)
- PyData Conference series on the Data Analytics and Python intersection

- PyCon Argentina (Argentina)

- PythonBrasil and Python Brazilian Community site (Brazil)

- SciPy conferences (Austin) – concentrate on scientific applications

- PyCon Canada (Ontario, Toronto, Canada)

- PyCarolinas (United States, North and South Carolina)

- PyOhio (Ohio, United States)

- PyTexas (Texas, United States)

- PyGotham (New York, United States)

- PyBay (California, United States)

Asia

- PyConAPAC

- PyConDhaka (Bangladesh)

- PyCon China (China)

- PyCon Hong Kong (Hong Kong)

- PyCon India (India)

- PyCon Indonesia (Indonesia)

- PyCon Iran (Iran)

- PyCon Japan (Japan)

- PyCon Singapore (Singapore)

- PyCon Korea (South Korea)

- PyCon Malaysia (Malaysia)

- PyCon Philippines (Philippines)

- PyCon Taiwan (Taiwan)

- PyCon Thailand (Thailand)

Australasia

- PyCon Australia

- Kiwi PyCon (New Zealand)

Europe

- EuroPython (Europe)

- EuroSciPy conference (Germany, France) - concentrate on scientific applications

- PyData (UK, Germany) - concentrate on the intersection of data analytics and

Python

- PyCon DE (Germany)

- PyCon FR (France)

- PyCon Ireland (Ireland)

- PyCon Italia (Italy)

- PyCon PL (Poland)

- PyCon UK (United Kingdom)

- RuPy (Poland) - a hybrid Python /Ruby conference

- Pycon UA (ex-USSR and Ukraine)

- Piter Py (Russia, Saint Petersburg)

- Moscow Python Conf (Russia, Moscow)

Open Source Conferences

Python has often featured in the following conference series and events:

- OSCON - features a Python track

- ConFoo Web Techno Conference - features a Python track

- EuroOSCON

- OSDC AU - a very strong Python track

PYTHON CODING STANDARDS

Follow PEP 8 plus the guidelines below for the Python code style.
Few strong Python code style links:
• Python guide from Hitchhiker's
• Style Guide for Google Python

How to label translation lines.

Use quotes only

• Use single quotes for literal text, for example, my identification, but use double quotes for strings that are more likely to include one quote characters (such as error messages or any text that includes natural language) as part of the string itself; e.g., "You have an error!."
• Single quotes are easier to read and write, but if a string contains single quotes it is safer to provide double quotes or cover the string in double-quotes.
• Single quotes are easier to read and write.

Imports

• Prevent generating loop imports only by importing more specialized modules than the one you change.
Instead of importing names directly, CKAN often uses code imported into a data structure. For example, only get action is used to access logic functions by CKAN controllers. This allows CKAN plugins to be customized.

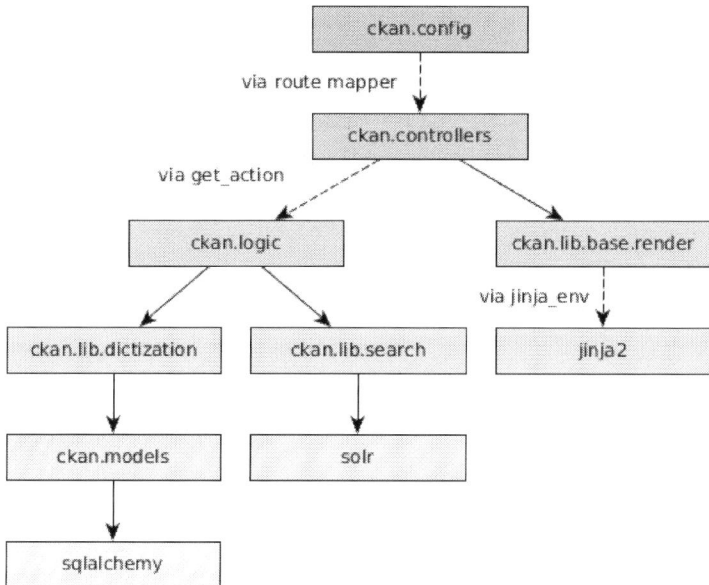

• Do not use the import module *. List the names you need specifically instead:

• from module import name1, name2

If the names are longer than one line, use parenthesis:

from module import (name1, name2, ...

   name12, name13)

Most of the existing CKAN code base only imports the modules and accesses names with the.name module. This makes circular imports in some cases and may even be appropriate for code exiting, but for new code is not recommended.

• Render all imports after the module docstring at the start of the file. Imports in the following order should be grouped:

1. Import standard library

2. Imports from third parties

3. imports of CKAN

Logging

We use the logging module from the Python Standard Library to log messages in CKAN, for example:

import logging

...

logger = logging.getLogger(__name__)

...

logger.debug('some debug message')

$#%^&^&)(*&(%(_+)_)*&^E#@$#%$^&*()

When logging:

• Keep log messages short.

• Do not include in the log message object representations. It is helpful, if possible, to provide a domain model identifier.

• Choose a suitable log level (INFO, DEBUG, WARNING ERROR, or CRITICAL).

Don't use the formatting of the old %s type, for example, "i am a %s" % sub. This layout of strings is not useful for internationalization.

Instead, use the new format() method and send meaningful names, for instance:

_(' ... {foo} ... {bar} ...').format(foo='foo-value', bar='bar-value')

Some useful tools for consistency of Python code

You can search your Python code for PEP8 compliance and general code quality with different tools. We suggest that you use them.

• pep8 can search your Python code for any of the PEP 8 Type Agreements. As mentioned above, only the master conducts style cleanups to prevent false mergers.

• Pylint analyzes Python source code to check for low-quality bugs and signals.

• Pyflakes also analyzes error detection programs in Python.

• Flake8 is a single tool that combines both pep8 and pyflakes.

• Syntastic is a Flake8, pyflakes, and pylint Vim plug-in.

CHAPTER THREE

PYTHON INTERPRETER

We want Python files to be generated in a text editor. Text editors are a personal matter of preference. Python won't mind as long as the indentation is clear. For those who do not already have an option of a shell editor, the Gedit Editor shown in Chapter 1 has a graphical user interface and is easy to use. Besides highlighting syntaxes, gedit manages automatic indentation and makes it easier to avoid errors in white space that could lead to Python failure.

The scripts of Python are .py files. For example, hello.py may be our first script. Try typing gedit hello.py to build a quick script in order to use gedit.

Python file layout

Formatting in Python is critical. A whitespace indentation is used by the Python interpreter to evaluate which pieces of code are grouped together in a particular way — for example as part of a method, loop, or class. How much space is usually used is not essential, provided it is consistent. If two spaces are first used for indenting, two spaces are then used for indentation.

Python Running Files

Let's comfortably write a fast and simple script with Python. Copy a text editor with the following code and save it as hello.py:

#! /usr /bin /python

user = "<your name>"

print "Hello " + user + "!"

This is described by line one as a Python script. This line is usually not required for scripts written in Windows, but it can be used irrespective of the platform for cross-compatibility. It gives the way to the executable Python that is running our software. Inline two, we allocate our name to a user variable. Then, we print the results and enter the text with the concatenation operator, a plus symbol, in the rest of the paragraph. Let's do it! Let's do it!

We may simply run our script in the shell window by typing python hello.py. In addition to running Python scripts, Linux or UNIX environments provide a second way: We can run a script in Chmod u+x hello.py and then ./hello.py. For now, let's make it happen with Kali!

You've seen a range of attacks and tactics in the earlier studies that can be used when you've encountered a weak program. You may have noted, however, that most of these attacks involve a wide range of requests for decent knowledge from the remote database. Depending on the case, you may need to fingerprint the remote database server correctly, and maybe hundreds (or even thousands) to get the data you are interested in. Manually preparing a large number of requests, but don't worry: many tools will automate the whole process, enabling you to relax when observing the tables on your computer.

Chart of the square

It is possibly "par excellence" at the time of this writing, thanks to its incredible list of features and very successful mailing list. In almost all cases, it will benefit you because it promotes the following DB technologies:

• SQL Server from Microsoft

• Access to Microsoft

• Oracle

• MySQL

• PostgreSQL

• SQLite

• Firebird

• Sybase

• MaxDB SAP

Not only is sqlmap an exploitation tool, but it can also help you identify weak injection points. When one or more SQL injections on the target host are detected, you can choose from different options (depending on your situation and privileges):

• Perform a comprehensive fingerprint back-end database server.

• Recover the user and client session of the database server.

• List users, hashes of password, rights, and databases.

• Dump all database server table/columns or individual database server table/columns, using different methods to maximize extraction and reduce the time required for an attack.

• Run custom SQL statements.

- Read arbitrary files.

- Execute operating system level commands.

Sqlmap is built in Python that separates the tool from the underlying code, so only the Python interpreter version of 2.4 is required. Sqlmap also applies different strategies for leveraging the vulnerability of SQL injection:

- UNION SQL injection query both when all rows are returned in one answer and when only one row is returned.

- Support for the stacked query.

- SQL inference injection. For each HTTP response, the tool calculates the value of the statement character output by character by making a comparison based on HTML page text hashes or string match. The bisection algorithm used in sqlmap to perform this technology will pick at most seven HTTP requests for each output character, this is the default SQL injection technique for sqlmap.

As its entry, sqlmap accepts a single aim URL, a list of goals from WebScarab or Burp log files, or a "Google dork" that searches the search engine and parses its results page. All the GET / POST parameters, HTTP cookies, HTTP User-Agent header values given are automatically checked by sqlmap, or by overriding the behavior and setting the parameters you need to test. Sqlmap also supports multi-threading to speed up blind SQL injection algorithms; it calculates the time to complete an assault according to the rate of requests performed, and it saves and retrieves the current session later. It also integrates with other open source security projects including Metasploit and w3af.

It can also be used to connect directly to a database and attack between them without a Web application (as long as the database credentials are available, of course).

Bobcat

Bobcat has various features, including the listing and dumping of connected servers, elevating privileges, brute forcing accounts, dumping data, and executing operating system commands, to help compromise a vulnerable application and help hack a database server. In Web applications, Bobcat is able to exploit SQL injection vulnerabilities regardless of its language but is reliant on the SQL server for the backend database. Local Microsoft SQL Server or Microsoft SQL Server Desktop Engine (MSDE) installation is also needed.

The Program also uses the erroneous way of leveraging SQL injection vulnerabilities, which allows for operation when an adequate egress filtering is given for a remote database server.

312

BSQL

BSQL, developed by Ferruh Mavituna, is a very interesting tool for Windows boxes. Even if its production appears discontinued in favor of Netsparker (commercial product), it operated extremely well under the OWASP SQLiBENCH project, an automated SQL injector benchmarking project that performs data extraction and thus deserves notice.

BSQL is published under GPLv2, runs on any installed .NET Framework 2 Windows computer, and is fitted with an automatic installer. It promotes error-based injection and blind injection and provides an interesting alternative solution to time-based injection in which time-outs are applied depending on the value of the character to be extracted so that with each request more than 1 bit can be extracted.

In the following databases, BSQL can locate SQL extract information and injection vulnerabilities:

• Oracle

• SQL Server

• MySQL

BSQL is multi-threaded and is very easy to configure by clicking on the Injection Wizard button in the window. The wizard will ask you to enter the target URL and the parameters in the request and then run a number of tests to identify vulnerabilities in the parameters checked. You will be informed if a vulnerable parameter is found and the actual extraction attack will begin.

Other Tools

You have a brief overview of some tools which can help you to efficiently extract data but keep in mind that several other tools can do an extremely good job. The following are among the most popular:

• FG-Injection Framework (http://sourceforge.net/projects/injection-fwk/)

• Havij (http://itsecteam.com/en/projects/project1.htm)

• SqlInjector (http://www.woanware.co.uk/?page_id=19)

• SQLGET (www.infobytecom.ar)

• Sqlsus (http://sqlsus.sourceforge.net/)

- Pangolin (http://www.nosec-inc.com/en/products/pangolin/)

- Absinthe (http://0x90.org/releases/absinthe/)

PYTHON BASICS

Python is one of today's most popular programming languages. It is commonly used in many market fields, such as programming, machine learning, web development, and data science. Considering its widespread use, it is not surprising that Python has exceeded Java as the top language for programming.

Python is a high-level structured programming language that is represented in plain terms. Python's father Guido van Rossum had clear objectives in mind when creating it, quick to look at readable, code and open source. Python is the 3rd most prominent language followed by JavaScript and Java in a 2018 survey of Stack Overflow, which demonstrates its development.

Python Features

Python is currently my favorite language for its simplicity, strong libraries and readability. You could be an old school coder or a totally new programmer, Python is the best way to start!

Python offers the following features:

- Simplicity: think less about language syntax and more about code.

- Open Source: a powerful language, free to use and change if necessary.

- Portability: Code Python can be shared and will function as expected. Seamless and unpleasant.

- Embedding & Extensible: Python may have other language snippets inside for certain functions.

- Interpreted: Python himself takes care of the issues about massive memory tasks and other heavy Processing tasks so you can just think about coding.

- Massive library volume: data science? You've studied Python. Web development? Web development? You already have Python protected. Still. Still.

- Object Orientation: Objects tend to interrupt complicated real-life problems in such a way that solutions can be encoded and solved.

To summarize, Python has a simple syntax, can be interpreted and has great support from the community. You may ask now, "What can you do if you know Python?" Okay, you have a range of choices.

- Data Scientist

- Artificial Intelligence and Machine Learning

- Internet of affairs

- Web development

- Analysis of data

- Automation

Now, if you know that Python is so awesome, why don't we start with the Python Basics?

Jump to the basics of Python

To get the Python Basics started, you need to install Python right first on your system? So now let's do that! You should be aware that most Linux and Unix distributions have a Python version out of their box these days. You can follow this step-by - step guide to set up yourself.

If you are set up, the first project has to be developed. Take the following steps:

- Creating Project, entering name and click create.

- Right-click on the folder of the project and use New->File->Python File to create a Python file and type the file name

OOPS

Older programming languages were designed to allow any code module to access the data. It could lead to potential security problems that lead developers to shift to object-oriented programming which could allow us to simulate real-world examples into code in order to obtain better solutions.

There are 4 OOPS concepts that are important to understand. They are as follows:

- Heritage: The heritage helps one to extract and alter attributes and techniques from the parent class. The simplest example would be for a car explaining the layout of a vehicle and explaining sports cars, sedans and so on.

Encapsulation: Encapsulation links data and objects together to prevent other objects and classes from accessing data. Python has private, secured and public forms whose names show what they are doing. To define private or secure keywords, Python uses '_' or '__'

- Polymorphism: This makes it possible for us to provide a similar interface for different types of data. You can have also more names with different data.

- Abstraction: Abstraction may be used by modeling classes relevant to the problem to simplify complex reality.

PYTHON SHELL

An easy way to run Python Node.js scripts with basic but efficient communication between processes and good error handling.

Characteristics

• Spawn Python scripts reliably in a child process

• JSON, Built-in text, and binary modes

• Specific parsers and formatters

• Simple and efficient stdin and stdout data transfers

• Extended tracks when a bug is thrown

Installation

npm install python-shell

To run the tests:

npm test

Documentation

Running python code:

```
import {PythonShell} from 'python-shell';
```

```
PythonShell.runString('x=1+1;print(x)', null, function (err) {
  if (err) throw err;
  console.log('finished');
});
```

If the script exits a non-zero code, an error is thrown.

Note the use of imports! If you're not using typescript ಠ_ಠ you can still get imports to work with this guide.

Or you can use require like so:

```
let {PythonShell} = require('python-shell')
```

Running a Python script:

```
import {PythonShell} from 'python-shell';

PythonShell.run('my_script.py', null, function (err) {
  if (err) throw err;
  console.log('finished');
});
```

If the script exits with a non-zero code, an error will be thrown.

Running a Python script with options and arguments:

```
import {PythonShell} from 'python-shell';

let options = {
  mode: 'text',
  pythonPath: 'path/to/python',
  pythonOptions: ['-u'], // get print results in real-time
  scriptPath: 'path/to/my/scripts',
  args: ['value1', 'value2', 'value3']
};

PythonShell.run('my_script.py', options, function (err, results) {
  if (err) throw err;
  // results is an array consisting of messages collected during execution
  console.log('results: %j', results);
});
```

Exchanging data between Python and Node:

```
import {PythonShell} from 'python-shell';
let pyshell = new PythonShell('my_script.py');
```

```
// sends a message to the Python script via stdin

pyshell.send('hello');


pyshell.on('message', function (message) {

  // received a message sent from the Python script (a simple "print" statement)

  console.log(message);

});


// end the input stream and allow the process to exit

pyshell.end(function (err,code,signal) {

  if (err) throw err;

  console.log('The exit code was: ' + code);

  console.log('The exit signal was: ' + signal);

  console.log('finished');

});
```

To send a message to the Python script use .send(message). Listen to messages emitted from the Python script when you attach the message event to

To quickly set up how data is sent and received between your Python and Node applications, use options.mode.

• use text mode for exchanging lines of text

• use json mode for exchanging JSON fragments

• use binary mode for anything else (data is sent and received as-is)

Error Handling and extended stack traces

If the process leaves a non-zero exit code, an error will be thrown. In addition, if "stderr" contains a formatted Python traceback, Python exception details including a concatenated stack track increase the error.

Sample error with traceback (from test/python/error.py):

Traceback (most recent call last):
  File "test/python/error.py", line 6, in <module>
    divide_by_zero()
  File "test/python/error.py", line 4, in divide_by_zero
    print 1/0
ZeroDivisionError: integer division or modulo by zero

would result into the following error:

{ [Error: ZeroDivisionError: integer division or modulo by zero]

  traceback: 'Traceback (most recent call last):\n File "test/python/error.py", line 6, in <module>\n   divide_by_zero()\n File "test/python/error.py", line 4, in divide_by_zero\n   print 1/0\nZeroDivisionError: integer division or modulo by zero\n',

  executable: 'python',

  options: null,

  script: 'test/python/error.py',

  args: null,

  exitCode: 1 }

and err.stack would look like this:

Error: ZeroDivisionError: integer division or modulo by zero
    at PythonShell.parseError (python-shell/index.js:131:17)
    at ChildProcess.<anonymous> (python-shell/index.js:67:28)
    at ChildProcess.EventEmitter.emit (events.js:98:17)
    at Process.ChildProcess._handle.onexit (child_process.js:797:12)
    ----- Python Traceback -----
    File "test/python/error.py", line 6, in <module>
      divide_by_zero()
    File "test/python/error.py", line 4, in divide_by_zero
      print 1/0

API Reference

PythonShell(script, options) constructor

319

Creates an instance of PythonShell and starts the Python process

- script: the path of the script to execute

- options: the execution options, consisting of:

o   mode: Configures how data is exchanged when data flows through stdin and stdout. The possible values are:

☐   text: each line of data (ending with "\n") is emitted as a message (default)

☐   json: each line of data (ending with "\n") is parsed as JSON and emitted as a message

☐   binary: data is streamed as-is through stdout and stdin

o   formatter: each message to send is transformed using this method, then appended with "\n"

o   parser: each line of data (ending with "\n") is parsed with this function and its result is emitted as a message

o   stderrParser: each line of logs (ending with "\n") is parsed with this function and its result is emitted as a message

o   encoding: the text encoding to apply on the child process streams (default: "utf8")

o   pythonPath: The path where to locate the "python" executable. Default: "python"

o   pythonOptions: Array of option switches to pass to "python"

o   scriptPath: The default path where to look for scripts. Default is the current working directory.

o   args: Array of arguments to pass to the script

Other options are forwarded to child_process.spawn.

PythonShell instances have the following properties:

- script: the path of the script to execute

- command: the full command arguments passed to the Python executable

- stdin: the Python stdin stream, used to send data to the child process

- stdout: the Python stdout stream, used for receiving data from the child process

- stderr: the Python stderr stream, used for communicating errors & logs

- childProcess: the process example created through child_process.spawn

- terminated: boolean indicating whether the method has exited

- exitCode: the process exit code, available after the process has ended

Example:

320

```
// create a new instance

let shell = new PythonShell('script.py', options);
```

PYTHON AUTO-COMPLETION

Python Version Support

Sublime Jedi Plugin	Branch	Jedi version	Sublime Text 2			Sublime Text 3		
Python 3.3			Python 2.6.x	Python 2.7.x	Python >3.3	Python 2.6.x	Python 2.7.x	Python >3.3
>= 0.14.0	master	>=0.13.2	✗	✓	✓	✗	✗	✓
>= 0.12.0	master	>=0.12.0	✗	✓	✓	✓	✗	✓
< 0.12.0	st2	0.11.1	✓	✓	✓	✓	✓	✓

Installation

with Git

cd ~/.config/sublime-text-2/Packages/

git clone https://github.com/srusskih/SublimeJEDI.git "Jedi - Python autocompletion"

with Sublime Package Control

- Open command pallet (default: ctrl+shift+p)
- Type package control install and select command Package Control: Install Package
- Type Jedi and select Jedi - Python autocompletion

Settings for the Python interpreter

By default, SublimeJEDI will use the default Python interpreter from the PATH. For each Sublime Project, you can also set different interpreters.

To configure the project-related Python interpreter, you must edit the settings file of your project. By default, the name of the file looks like the name of the group.

For example, you can set Python interpreters and external python package directories by using:

```
# <project name>.sublime-project
{
  // ...

  "settings": {
    // ...
    "python_virtualenv": "$project_path/../../virtual/",
    "python_interpreter": "$project_path/../../virtual/bin/python",

    "python_package_paths": [
      "$home/.buildout/eggs",
      "$project_path/addons"
    ]
  }
}
```

SublimeREPL integration

SublimeREPL was turned off by default completion for. If you want use autocompletion feature of SublimeJEDI in a repl, please set enable_in_sublime_repl: true in User/sublime_jedi.sublime-setting or in your project setting.

Autocomplete on DOT

If you want a dot to automatically complete, you can specify a trigger for the Python preferences or Sublime User :

```
# User/Preferences.sublime-settings or User/Python.sublime-settings
{
  // ...
```

```
    "auto_complete_triggers": [{"selector": "source.python", "characters": "."}],
}
```

If you want auto-completion only with dot and not during typing, you can set it (in addition to the above trigger):

User/Preferences.sublime-settings or User/Python.sublime-settings

```
{
    // ...
    "auto_complete_selector": "-",
}
```


Find Related Names ("Find Usages")

Find function / method / variable / class usage, definition.

Shortcut: ALT+SHIFT+F.

There are two settings related to finding usages:

highlight_usages_on_select: highlights usages of symbol in file when symbol is selected (default false)

highlight_usages_color: color for highlighted symbols (default "region.bluish")

other available options are "region.redish", "region.orangish", "region.yellowish", "region.greenish", "region.bluish", "region.purplish", "region.pinkish", "region.blackish"

these colors are actually scopes that were added to Sublime Text around build 3148.

Show Python Docstring

Show docstring as tooltip.

For ST2: Show docstring in output panel.

Shortcut: CTRL+ALT+D.

Styling Python Docstring

When mdpopups are available, docstring tooltips are displayed. To change the theme, follow the styling guide of mdpopups.

Basically a Packages/User/mdpopups.css is required to define your own style.

To specify rules which apply to Jedi tooltips only, use .jedi selector as displayed in the following example.

```
/* JEDI's python function signature */
.jedi .highlight {
    font-size: 1.1rem;
}


/* JEDI's docstring titles


  h6 is used to highlight special keywords in the docstring such as


  Args:
  Return:
*/
.jedi h6 {
    font-weight: bold;
}
```

Logging

The plugin uses Python to log all libs. It allows proper data to be obtained correctly rather than print()-ing to a sublime terminal. To make logging more helpful, it can allow stream logs into file/console / etc to support ST Plugin Logging Power. You can find great documentation on the github website, how you can use it.

```
{
    "logging_enable_on_startup": false,
    "logging_use_basicConfig": false,
    "logging_root_level": "DEBUG",
```

```
    "logging_console_enabled": true,

    "logging_console_level": "INFO",     // Only print warning log messages in the console.

    "logging_file_enabled": true,

    "logging_file_level": "DEBUG",

    "logging_file_datefmt": null,

    "logging_file_fmt": "%(asctime)s %(levelname)-6s - %(name)s:%(lineno)s -
%(funcName)s() - %(message)s",

    "logging_file_path": "/tmp/sublime_output.log",

    "logging_file_rotating": false,

    "logging_file_clear_on_reset": false
}
```

CHAPTER FOUR

PYTHON MAGIC COMMANDS

Magic commands or magic functions are an important improvement compared to the standard Python shell that IPython provides. These magic commands are designed to solve common problems in Python data analysis. In reality, they regulate IPython 's behavior.

Magic commands serve as easy functions in which the most normal syntax of Python is not. They are useful for integrating invalid python syntax into your workflow.

Magic Command forms

Two types of magic commands exist −

• The magic of the line

• The magic of cells

Magic of Line

They are similar to calling on the command line. They begin with a % character of percent. The remainder of the line is the argument passed without parentheses or citations. Line magics can be used as an expression and the attribute can be given their return value.

Magic of cells

They have a %% character prefix of one. They can run on several lines below their call, unlike line magic functions. In reality, they can make arbitrary changes to the input they obtain which do not even have to be a valid Python code. The entire block is received as a single string.

Using the magic command to learn more about magic features, built-in magic, and their docstrings. Is knowledge of a particular magic function obtained by %magicfunction? Command.

Pasting Code Blocks: %paste and %cpaste

One popular gocha is to paste multi-line code blocks while functioning in the IPython interpreter, particularly while indentation and interpreters are involved. One common case is that you will find a sample code on a website and would like to paste it into your interpreter. Take the following basic function:

```
>>> def donothing(x):
...     return x
```

The code is written as shown in the Python interpreter, and if you directly copy it into IPython, an error occurs:

```
In [2]: >>> def donothing(x):
   ...:    ...     return x
   ...:
  File "<ipython-input-20-5a66c8964687>", line 2
    ...     return x
           ^
SyntaxError: invalid syntax
```

The translator is frustrated with the additional prompt characters in the direct paste. But never fear – the magic %Paste feature of IPython is built to handle this particular type of marked multi-line input:

```
In [3]: %paste
>>> def donothing(x):
...     return x
```

326

-- End pasted text –

The %paste command enters and implements the code, so the function is will be ready to use:

In [4]: donothing(10)

Out[4]: 10

A related command is a %cpaste that opens an interactive multi-line prompt in which one or more parts of code can be pasted for execution in a batch:

In [5]: %cpaste

Pasting code; enter '--' alone on the line to stop or use Ctrl-D.

:>>> def donothing(x):

:...   return x

:--

Like others we can see, these magic commands provide features that would be difficult or even impossible in a standard Python interpreter.

Running External Code: %run

When you start creating a more detailed code, you'll probably be using both IPython for collective exploration and a text editor to save code you want to reuse. Instead of running this code in a new window, running it in your IPython session is easy. This can be done with the magic of the %run.

For instance, imagine creating a myscript.py file that contains the following contents:

```
#-------------------------------------
# file: myscript.py


def square(x):
    """square a number"""
    return x ** 2
```

```
for N in range(1, 4):
    print(N, "squared is", square(N))
```

From your IPython session you may perform this as follows:

In [6]: %run myscript.py

1 squared is 1

2 squared is 4

3 squared is 9

PYTHON SCALAR TYPES

Scalars

Python describes only one version of a specific data class (only one version of integer, one type of floating-point, etc.). This is useful for applications that do not have to deal with all the ways data can be displayed on a computer. However, more control is often required for scientific computing.

There are 24 new simple Python forms in NumPy to define multiple kinds of scalars. These type descriptors are based mainly on the C-language forms that are written into the CPython, with some other Python-compatible forms.

Array scalars have the same methods and properties as ndarrays. This allows you to treat array items on the same basis as arrays, smoothing out rough edges that result when mixing scalars and arrays.

The array scalars reside in the hierarchy of data types (see Figure below). They can be detected using hierarchy. For instance, if val is an array scalar object, isinstance(val, np.generic) will return true. Alternatively, it can be calculated what type of scalar array is present with the aid of other data type members. For example, if val is a complex-valued type, isinstance(val, np.complexfloating), while isinstance(val, np.flexible) returns true, if val is one of the flexible element array types (string, unicode, void).

PYTHON BUILT-IN DATA

Built-in Types

The following parts define the typical forms implemented in the interpreter.

Sequences, numerics, mappings, instances, classes, and exceptions are the key built-in styles.

Some groups in the set are mutable. The methods by which their members are inserted, subtracted, or rearranged and no particular item is returned will never return the set instance itself but none.

Some operations can be supported by various object types; in particular, almost all objects can be compared for equality, truth-tested, and transformed into a string (with the repr() function or with slightly different str() method). The latter function is used implicitly when the print() function is written to an object.

Truth Value Testing

Any object can be checked for the true value, for use as an operand of the following Boolean operations, or in a state.

By default, an item is considered true unless its class specifies a __bool__() returning False method or __len__() returning zero when called by the item. 1 Most interconnected artifacts are considered false here: 1

constants defined to be false: None and False.

zero of any numeric type: 0, 0.0, 0j, Decimal(0), Fraction(0, 1)

empty sequences and collections: '', (), [], {}, set(), range(0)

A type of data is a set of values and a set of operations on these values. Many forms of data are integrated into the Python language. In this section we look at Python's built-in data types str (for sequences of characters) float (for floating-point numbers), int (for integers), and bool (for true-false values).

type	set of values	common operators	sample literals
int	integers	+ - * // % **	99 12 2147483647
float	floating-point numbers	+ - * / **	3.14 2.5 6.022e23
bool	true-false values	and or not	True False
str	sequences of characters	+	'AB' 'Hello' '2.5'

Basic built-in data types

We need to use some terms to speak about data types. To do this, we begin with the above code fragment:

a = 1234

b = 99

c = a + b

Python has either the above standard or integrated data types:

GETTING STARTED WITH PANDAS

We will explain in this section how Pandas in Python can be used. Pandas are one of the most common python modules that can be used with python for data handling and analysis. In essence, it offers a simple interface for communicating with flowing knowledge and transforming it on the go. This module is subject to the BSD license and can be used free of charge. This module can be downloaded via the website or the python package manager.

Pandas offer us a variety of data analysis options, such as reading data from files and databases, introducing different transformations across data frames, cutting and dicing data, and then writing the data back to a database or preparing the data for use as a visualization tool. In the python framework, Pandas can also visualize the data by importing other modules named matplotlib and showing stunning visuals. However, we will only continue to learn Pandas in python for the purpose of this chapter.

What can be done in python with Pandas?

For your data applications, it can be considered as bread and butter. Whenever you think about playing with python data, the first thing you can think about is using Pandas to wrangle the data into your sandbox. The cleaning of the data can be started by eliminating unnecessary data, transforming the data through the use of business logic, and then preparing the data for display.

Let's take an example where you want to read data from a CSV file on your device or on a shared network site. Using Pandas, you can easily link and obtain information from the CSV file and build a data frame in your python environment.

If the data is in the python, you can perform several operations, some of them as follows.

If the data is in the python, you can perform several operations, some of them as follows.

• The basic statistics of your dataset can be measured and answered common questions such as the mean, median, minimum and maximum values

• A link between two or more columns can also be found on the dataset

• Clean data by deleting incomplete and blank values and filter registrations based on a criterion

• Visualize data through other modules such as matplotlib, seaborn, etc.

• Save cleaning data frame into a CSV or your preference database

How does it fit into the world of data?

If you work as a computer engineer or data scientist, you might have encountered Pandas during the production of applications already. However, for a beginner, we recommend that you understand essentially how Python runs, the different data structures in Python, including iterations, lists, tuples of dictionaries, etc.

The Pandas module was built on top of a common NumPy module. This indicates that there are very similar data structures between these two modules. The data in Pandas can be used to supply other packages like SciPy, for scientific analysis or for Matplotlib to visualize, etc. It can also be used in machine learning modules such as Scikit-learn as a source.

Installation and configuration of Pandas

Up until now, we've learned what Pandas library is in python and different stuff. Now let's go ahead and see how we can install this on our computer and start using it.

Creating Python Data Frames Pandas

The data structure is the fundamental structure of a Pandas library. The data frame is essentially a 2-D array representation. The data frame can also be interpreted as a memory table where you can perform all operations as previously mentioned. Whenever we operate with the Pandas module, we can try to fit the data into a data structure so that all built-in methods can be used directly.

There are many ways to construct a data frame. Let us try and create the similar from two dictionaries for the sake of this segment. Remember, for example, we have a list of staff and their respective divisions. We can therefore construct a simple dictionary with two lists containing the details. To build the dictionary, you can use the code below.

```
data = {
    'employees':['Bob','Jack'],
```

'department':['IT','Customer Service']

}

Descriptive statistics

Descriptive statistics (mean, standard deviation, number of observations, minimum, maximum, and quartile) can be determined with the .describe() techniques that return a descriptive statistic pandas data frame.

In [1]: df = pd.DataFrame({'A': [1, 2, 1, 4, 3, 5, 2, 3, 4, 1],

'B': [12, 14, 11, 16, 18, 18, 22, 13, 21, 17],

'C': ['a', 'a', 'b', 'a', 'b', 'c', 'b', 'a', 'b', 'a']})

In [2]: df
Out[2]:

```
   A   B  C
0  1  12  a
1  2  14  a
2  1  11  b
3  4  16  a
4  3  18  b
5  5  18  c
6  2  22  b
7  3  13  a
8  4  21  b
9  1  17  a
```


In [3]: df.describe()
Out[3]:

```
              A          B
count  10.000000  10.000000
mean    2.600000  16.200000
```

std	1.429841	3.705851
min	1.000000	11.000000
25%	1.250000	13.250000
50%	2.500000	16.500000
75%	3.750000	18.000000
max	5.000000	22.000000

Note that since C is not a numerical column, it is excluded from the output.

In [4]: df['C'].describe()

Out[4]:

```
count    10
unique    3
freq      5
Name: C, dtype: object
```

The process summarizes the categorical data, in this case, by the number of observations, the number of unique elements, mode, and mode frequency.

If Pandas is installed, you can check if it works properly by constructing a randomly distributed value dataset.

```
import pandas as pd  # This is always assumed but is included here as an introduction.

import numpy as np

import matplotlib.pyplot as plt


np.random.seed(0)


values = np.random.randn(100) # array of normally distributed random numbers

s = pd.Series(values) # generate a pandas series

s.plot(kind='hist', title='Normally distributed random values') # hist computes distribution

plt.show()
```

CHAPTER FIVE

DATA PREPARATION

Good data planning facilitates accurate analysis, reduces inaccuracies and errors that can be recorded in data processing, and improves user usability to all processed data. The new tools that allow any user to clean and apply data on their own have made it easier.

What is Data Preparation?

The method of data collection before processing and analysis is the method of cleaning and processing raw data. It is an important step before processing and frequently includes data reformatting, correcting data, and merging data sets to expand data.

Data preparedness is always a long undertaking for data practitioners or business users, but it is important to place data in perspective so that information can be translated and prejudices from poor data quality are removed.

For example, standardization of enriching source data, data formats, and/or eliminating outliers typically require the data preparation process.

Data planning benefits + the cloud

76 percent of data scientists agree that data processing is the hardest aspect of their work, but clean data can only be used for effective, reliable business decisions. Helps data preparation:

• Fix errors fast — Data planning helps to detect errors prior to processing. These errors become harder to understand and correct after data has been separated from its actual source.

• Deliver top-quality data — Datasets are cleaned and reformatted to ensure the high quality of the data used in analytics.

• Taking better business decisions — better data collection and analysis will lead to accurate, reliable, and high-quality business choices, quicker and more effective.

Moreover, as data and data processing moves into the cloud, data planning moves to further gain, for example:

• Superior scalability — The preparation of cloud data will expand at the company pace. The organization does not have to worry or attempt to predict the decisions about the underlying infrastructure.

• Future proof – Cloud data planning automatically updates to allow new features or issue fixes to be enabled once released. This helps companies to remain ahead without interruption even with increased costs of the innovation curve.

• Accelerated data use and collaboration — Processing data in the cloud ensures that it is already available, does not need software implementation, and encourages teams to work together to produce quicker performance.

A nice, cloud-based data preparation tool can also give other advantages (such as an intuitive and easy-to-use GUI) for faster and effective preparation.

The data preparation method details differ according to sector, organization, and needs, but essentially the same structure remains.

1. Collect data

The phase of data processing starts with the correct data. This can be accessed from an existing data set or incorporated ad hoc.

2. Find and test data

After data collection, it is critical that each dataset is discovered. This step is to study the data and to understand what needs to be done before the data are useful in a given context.

Discovery is a major challenge, but the data preparation framework from Talend provides visualization tools that help users identify and navigate their data.

3. Clean and validate data

Data cleaning is typically the most time-consuming aspect of data preparation, but it is important to delete obsolete data and fill in gaps.

Relevant tasks here are:

•   Removing extraneous data and outliers.

•   Filling in missing values.

•   Conforming data to a standardized pattern.

•   Masking private or sensitive data entries.

If the data has been cleaned, it must be checked to this stage by checking for errors in data preparation. Sometimes, a system error becomes evident in this phase and must be corrected before continuing.

4. Transforming and enriching data

Data transformation means the process of changing the format or value entries to achieve a well-defined result or to make it easier for a broader audience to understand the data. Enhancing data involves incorporating and linking data to other relevant information for more in-depth analysis.

5. Data storage

After the data has been compiled, it can be processed or transmitted to a third-party program, such as a business intelligence platform, which can determine the means of processing and analysis.

Data Preparation tools for self-service

Data preparation is a very effective process but often involves intensive resource expenditure. Data researchers and data analysts estimate that 80% of their time is spent on data preparation rather than analysis.

Does the data team have time to test the data thoroughly? What about companies with no data scientists or data analysts?

This is where self-service platforms such as Talend Data Preparation are implemented. Cloud-native learning systems simplify the data preparation process. Instead of cleaning up, data scientists and business users should concentrate on analyzing the results.

However, it also helps businesses that lack specialized IT expertise to manage the process themselves. This makes the preparation of data more a team activity instead of spending scarce time and cycles on the teams.

To get the best value from a self-service data preparation tool, look for a platform with:

• Data access and exploration from any dataset — from files in Excel and CSV to data stores, data lakes, and cloud applications like Salesforce.com.

• Works for washing and enrichment.

• Auto-discovery, standardization, classification, insightful feedback, and data show.

• Export file functions (Excel, Server, Tableau, etc.) alongside managed export to data storage facilities and corporate applications.

• Data processing and data sets are exchanged.

• Automatic reporting, versioning, and operationalization functionality in ETL processes.

Data Planning Future

At first, data preparation was focused on analysis and has expanded to cover a wider set of applications and can be used by a wider range of users.

It has developed into a platform that promotes cooperation between data experts, IT professionals, and business users, even if it increases the personal productivity of anyone who uses it.

Begin with the preparation of data

Data planning produces higher quality analysis data and other related activities of data management by error eradication and raw data normalization before processing. It is important, but requires a lot of time and may require certain skills.

Now, with an advanced data preparation platform, the process has become quicker and more user-friendly.

The five D's of data preparation

The processing of data is a structured component of many organization processes and IT-maintained applications, such as data management and business intelligence. But the business is also an informal activity of ad hoc reporting and analytics which routinely burden IT and more technologically advanced business users (e.g. data scientists) with personalized data preparation applications. There is growing interest these days to allow business users to access and manipulate data sources on their own without the use of SQL, Python, or SAS ® technology tools for data preparation.

One way to understand the data preparation inside and outside is to look at these five D's: discover, distill, document, detain, and deliver. Let's take a closer look at these things.

1. Discover

Discover is to find the data that best serves a particular function. Many users consider this as an activity that takes time and time. A robust, well-recorded data catalog (i.e. metadata repository) is important for efficient discovery. The data catalog includes a detailed index showing the location of available data, along with statistics on data profiling and other contents.

Data profiling is important for enhancing the understanding of this data as it offers high-level data quality statistics (such as row counts, column-specific data types, min, max and median column values, and zero counts). This allows the option of several available data sets.

It is important to remember that exploration should not only be about finding the required data right now. It should also promote later seeking data when similar needs occur. The data catalog should be modified, as the company meets new data sources, particularly external to the organization. This is valid even if there are no further measures in data preparation immediately.

2. Detain

The issue of detention is to collect the selected data during the discovery. The term "detention" evokes the idea that a copy of the data feeding the rest of the preparation process is temporarily imprisoned. The cells of a table hold data indefinitely both during and after planning for too many organizations. For the processing in the "distill" stage of data preparation a time-limited staging area or working area is required. If persistent data retention is required, shared and controlled storage – a link database, a network file system, or a large-scale repository, such as a Hadoop data lake – should be used. A new technique involves the use of storage in-memory areas (or the cloud) for much faster mixing and creating data in real-time before it is sent to other processes.

3. Distill

Distill aims to refine the collected data during the data preparation detention process. You must decide, in the process of processing data, how appropriate the data is for its intended aim or use. This is an underlying aspect of data quality – integrating data quality into the preparation of data. The amount of data quality functions such as validation, deduction, and improved functions can often be based on the ability to reuse elements from other implementations.

For example, transformations and quality regulations are implemented in data storage and business intelligence, thus combining multiple data sources into a unified data model optimized for query processing and standard reporting. It's all about: don't reinvent the wheel, reuse what is there. The more reusable the distillation methods are, the less IT relies on your company to produce customized processes.

The organization should preferably aim to make components of data quality a library of features and rules which can be reused to clean data. Aggregating and filtering data to create personalized views or to change presentation information may also include distilled data. Some analytical tool enables this distillation aspect through in-house data processing to prevent the continuous storage of contrary viewpoints of the provided data.

4. Document

The document consists of the documentation of both commercial and technical information on the data detected, distilled, and detained   including:

- Technical definitions.
- Business terminology.
- Source data lineage.

- History of changes applied during distillation.
- Relationships to other data.
- Data usage recommendations.
- Associated data governance policies.
- Identified data stewards.

All these metadata are exchanged through the data repository. The processing of manual data, often by wranglers, is not only time consuming but often redundant. This is because various users (or even the same user) can do the same job and don't produce the same results every time. Shared metadata allows faster and reliably replicated data preparation. Shared metadata also allows efficient cooperation in various aspects of data preparation when several users are involved.

5. Deliver

Delivery consists of structuring the distilled data in the format required by the processor used. The supplied data set(s) should also be tested for permanent detention and the supporting metadata applied to the data catalog if detained. These steps allow other users to discover the data.

The distribution must also comply with policies for data governance, such as those which reduce sensitive information exposure. It is important to note that this may not be a single delivery. The successful delivery of new or changed data which require scheduled or on-demand data preparation. In addition, the use of the data supplied should be checked after a certain period of time (and the related entries in the data catalog should be deleted) – and unused data discarded.

Prepare data for a repeatable process

Data preparation must become a formalized best practice for an organization. Shared metadata, continuous storage, and reusable transformation/cleansing logic make the data preparation a routine and productive operation. Users will in turn find the necessary data more easily – and they will be prepared with the information they need to efficiently use the data. Business users can deal with data on their own and free up IT for other activities with self-service data preparation software. The whole company becomes more efficient in this process.

Organizations are better supported by the reuse and implementation of data preparation elements in operating systems and development areas. As data collection makes it possible for you to find, store, distill, record, and distribute data, it allows the whole organization to use its valuable data assets to the best advantage.

Understanding the method of data preparation

Research indicates that up to 80 % of the total processing period is spent in the data preparation process. For companies, this remains a significant obstacle to fast and reliable research. The process of data processing helps you to easily translate raw data from different sources into distilled information to be used for reliable analysis and useful business insights. The process of self-service data preparation is increasingly evolving into a skill needed for a growing number of data analysts, data scientists, and business users. These people have learned and embraced this new skill to support their everyday business intelligence and analytical initiatives. To date, the data processing methods available were mostly restricted to Excel or other spreadsheet programs. As a result, the process of preparing the data, who is responsible for it, and how it suits the current analytical methodology is not necessarily clear.

Production of data

In general, six data analysis steps are needed for most analysts to use data. The precise figure of processing stages and processes will differ depending on the available tools and software, but these six processing steps are the overview for the processing of data:

• Collection of data. Data would be taken from clouds, data lakes, and other networks with a processor to build a broad database.

• Preparation of data. The data must be cleaned and arranged after the collection point. The raw data is reviewed for errors and any bad data is deleted.

• Input of data. The cleaned data are loaded into its target database and translated into usable information.

• Collection of data preparation. The data is interpreted using algorithms or other processing tools. This phase can vary depending on the type and use of the data.

• Analysis of results. Data are gathered and transformed into a functional form like a graph, graph, video, or text.

• Storage of data. The final step is to archive the data both on the computer and in a database for future use. For enforcement, data storage is also required.

The analysis of data preparation takes a long time to analyze, so researchers look for new approaches and techniques to shorten it. Trifacta provides a modern way of redirecting data to easily construct usable data.

A wonderful way to wrangle Trifacta data

The data preparation process, also known as the data challenge, is a radically new way of managing and cleaning data on any volume and format into a functional and dependable analytical tool. Trifacta Wrangler is a simple, self-service data preparation platform for easily explore, clean, and turn diverse data of all types and sizes through IT, business users, and data analyzers. Trifacta 's data planning methods are a new approach to process automation.

DATA PREPARATION AND ANALYSIS

Preparation and review of data

The data to be analyzed must be prepared by the researcher after data collection. Right arrangement of the data will save a lot of time and avoid errors. Most researchers tend to use a database or a statistical analysis program (e.g. Microsoft Excel, SPSS) to format to fit their requirements and efficiently organize their results. If the data is entered, it is necessary for the researcher to analyze the data for accuracy. You can do this by testing a random collection of participant data classes, but this is not as successful as the second re-entry and search for discrepancies. This approach is especially simple to do with numerical data since the researcher can simply use the database software to summarize the columns of the table and then check variations in the totals. A specialist computer program that monitors double-entry data for anomalies is one of the best methods of verification of accuracy.

Statistics descriptive

Descriptive statistics identify but do not draw data conclusions. Each statistical summary summarizes several discrete data sets using a specific figure. You may tell the researcher the central tendency of the variable, which means a participant's average score of a given study scale. The investigator may also assess the distributions of scores on a particular study measure or the range of scores. Descriptive statistics may also be used to tell the researcher how often a study test results in such answers or ratings. For instance, the researchers should note in the previous example about the efficacy of corrective lenses with regard to economic efficiency that a person with a corrected vision has an average dollar per week of $500, compared to $450 for a person without a corrected vision, which has an average of DPW. This amount of knowledge is not adequate to conclude that the correction of vision affects economic growth. These conclusions must be reached by inferential statistics. In addition, descriptive statistics might inform researchers that the DPW distribution for the entire sample is $351-$640 and that the average DPW for the sample is $445.

Correlation

Correlation is one of the most common forms of descriptive statistics (and most frequently misused). It can be defined better as "single numbers representing the degree of relationship between two variables." If two variables appear to be 'correlated,' that means that the rating of a participant on one variable tends to differ by rating on the other. For instance, the height and size of people seem to correlate positively. This means that most people, when they are tall, will probably have a large shoe and, if they are short, will probably have a smaller shoe size. Correlation can be negative, too. For instance, warmer outside temperatures can be adversely linked to the amount of hot chocolates sold in a local coffee shop. This means that hot chocolate sales begin to decline as the temperature increases. Although causality may seem apparent in this case , it is important to note that correlation does not require cause at a statistical level. A good researcher recognizes that there is no way to determine the causal relationship between two variables from correlation alone. To conclude that "X induced Y," a study with control groups and random sampling procedures should be experimental. Determining cause is difficult and establishing a cause-and - effect relationship is a common mistake if the methodology of the analysis does not support this claim.

Statistics inferential

Inferential statistics allow the scientist to start making hypothesis inferences based on the collected data. This means that the researcher draws conclusions about the general population when applying inferential statistics to results. Inferential statistics tend to generalize trends that potentially occur in the target population outside the data in the sample. This course will not deal with the particular types of inferential statistics the researcher may use but rather a short and practical overview, complete with step-by - step examples and helpful explanations.

Significance Statistical

Researchers can not necessarily assume that there is a difference in a well-constructed analysis between two groups. This discrepancy must be attributed to the independent variable manipulation. Regardless of how well a researcher designs the analysis, the findings are often mistakes. This mistake can occur because of individual differences between and within experimental groups, or because of systemic differences in the sample of the researcher. Regardless of its source, this error acts as a "noise" in data, affecting the study measures results of the participants even if it is not the variable of interest. The statistical value seeks to assess the likelihood of the observed analysis arising from the consequence of something other than chance. At a certain amount, a result is "statistically important." For instance, at $p < .05$ a result may be important. "P" represents the likelihood that the outcome was due to chance and .05 represents a 5 percent chance. In a well-run analysis, $p < .05$ therefore indicates that inferential statistical analyzes have shown that the observed effects are more than 95% likely to be produced by the effect of the independent variable. The 5% reduction is commonly considered the norm for most scientific study. It is technically difficult to be completely sure that our observations are not due to chance, since the essence of science is that of studying patterns and testing theories and not definitive proof.

WHAT IS DATA AGGREGATION?

Data aggregation is the data collection process and is presented in a simplified format. The data may be compiled from different data sources to integrate them into a description of the analysis of the data. This is a critical step because the precision of data analysis insights primarily depends on the quantity and the consistency of the data used. It is necessary to collect high-quality accurate data and to produce enough results. For anything from financial or business planning decisions to product, price, operational, and marketing strategies, data aggregation is useful.

Business decisions today are focused on large quantities of data, making easy access to information vital to the right decision-making at the right time. The emergence of big data and the proliferation of data sources are a rich source of knowledge for organizations and data scientists. However, collecting useful data is still a problem that makes it necessary to aggregate data. How important? Let's find out.

Data collection helps companies meet clear business goals or perform process / human research, in a process in which data are searched, collected, and delivered in a simplified, report-based form. Data aggregation is a step between data and analysis using various methods to search for and collect data. The collection of data is a critical component of efficient data management and here are the reasons.

What is important for data aggregation

Although organizations recognize the value of data collection and data quality, data processing in data management is often overlooked. This can be negative. For instance, numerous financial uncertainty during the recession and in other periods of economic downturns has shown that risk accumulation is one of the weakest links in most businesses' technology and risk architecture.

This impedes efficient and successful risk-based decision-making, which helps companies to strengthen their responses to both internal and external disasters. For this reason, it is recommended that financial institutions – especially banks – aggregate risks across different spectrums.

This means that risks, such as credit risk for trading, presented at each level must be assessed, controlled, and supervised through companies and potential legal entities. In short, companies must evaluate and analyze all risks in order to assess their overall company risk. This is important for efficient risk management.

In addition to risk management, data collection may also lead to the reporting of key performance indicators (KPI). The aggregation of data minimizes the number of rows to be submitted to get the KPI values. This reduces the time needed to update the KPI dashboards significantly, which in turn decreases resource usage and users' wait time.

The collection of data consolidates here huge volumes of quantitative data into higher hierarchy levels of dimension. For example, every single transaction is no longer needed to be processed. You can only group large sets of transaction rows in a few rows depending on the form of transaction and the month they occurred. This makes data processing simpler.

The solution to pick an appropriate data aggregation

Because 90 percent of all reports contain aggregate information, a solution to aggregate data will allow you to generate major performance benefits while improving your data analysis and reporting ability. However, how do you select an efficient solution for aggregation? By checking for the following seven qualities:

· Class solution that supports complex market environments

Flexible architecture

· Superior performance with quality, speed, and application responsiveness

 scalability

· Quick implementation

· Effective use of the tools of hardware and software

· Efficiency of cost

What is an example of aggregate data?

Here is an example of company aggregate data:

Companies also gather information from their online clients and visitors to their websites. The aggregate data will include consumer population statistics and behavioral metrics, such as transaction numbers or average age.   The marketing team will use this aggregated data to personalize content, deals, and more in the digital experience of the customer with the brand. The product team will also learn which products are popular and which are not popular. The data can also be used by managers and financial departments to help them determine how the budget should be allocated to product development or marketing strategies.

What is data aggregation in the financial and investing sectors?

Finance and investment companies are largely focused on alternative data for their recommendations. Many of this data comes from the press, as investors need to keep up to date on the financial developments of the market and the business. Financial companies also will use data mining to capture news and copy articles and use this data for predictive analytics, to detect trends, events, and changing views that may impact the finances of their monitoring companies and goods.

This knowledge can be found free of charge on news websites but is circulated via hundreds of websites. It takes time manually to merge each individual website and may generate inaccurate data sets because of missing data.

What is data aggregation in the retail industry?

The retail and e-commerce industries have several possible data aggregation applications. One is efficient price surveillance. Specific research in the field of e-commerce and retail is required to succeed. Companies must know what they face. Thus, they must constantly obtain new knowledge about the goods, promotions, and prices of their rivals. This information can be accessed from the websites of rivals or from other websites where their goods are identified. To obtain accurate information, data from each different source must be aggregated. This is a major order for manual review of web results.

 Another way to use data aggregations for retail and eCommerce companies is to collect product descriptions and images on their websites. Sometimes they come from suppliers, and borrowing the original photos and details from them is much simpler than making your own. Collecting product lists or competitor rates manually takes time and makes it virtually difficult to make sure it is up to date regularly. After looking at travel, we'll tell you how retail and digital companies can more effectively aggregate and combine data.

What is data aggregation in the travel industry?

Data collection in the travel industry may be used for a wide variety of purposes. Competitive pricing tracking, industry studies, market intelligence, consumer feelings analysis, and the collection of pictures and explanations of the services on their web pages. Online competition is intense so the collection of data or lack of it will make or break up a travel business.

Travel companies must manage the ever-changing cost of travel and the availability of land. You will need to learn which destinations are popular and which markets you can target with your offer to fly. The data required for these observations are scattered across many areas of the internet, making it difficult to collect them manually. That is where our Network Data Integration data collection and aggregation service comes in.

Data Aggregation with Web Data Integration

Web Data Integration (WDI) is a cure for web data mining's time-consuming nature. WDI can extract data from every website you need to access. Applied to previously mentioned use cases, or to any area, the Web data integration can cut data to minutes by eradicating human error during data aggregation. This enables businesses to access the data they need from anywhere they need it. Both with automated quality management to ensure precision.

WDI not only collects and aggregates the data you need but also prepares and cleans the data for integration, analysis, and discovery in a consumable format. So web data integration is ideal for you if your business needs reliable, up-to-date web data.

Data Aggregation in the Context of Middleware

There are three common tasks and functions for marketing analytics middleware.

In short, we call them ETV (Transforming, processing and visualizing). Together, this is the process for data extraction and preparation for analysis from SaaS applications.

There is a software layer for each of these three stages, meaning that there are companies whose only focus is on supporting marketers at each level.

1. Extract — Data extraction layer

2. Transform — Data preparation layer

3. Analyze/Visualize — Analytics and Visualization layer

We at Improvado believe it is necessary to offer marketers the freedom to use tools to incorporate and analyze their data without the intervention of engineers.

In this section, we address the extraction process of analytics middleware — take all of the data contained in your various marketing databases and convert it into an analysis platform.

Manual Data Aggregation vs. Automated Data Aggregation

Aggregating data can be a highly manual operation, particularly in the early stages of your business.

Click Export.   Sort by an excellent board. Reformat it to appear like other sources of knowledge. Develop charts to compare the different marketing campaigns' performance/budget/advance.

Sounds like a routine familiar? You definitely aren't alone.

For all marketers, data aggregation is an essential operation. It's the only able to determine how campaigns operate. This export/sort/reformatting method is not a special or fresh-every marketer has had it at some point.

Fortunately, we now have the option of automating data aggregation. Exactly what does it look like?

It looks like installing third-party applications, often referred to as Middleware, which can automatically pull the data from your marketing tools.

The collection of data is the first step in an effective marketing strategy review and you must therefore take this step in the right direction. Automating the marketing performance and ROI would improve because it takes too long to concentrate on other aspects of the analytical marketing process.

Data aggregation levels

Three data aggregation levels were established – beginner, intermediate, and MASTER. Identify which one you are and how you can leap to the next step.

Novice at Data Aggregation

A data aggregation novice does not necessarily aggregate any data. You look through your marketing channels to obtain marketing insights.

You can log in to Google Analytics and see that one page is particularly busy. This knowledge is used to build more options for clicking through the page for your customers (and stay on your website).

You make educated decisions about "information," but you don't actually collect the data to do so, so much of the big picture is missing.

A comparison of multiple channel data is important to make intelligent marketing decisions. How else would you know what marketing campaigns for your company are working for? If you just look at the data on the website, you skip it.

Data aggregation for intermediate

You have a dashboard for ads. It's in Google's tablet or an outstanding one. You're updating it ... every week? Monthly?

Whenever you update the dashboard, you could see how your marketing strategies are doing and compare data-driven decisions across platforms.

Now it's difficult to build a marketing dashboard, so kudos to you at this point.

Is this model a problem? Creating a dashboard takes time and holding its perspective is much more critical.

Novice at Data Aggregation

You have seen at this stage how boring marketing dashboards can be and how repetitive you are.

How can you speed this up? Via automation. Data Collection Masters have an automated pipeline in place so that they have real-time feedback from their marketing results.

Marketing data collection applications such as Improvado will pipe your data from marketing channels and send them to your warehouse, tablet, or visualization app, however, you wish.

As it's mentioned above, you spend more time updating a marketing dashboard and clicking on various tabs and apps, so you can make educated ROI-driven marketing decisions.

Who are the main players in applications for data aggregation?

Improvado

What is Improvado

Improvado has been developed by marketers, for marketers, as an extremely helpful data collection method. This platform helps you to capture all campaign data in real-time into a single dashboard, along with the ability to display them in automated reports and well-designed custom dashboards.

Who should use use Improvado?

The method is suitable for marketers, specially developed to concentrate on the marketing problem. Improvado offers a gateway to any marketing tool you can use. Also, the integrations with the platform go very far and draw granular data from the keyword and ad level to allow marketers to see the entire image.

Perhaps one of the main advantages of using the improvado network is its outstanding customer service personnel. They will help you develop any custom dashboards and integrations you want. Improved data can also be used in any BI tool like Tableau or Looker and in the dashboard of the app.

Improvado pricing

Improvado pricing is carried out on a personalized basis. The company will determine your business needs and provide you with pricing information during a call.

Domo is data analysis and organizational intelligence applications.

Who should use Domo?

Domo is ideally suited to C-level managers in organizations looking for a company-wide (non-marketing) BI platform to build executive dashboards.

The crucial thing to remember is that marketing data and business data in general, are not directly focused. That means it's capable of aggregate and displaying marketing data through executive dashboards a business intelligence but, since marketing integrations are small, the connectors don't run so thoroughly and the tool overall can be too big for the use of the marketing team alone.

What is Stitch?

Stitch is the first cloud-focused development platform for quick transfer of data. The app helps you to add your data in minutes whenever you want it.

Who should use Stitch?

The interface for data teams is a simple and extensible ETL. Users can collect data from several sources, load data into leading data platforms, and analyze it using leading instruments.

ADVANCED PANDAS

Python Data Analysis Bibliothek Pandas is currently widely used worldwide. It began initially as a data discovery and testing tool but eventually became used in a production-like environment. It is used for example in scheduled data extraction and model creation through airflow or even streaming to prepare data for model inference. Pandas or Python may argue that they are not acceptable methods for production environments. However, it is important to know how to make the most of it.

Pandas are a strong tool but needs to be perfected to achieve optimum efficiency. In the following segment you will learn how to maximize processing speed and the use of memory:

1. Index Optimization

2. Vectorize Operations

3. Memory Optimization

4. Filter Optimization

Index Optimization: Pandas have optimized strong reliance on indices that allow for quick search or fusion of indexed tables. In the examples below, we combine the summary table with the listing table, use a column, and then use the index.

```
%%timeit
listings.merge(reviews, on='listing_id')
# 439 ms ± 24.5 ms per loop (mean ± std. dev. of 7 runs, 1 loop each)

%%timeit
reviews_ = reviews.set_index('listing_id')
listings_ = listings.set_index('listing_id')
listings_.merge(reviews_, left_index=True, right_index=True)
# 393 ms ± 17.4 ms per loop (mean ± std. dev. of 7 runs, 1 loop each)
```

Even when the index has to be set, combining with indices is easier. When looking for value, let's see the differences.

```
listings = listings.set_index('listing_id', drop=False)
```

```
%%timeit
```

```
listings.loc[29844866, 'name']
```

```
# 10.1 µs ± 1.25 µs per loop (mean ± std. dev. of 7 runs, 100000 loops each)
```

```
%%timeit
```

```
listings.at[29844866, 'name']
```

```
# 5.34 µs ± 474 ns per loop (mean ± std. dev. of 7 runs, 100000 loops each)
```

```
listings = listings.reset_index(drop=True)
```

```
%%timeit
```

```
listings.loc[listings['listing_id'] == 29844866, 'name']
```

```
# 593 µs ± 30 µs per loop (mean ± std. dev. of 7 runs, 1000 loops each)
```

```
%%timeit
```

```
listings.iloc[22529]['name']
```

```
# 252 µs ± 45.9 µs per loop (mean ± std. dev. of 7 runs, 1000 loops each)
```

Simple searches that use indices outperform other approaches to a significant degree. If you need a single value, it is easier to use .at[] than to use .loc[].

Vectorize Operations: Vectorization is the execution of operations on whole arrays. Similar to NumPy, Pandas has developed vectorized operations optimizations. It is recommended that loops be avoided when dealing with data frames, as reading and writing is expensive. However, vectoring cannot always be feasible, so we'll also demonstrate what is the best iterative method for pandas by comparing .iterrows(),.loc[].iloc[],and.map()/.apply().

In the following example, the price column will be normalized between 0 and 1 using the various operations mentioned above.

```
# .iloc[]

%%timeit

norm_prices = np.zeros(len(listings,))

for i in range(len(listings)):

    norm_prices[i] = (listings.iloc[i]['price'] - min_price) / (max_price - min_price)

listings['norm_price'] = norm_prices
```

```
# 8.91 s ± 479 ms per loop (mean ± std. dev. of 7 runs, 1 loop each)
```

```
# Iterrows()
```

```
%%timeit
```

```
norm_prices = np.zeros(len(listings,))
```

```
for i, row in listings.iterrows():

    norm_prices[i] = (row['price'] - min_price) / (max_price - min_price)
```

```
listings['norm_price'] = norm_prices
```

```
# 3.99 s ± 346 ms per loop (mean ± std. dev. of 7 runs, 1 loop each)
```

```
# .loc[]
```

```
%%timeit
```

```
norm_prices = np.zeros(len(listings,))
```

```
for i in range(len(norm_prices)):

    norm_prices[i] = (listings.loc[i, 'price'] - min_price) / (max_price - min_price)
```

```
listings['norm_price'] = norm_prices
```

```
# 408 ms ± 61.2 ms per loop (mean ± std. dev. of 7 runs, 1 loop each)
```

```
# .map()
```

```
%%timeit
```

```
listings['norm_price'] = listings['price'].map(lambda x: (x - min_price) / (max_price -
min_price))
```

```
# 39.8 ms ± 2.33 ms per loop (mean ± std. dev. of 7 runs, 10 loops each)
```

```
# Vectorize
```

```
%%timeit
```

```
listings['norm_price'] = (listings['price'] - min_price) / (max_price - min_price)
```

```
# 1.76 ms ± 107 μs per loop (mean ± std. dev. of 7 runs, 100 loops each)
```

The calculation speed gap is huge, with the vectorized solution ~82,000 times faster than using .iloc[].

While this is a very easy example, it is important more with these basic operations, which cover most of the calculation time.

It can be difficult to write a vectorized code for complex problems. Intermediate solutions, which can be an inefficient memory, also have to be stored in the data frame. The data are taken out of the data frame and loop into NumPy arrays as a good alternative for complex operations. Consider an example where we use business rules to decide the most appropriate Airbnb for us, first by looping with .loc[], [then transforming it into NumPy arrays and finally by making use of some Pandas vectorization magic.

```
room_type_scores = {'Entire home/apt': 1,

            'Private room': 0.7,

            'Shared room': 0.2}


%%timeit


scores = np.zeros(len(listings))


for i in range(len(listings)):

    row = listings.loc[i]

    if row['availability_365'] == 0:
        .
        scores[i] = 0

    elif row['price'] > 100:

        scores[i] = 0
```

```python
    else:

        room_type_score = room_type_scores[row['room_type']]

        price_score = (100 - row['price']) / 100

        review_score = 1 if row['number_of_reviews'] > 50 else 0.5

        scores[i] = room_type_score * price_score * review_score

listings['score'] = scores

# 5.64 s ± 194 ms per loop (mean ± std. dev. of 7 runs, 1 loop each)
```

.loc[]

```python
%%timeit

prices = listings['price'].values

nr_reviews = listings['number_of_reviews'].values

availability = listings['availability_365'].values

room_types = listings['room_type'].values

scores = np.zeros(len(listings))
```

```python
for i in range(len(listings)):

    if availability[i] == 0:

        scores[i] = 0

    elif prices[i] > 100:

        scores[i] = 0

    else:

        room_type_score = room_type_scores[room_types[i]]

        price_score = (100 - prices[i]) / 100

        review_score = 1 if nr_reviews[i] > 50 else 0.5

        scores[i] = room_type_score * price_score * review_score

listings['score'] = scores

# 41.4 ms ± 2.31 ms per loop (mean ± std. dev. of 7 runs, 10 loops each)
```

Numpy

```
%%timeit

listings.loc[listings['room_type'] == 'Entire home/apt', 'room_type_score'] = 1

listings.loc[listings['room_type'] == 'Private room', 'room_type_score'] = 0.7

listings['room_type_score'].fillna(0.2, inplace=True)

listings.loc[listings['number_of_reviews'] > 50, 'review_score'] = 1

listings['review_score'].fillna(0.5, inplace=True)

listings['price_score'] = (100 - listings['price']) / 100

listings['score'] = listings['room_type_score'] * listings['price_score'] * listings['review_score']

listings.loc[(listings['availability_365'] == 0) |

        (listings['price'] > 100), 'score'] = 0

# 17.5 ms ± 668 µs per loop (mean ± std. dev. of 7 runs, 100 loops each)
```

We see that NumPy arrays are a quick option to vectorized operations, which is helpful when vectorizing is too complex. The computation time with NumPy for a limited number of samples is lower than a vectorized method.

Memory Optimization: One of the Pandas' disadvantages is that data frame memory consumption is inefficient by design. The column type is deduced when the csv or json file reads and is defaulted to the largest form of data (int64, float64, object).

Our DataFrame listings are built via a csv with the following characteristics:

```
listings.info()

<class 'pandas.core.frame.DataFrame'>
RangeIndex: 22552 entries, 0 to 22551
Data columns (total 16 columns):
id                              22552 non-null int64
name                            22493 non-null object
host_id                         22552 non-null int64
host_name                       22526 non-null object
neighbourhood_group             22552 non-null object
neighbourhood                   22552 non-null object
latitude                        22552 non-null float64
longitude                       22552 non-null float64
room_type                       22552 non-null object
price                           22552 non-null int64
minimum_nights                  22552 non-null int64
number_of_reviews               22552 non-null int64
last_review                     18644 non-null object
reviews_per_month               18638 non-null float64
calculated_host_listings_count  22552 non-null int64
availability_365                22552 non-null int64
dtypes: float64(3), int64(7), object(6)
memory usage: 2.8+ MB
```

All columns have the largest data types previously indicated. We can see here some noticeable changes, such as the availability 365 has only 365 potential values, so it can be reduced to an int16 (-32,768 to +32,767).

We have specified some features that automatically download columns to the smallest datatype possible without losing details. We use pandas for strings when the quantity of strings is less than half the total quantity of strings. This should be adapted to your needs since the concept of a category limits the inclusion of unknown values in this section. We cast the columns on the DateTime dtype of the pandas. It does not minimize the use of memory but makes time-based operations.

```python
import pandas as pd

from typing import List

def optimize_floats(df: pd.DataFrame) -> pd.DataFrame:

    floats = df.select_dtypes(include=['float64']).columns.tolist()

    df[floats] = df[floats].apply(pd.to_numeric, downcast='float')

    return df

def optimize_ints(df: pd.DataFrame) -> pd.DataFrame:

    ints = df.select_dtypes(include=['int64']).columns.tolist()

    df[ints] = df[ints].apply(pd.to_numeric, downcast='integer')

    return df

def optimize_objects(df: pd.DataFrame, datetime_features: List[str]) -> pd.DataFrame:

    for col in df.select_dtypes(include=['object']):

        if col not in datetime_features:

            num_unique_values = len(df[col].unique())
```

```python
        num_total_values = len(df[col])

        if float(num_unique_values) / num_total_values < 0.5:

            df[col] = df[col].astype('category')

    else:

        df[col] = pd.to_datetime(df[col])

    return df

def optimize(df: pd.DataFrame, datetime_features: List[str] = []):

    return optimize_floats(optimize_ints(optimize_objects(df, datetime_features)))
```

Now we can easily optimize our data framework by calling

```python
optimized_listings = optimize(listings, ['last_review'])
```

This results in the following dataframe:

```
optimized_listings.info()
```

```
<class 'pandas.core.frame.DataFrame'>
RangeIndex: 22552 entries, 0 to 22551
Data columns (total 16 columns):
listing_id                      22552 non-null int32
name                            22493 non-null object
host_id                         22552 non-null int32
host_name                       22526 non-null category
neighbourhood_group             22552 non-null category
neighbourhood                   22552 non-null category
latitude                        22552 non-null float32
longitude                       22552 non-null float32
room_type                       22552 non-null category
price                           22552 non-null int16
minimum_nights                  22552 non-null int16
number_of_reviews               22552 non-null int16
last_review                     18644 non-null datetime64[ns]
reviews_per_month               18638 non-null float32
calculated_host_listings_count  22552 non-null int8
availability_365                22552 non-null int16
dtypes: category(4), datetime64[ns](1), float32(3), int16(4), int32(2), int8(1), object(1)
memory usage: 1.3+ MB
```

Only two columns have the same types as before, which is worth optimizing. The total memory usage decreased from 2.8 MB to 1.3 MB and improved by more than 50%. It is not necessary, but very useful for large data frames for this toy example.

This requires knowledge of the ranges of values per column.

To preserve the new column types, the data frame can be stored in a type that contains column type information like a pickle. The physical size of the file as shown in the example below will also be reduced.

listings	23-8-2019 16:28	CSV File	3.934 KB
listings.pkl	23-8-2019 16:19	PKL File	3.213 KB
optimized_listings	23-8-2019 16:27	CSV File	3.548 KB
optimized_listings.pkl	23-8-2019 16:20	PKL File	1.813 KB

When chaining differece operations, it is worth considering which operations to carry out first. Filter steps should be performed as soon as possible.

Even when making internal connections between data frames, it's worth filtering before fusion. If we sample our lists with .sample(frac=0.2) and merge the reviews, we can see that they will filter the reviews first more efficiently.

listings = listings.sample(frac=0.2, random_state=1337)

363

```python
def optimized_merge(df1, df2, merge_column):
    df2 = df2[df2[merge_column].isin(df1[merge_column])]
    return df1.merge(df2, on=merge_column)
```

```python
%%timeit
listings.merge(reviews, on='listing_id')
# 106 ms ± 2.46 ms per loop (mean ± std. dev. of 7 runs, 10 loops each)
```

```python
%%timeit
optimized_merge(listings, reviews, 'listing_id')
# 69.6 ms ± 761 µs per loop (mean ± std. dev. of 7 runs, 10 loops each)
```

Advanced Features of Pandas and How to Use Them

(1) Options and Settings Configuration

Pandas come with a set of options and settings that you can configure. They are enormous productivity boosters because you can customize your Pandas environment according to your needs.

For example, we can modify some of the display settings of Pandas to change the number of rows and columns displayed and the number of floating-point accuracy.

```python
import pandas as pd

display_settings = {
    'max_columns': 10,
    'expand_frame_repr': True,  # Wrap to multiple pages
    'max_rows': 10,
    'precision': 2,
    'show_dimensions': True
```

```
}
```

```
for op, value in display_settings.items():

    pd.set_option("display.{}".format(op), value)
```

The above code ensures that Pandas displays a maximum of 10 rows and 10 columns at a maximum of 2 decimal places. This way, when we try to print out a large DataFrame, our terminal or Jupyter Notebook will not look like a mess!

This is only a fundamental example. Beyond the simple display settings, there is much more to explore. All options can be checked in the official documentation.

(2) DataFrames Combination

A relatively unknown feature of Pandas DataFrames is that they exist in two ways.

Each method produces a different result, so it is very important to select the correct one based on what you want to achieve. They also contain lot parameters that further adapt the fusion. Let's check them out. Let's check them out.

Concatenating

Concatenation is the best-known method for combining data frames and can intuitively be understood as "stacking." Stacking can be done horizontally or vertically.

Imagine you have a huge CSV dataset. It is worth dividing it into several files to make it easier to handle (this is common practice for large data sets known as sharding).

When loaded into pandas, the DataFrame of each CSV can be vertically stowed to create one large DataFrame for each data. For example, if we have three shards, each with 5 Million rows, then our final data frame will have 15 million rows, once we have all stacked them vertically.

The code below illustrates how dataframes can be concatenated vertically in pandas.

```
# Vertical concat

pd.concat([october_df, november_df, december_df], axis=0)
```

Something similar can be done by splitting the dataset by column rather than rows — a few columns per CSV file (including all rows). It is like we break the characteristics of the dataset into different shards. You would then stack these columns/features horizontally to merge them.

```
# Horizontal concat

pd.concat([features_1to5_df, features_6to10_df, features_11to15_df], axis=1)
```

Merging

Merging is more complicated yet more efficient, combining Pandas DataFrames in a SQL-like style, i.e., some common attributes enter the Dataframes.

Imagine having two DataFrames that explain your YouTube channel. One includes a list of user IDs and how much time every user spent on your site. The other contains the same list of user IDs and the number of videos each user saw. The combination of 2 data frames enables us to merge into one data frame, matching user IDs, and then placing the ID, time, and video counts in one row for each user.

The merge feature is used to merge two DataFrames in Pandas. An example of how it operates can be seen in the code below. The right and left parameters refer to the two DataFrames you want to combine, while the corresponding column is defined.

```
pd.merge(left=ids_and_time_df,

        right=ids_and_videos_df,

        on="id")
```

If you want to go even further into emulating SQL connections, how you can select the type of SQL-style you want to join: within, outside, left, or right.

(3) Dataframes reshaping

Pandas DataFrames are restructured and restructured in a number of ways. These vary from basic, basic, powerful, and complicated. Let's look at the three most popular. For all of the following examples, we will use this Superheroes Dataset!

```
import pandas as pd


players_data = {'Player': ['Superman', 'Batman', 'Thanos', 'Batman', 'Thanos',

    'Superman', 'Batman', 'Thanos', 'Black Widow', 'Batman', 'Thanos', 'Superman'],
```

```
'Year': [2000,2000,2000,2001,2001,2002,2002,2002,2003,2004,2004,2005],

'Points':[23,43,45,65,76,34,23,78,89,76,92,87]}


df = pd.DataFrame(players_data)


print(df)


"""
        Player  Year  Points

0      Superman  2000      23

1        Batman  2000      43

2        Thanos  2000      45

3        Batman  2001      65

4        Thanos  2001      76

5      Superman  2002      34

6        Batman  2002      23

7        Thanos  2002      78

8   Black Widow  2003      89

9        Batman  2004      76

10       Thanos  2004      92

11     Superman  2005      87
"""
```

Transpose

The best of all of them. Swaps the rows of the DataFrame with its columns. You will have 10 rows and 5000 columns if you have 5000 rows and 10 columns and then transpose the dataFrame.

import pandas as pd

players_data = {'Player': ['Superman', 'Batman', 'Thanos', 'Batman', 'Thanos',

  'Superman', 'Batman', 'Thanos', 'Black Widow', 'Batman', 'Thanos', 'Superman'],

```python
'Year': [2000,2000,2000,2001,2001,2002,2002,2002,2003,2004,2004,2005],
'Points':[23,43,45,65,76,34,23,78,89,76,92,87]}

df = pd.DataFrame(players_data)

print(df)

"""
        Player  Year  Points
0      Superman  2000      23
1        Batman  2000      43
2        Thanos  2000      45
3        Batman  2001      65
4        Thanos  2001      76
5      Superman  2002      34
6        Batman  2002      23
7        Thanos  2002      78
8   Black Widow  2003      89
9        Batman  2004      76
10       Thanos  2004      92
11     Superman  2005      87
"""
```

Groupby

The main use of Groupby is to break DataFrames into many pieces based on certain keys. If the DataFrame is separated into parts, certain operations on every component can be performed independently.

For instance, we can see how a DataFrame of players with the corresponding years and points was generated in the code below. Then we broke up the DataFrame according to the player into several pieces. Each player gets his or her own party, which indicates how many points the player has been involved in each year.

```python
groups_df = df.groupby('Player')
```

```python
for player, group in groups_df:
    print("----- {} -----".format(player))
    print(group)
    print("")


### This prints out the following
"""
----- Batman -----
    Player  Year  Points
1   Batman  2000      43
3   Batman  2001      65
6   Batman  2002      23
9   Batman  2004      76
----- Black Widow -----
        Player  Year  Points
8  Black Widow  2003      89
----- Superman -----
      Player  Year  Points
0   Superman  2000      23
5   Superman  2002      34
11  Superman  2005      87
----- Thanos -----
    Player  Year  Points
2   Thanos  2000      45
4   Thanos  2001      76
7   Thanos  2002      78
10  Thanos  2004      92
"""
```

Stacking

Stacking converts the DataFrame into a multi-level index, i.e. every row has multiple subsections. These subsections are generated with columns of the DataFrame and compressed into a multi-index. All in all, stacking can be interpreted as multi-index rows compressing columns.

The best illustration of this is an example shown below.

df = df.stack()

print(df)

"""

0	Player	Superman
	Year	2000
	Points	23
1	Player	Batman
	Year	2000
	Points	43
2	Player	Thanos
	Year	2000
	Points	45
3	Player	Batman
	Year	2001
	Points	65
4	Player	Thanos
	Year	2001
	Points	76
5	Player	Superman
	Year	2002
	Points	34
6	Player	Batman
	Year	2002

```
      Points         23
7   Player        Thanos
     Year          2002
     Points         78
8   Player     Black Widow
     Year          2003
     Points         89
9   Player        Batman
     Year          2004
     Points         76
10  Player        Thanos
     Year          2004
     Points         92
11  Player       Superman
     Year          2005
     Points         87
"""
```

(4) Dealing with data on time

The Python Datetime Library is a staple. Whenever you deal with something that has to do with details on real-world date and time, it's your library. And luckily for us, Pandas also has the option to use Datetime artifacts.

Let's take an illustration to explain it. Throughout the code above, we first build a dataframe with 4 columns: Day, Month, Year, and data, . As you can see, it is very chaotic; we use 3 columns to just save the date when we know in reality that the calendar date is only one value

```
from itertools import product

import pandas as pd

import numpy as np


col_names = ["Day", "Month", "Year"]
```

```python
df = pd.DataFrame(list(product([10, 11, 12], [8, 9], [2018, 2019])),
            columns=col_names)


df['data'] = np.random.randn(len(df))


df = df.sort_values(['Year', 'Month'], ascending=[True, True])


print(df)



"""
    Day  Month  Year      data
0   10      8  2018  1.685356
4   11      8  2018  0.441383
8   12      8  2018  1.276089
2   10      9  2018 -0.260338
6   11      9  2018  0.404769
10  12      9  2018 -0.359598
1   10      8  2019  0.145498
5   11      8  2019 -0.731463
9   12      8  2019 -1.451633
3   10      9  2019 -0.988294
7   11      9  2019 -0.687049
11  12      9  2019 -0.067432
"""
```

With DateTime, we can clean stuff up.

Pandas come conveniently with a function named to DateTime) (which enables multiple DataFrame columns to be compressed and converted into a single entity. When it's in this format, the Datetime library has all the versatility at your disposal.

To use the function to_datetime(), (all the "date" data from the corresponding columns must be passed on. That's the columns "Day," "Month," and "Year." When we have Datetime stuff we don't need the other columns and can just remove them. See the code above to see how it works!

```python
from itertools import product

import pandas as pd

import numpy as np


col_names = ["Day", "Month", "Year"]


df = pd.DataFrame(list(product([10, 11, 12], [8, 9], [2018, 2019])),
            columns=col_names)


df['data'] = np.random.randn(len(df))


df = df.sort_values(['Year', 'Month'], ascending=[True, True])


df.insert(loc=0, column="date", value=pd.to_datetime(df[col_names]))
df = df.drop(col_names, axis=1).squeeze()


print(df)


"""
        date      data
0  2018-08-10 -0.328973
4  2018-08-11 -0.670790
8  2018-08-12 -1.360565
2  2018-09-10 -0.401973
6  2018-09-11 -1.238754
10 2018-09-12  0.957695
```

```
1  2019-08-10  0.571126

5  2019-08-11 -1.320735

9  2019-08-12  0.196036

3  2019-09-10 -1.717800

7  2019-09-11  0.074606

11 2019-09-12 -0.643198

"""
```

(5) Category mapping of objects

Mapping is a good trick to assist with categorical data organization. Imagine, for example, that we have a massive DataFrame with thousands of rows where we have objected to categorizing one of the columns. This simplifies both the preparation of machine learning models and the usefulness of data visualization.

See the code below for a small example with a list of foods we want to categorize.

In the above code, we put our list in a sequence of pandas. We have also built a dictionary showing the kind of mapping that we want to categorize any food item like a "protein" or a "carb." That is a toy example, but if this sequence were to be a large-scale one, then suggesting that a length of 1,000,000 items would not work.

Instead of the simple for-loop, a function can be written with the integrated Pandas function.map) (to simplify the mapping. Check the code below to see how the function is implemented.

In this feature, we first loop via our dictionary to construct a new dictionary in which the keys represent every possible element in the pandas sery and the values represent the new mapped object, "Carbs" or "Protein"

CONCLUSION

The huge popularity shows the effectiveness of Python as a modern language of programming. At the same time, developers around the world are currently using Python 3 to create a variety of GUI, web, and mobile applications on their desktop. There are also a number of reasons why Python's enormous success and market share will remain intact for a longer time.

Python is known for being an extensive language that is part of the standard library with extensive functionality. But Python's growing popularity has led to a wide range of third-party packages or modules that expand Python's functionality and enable the language to address unique programming challenges. Modules for handling non-standard database interactions and advanced cryptography features are available, for example. Modules for handling common tasks such as rendering charts, reading file metadata, and compiling Python applications in standardized executable applications are also available. Due to the availability of many web-centric modules, Python Web programming is made easier to handle tasks, such as e-mail, HTTP status maintenance, JavaScript interaction, or other common web development tasks.

The standard Python library provides developers with a variety of features that are comparable to more complex languages like C++ while maintaining simple, accessible language syntax. Comprehensive file-based I / O, database interactivity, advanced exception management, and a host of data types made Python suitable for web applications as well as general purposes. Python's web programming is an easy task for application developers who seek to develop web applications.

Printed in Great Britain
by Amazon